NORWEGIAN
VOCABULARY

ENGLISH-NORWEGIAN

The most useful words
To expand your lexicon and sharpen
your language skills

7000 words

Norwegian vocabulary for English speakers - 7000 words
By Andrey Taranov

T&P Books vocabularies are intended for helping you learn, memorize and review foreign words. The dictionary is divided into themes, covering all major spheres of everyday activities, business, science, culture, etc.

The process of learning words using T&P Books' theme-based dictionaries gives you the following advantages:

- Correctly grouped source information predetermines success at subsequent stages of word memorization
- Availability of words derived from the same root allowing memorization of word units (rather than separate words)
- Small units of words facilitate the process of establishing associative links needed for consolidation of vocabulary
- Level of language knowledge can be estimated by the number of learned words

T&P Books Publishing
www.tpbooks.com

ISBN: 978-1-78492-012-8

This book is also available in E-book formats.
Please visit www.tpbooks.com or the major online bookstores.

NORWEGIAN VOCABULARY
for English speakers

T&P Books vocabularies are intended to help you learn, memorize, and review foreign words. The vocabulary contains over 7000 commonly used words arranged thematically.

- Vocabulary contains the most commonly used words
- Recommended as an addition to any language course
- Meets the needs of beginners and advanced learners of foreign languages
- Convenient for daily use, revision sessions, and self-testing activities
- Allows you to assess your vocabulary

Special features of the vocabulary

- Words are organized according to their meaning, not alphabetically
- Words are presented in three columns to facilitate the reviewing and self-testing processes
- Words in groups are divided into small blocks to facilitate the learning process
- The vocabulary offers a convenient and simple transcription of each foreign word

The vocabulary has 198 topics including:

Basic Concepts, Numbers, Colors, Months, Seasons, Units of Measurement, Clothing & Accessories, Food & Nutrition, Restaurant, Family Members, Relatives, Character, Feelings, Emotions, Diseases, City, Town, Sightseeing, Shopping, Money, House, Home, Office, Working in the Office, Import & Export, Marketing, Job Search, Sports, Education, Computer, Internet, Tools, Nature, Countries, Nationalities and more ...

T&P BOOKS' THEME-BASED DICTIONARIES

The Correct System for Memorizing Foreign Words

Acquiring vocabulary is one of the most important elements of learning a foreign language, because words allow us to express our thoughts, ask questions, and provide answers. An inadequate vocabulary can impede communication with a foreigner and make it difficult to understand a book or movie well.

The pace of activity in all spheres of modern life, including the learning of modern languages, has increased. Today, we need to memorize large amounts of information (grammar rules, foreign words, etc.) within a short period. However, this does not need to be difficult. All you need to do is to choose the right training materials, learn a few special techniques, and develop your individual training system.

Having a system is critical to the process of language learning. Many people fail to succeed in this regard; they cannot master a foreign language because they fail to follow a system comprised of selecting materials, organizing lessons, arranging new words to be learned, and so on. The lack of a system causes confusion and eventually, lowers self-confidence.

T&P Books' theme-based dictionaries can be included in the list of elements needed for creating an effective system for learning foreign words. These dictionaries were specially developed for learning purposes and are meant to help students effectively memorize words and expand their vocabulary.

Generally speaking, the process of learning words consists of three main elements:

- Reception (creation or acquisition) of a training material, such as a word list
- Work aimed at memorizing new words
- Work aimed at reviewing the learned words, such as self-testing

All three elements are equally important since they determine the quality of work and the final result. All three processes require certain skills and a well-thought-out approach.

New words are often encountered quite randomly when learning a foreign language and it may be difficult to include them all in a unified list. As a result, these words remain written on scraps of paper, in book margins, textbooks, and so on. In order to systematize such words, we have to create and continually update a "book of new words." A paper notebook, a netbook, or a tablet PC can be used for these purposes.

This "book of new words" will be your personal, unique list of words. However, it will only contain the words that you came across during the learning process. For example, you might have written down the words "Sunday," "Tuesday," and "Friday." However, there are additional words for days of the week, for example, "Saturday," that are missing, and your list of words would be incomplete. Using a theme dictionary, in addition to the "book of new words," is a reasonable solution to this problem.

The theme-based dictionary may serve as the basis for expanding your vocabulary.

It will be your big "book of new words" containing the most frequently used words of a foreign language already included. There are quite a few theme-based dictionaries available, and you should ensure that you make the right choice in order to get the maximum benefit from your purchase.

Therefore, we suggest using theme-based dictionaries from T&P Books Publishing as an aid to learning foreign words. Our books are specially developed for effective use in the sphere of vocabulary systematization, expansion and review.

Theme-based dictionaries are not a magical solution to learning new words. However, they can serve as your main database to aid foreign-language acquisition. Apart from theme dictionaries, you can have copybooks for writing down new words, flash cards, glossaries for various texts, as well as other resources; however, a good theme dictionary will always remain your primary collection of words.

T&P Books' theme-based dictionaries are specialty books that contain the most frequently used words in a language.

The main characteristic of such dictionaries is the division of words into themes. For example, the *City* theme contains the words "street," "crossroads," "square," "fountain," and so on. The *Talking* theme might contain words like "to talk," "to ask," "question," and "answer".

All the words in a theme are divided into smaller units, each comprising 3–5 words. Such an arrangement improves the perception of words and makes the learning process less tiresome. Each unit contains a selection of words with similar meanings or identical roots. This allows you to learn words in small groups and establish other associative links that have a positive effect on memorization.

The words on each page are placed in three columns: a word in your native language, its translation, and its transcription. Such positioning allows for the use of techniques for effective memorization. After closing the translation column, you can flip through and review foreign words, and vice versa. "This is an easy and convenient method of review – one that we recommend you do often."

Our theme-based dictionaries contain transcriptions for all the foreign words. Unfortunately, none of the existing transcriptions are able to convey the exact nuances of foreign pronunciation. That is why we recommend using the transcriptions only as a supplementary learning aid. Correct pronunciation can only be acquired with the help of sound. Therefore our collection includes audio theme-based dictionaries.

The process of learning words using T&P Books' theme-based dictionaries gives you the following advantages:

- You have correctly grouped source information, which predetermines your success at subsequent stages of word memorization
- Availability of words derived from the same root (lazy, lazily, lazybones), allowing you to memorize word units instead of separate words
- Small units of words facilitate the process of establishing associative links needed for consolidation of vocabulary
- You can estimate the number of learned words and hence your level of language knowledge
- The dictionary allows for the creation of an effective and high-quality revision process
- You can revise certain themes several times, modifying the revision methods and techniques
- Audio versions of the dictionaries help you to work out the pronunciation of words and develop your skills of auditory word perception

The T&P Books' theme-based dictionaries are offered in several variants differing in the number of words: 1.500, 3.000, 5.000, 7.000, and 9.000 words. There are also dictionaries containing 15,000 words for some language combinations. Your choice of dictionary will depend on your knowledge level and goals.

We sincerely believe that our dictionaries will become your trusty assistant in learning foreign languages and will allow you to easily acquire the necessary vocabulary.

TABLE OF CONTENTS

PRONUNCIATION GUIDE

Letter	Norwegian example	T&P phonetic alphabet	English example
Aa	plass	[ɑ], [ɑ:]	bath, to pass
Bb	bøtte, albue	[b]	baby, book
Cc [1]	centimeter	[s]	city, boss
Cc [2]	Canada	[k]	clock, kiss
Dd	radius	[d]	day, doctor
Ee	rett	[e:]	longer than in bell
Ee [3]	begå	[ɛ]	man, bad
Ff	fattig	[f]	face, food
Gg [4]	golf	[g]	game, gold
Gg [5]	gyllen	[j]	yes, New York
Gg [6]	regnbue	[ŋ]	English, ring
Hh	hektar	[h]	humor
Ii	kilometer	[ɪ], [i]	tin, see
Kk	konge	[k]	clock, kiss
Kk [7]	kirke	[h]	humor
Jj	fjerde	[j]	yes, New York
kj	bikkje	[h]	humor
Ll	halvår	[l]	lace, people
Mm	middag	[m]	magic, milk
Nn	november	[n]	name, normal
ng	id_langt	[ŋ]	English, ring
Oo [8]	honning	[ɔ]	bottle, doctor
Oo [9]	fot, krone	[u]	book
Pp	plomme	[p]	pencil, private
Qq	sequoia	[k]	clock, kiss
Rr	sverge	[r]	rice, radio
Ss	appelsin	[s]	city, boss
sk [10]	skikk, skyte	[ʃ]	machine, shark
Tt	stør, torsk	[t]	tourist, trip
Uu	brudd	[y]	fuel, tuna
Vv	kraftverk	[v]	very, river
Ww	webside	[v]	very, river
Xx	mexicaner	[ks]	box, taxi
Yy	nytte	[ɪ], [i]	tin, see
Zz [11]	New Zealand	[s]	star, cats
Ææ	vær, stær	[æ]	chess, man

Letter	Norwegian example	T&P phonetic alphabet	English example
Øø	ørn, gjø	[ø]	eternal, church
Åå	gås, værhår	[o:]	fall, bomb

Comments

[1] before **e, i**
[2] elsewhere
[3] unstressed
[4] before **a, o, u, å**
[5] before **i** and **y**
[6] in combination **gn**
[7] before **i** and **y**
[8] before two consonants
[9] before one consonant
[10] before **i** and **y**
[11] in loanwords only

ABBREVIATIONS
used in the vocabulary

English abbreviations

ab.	-	about
adj	-	adjective
adv	-	adverb
anim.	-	animate
as adj	-	attributive noun used as adjective
e.g.	-	for example
etc.	-	et cetera
fam.	-	familiar
fem.	-	feminine
form.	-	formal
inanim.	-	inanimate
masc.	-	masculine
math	-	mathematics
mil.	-	military
n	-	noun
pl	-	plural
pron.	-	pronoun
sb	-	somebody
sing.	-	singular
sth	-	something
v aux	-	auxiliary verb
vi	-	intransitive verb
vi, vt	-	intransitive, transitive verb
vt	-	transitive verb

Norwegian abbreviations

f	-	feminine noun
f pl	-	feminine plural
m	-	masculine noun
m pl	-	masculine plural
m/f	-	masculine, neuter
m/f pl	-	masculine/feminine plural
m/f/n	-	masculine/feminine/neuter

m/n	-	masculine, feminine
n	-	neuter
n pl	-	neuter plural
pl	-	plural

BASIC CONCEPTS

Basic concepts. Part 1

1. Pronouns

I, me	jeg	['jæj]
you	du	[dʉ]
he	han	['han]
she	hun	['hʉn]
it	det, den	['de], ['den]
we	vi	['vi]
you (to a group)	dere	['derə]
they	de	['de]

2. Greetings. Salutations. Farewells

Hello! (fam.)	Hei!	['hæj]
Hello! (form.)	Hallo! God dag!	[ha'lʊ], [gʊ 'da]
Good morning!	God morn!	[gʊ 'mɔːn]
Good afternoon!	God dag!	[gʊ'da]
Good evening!	God kveld!	[gʊ 'kvɛl]
to say hello	å hilse	[ɔ 'hilsə]
Hi! (hello)	Hei!	['hæj]
greeting (n)	hilsen (m)	['hilsən]
to greet (vt)	å hilse	[ɔ 'hilsə]
How are you? (form.)	Hvordan står det til?	['vʊːdan stoːr de til]
How are you? (fam.)	Hvordan går det?	['vʊːdan gor de]
What's new?	Hva nytt?	[va 'nʏt]
Goodbye! (form.)	Ha det bra!	[ha de 'bra]
Bye! (fam.)	Ha det!	[ha 'de]
See you soon!	Vi ses!	[vi sɛs]
Farewell!	Farvel!	[far'vɛl]
to say goodbye	å si farvel	[ɔ 'si far'vɛl]
So long!	Ha det!	[ha 'de]
Thank you!	Takk!	['tak]
Thank you very much!	Tusen takk!	['tʉsən tak]
You're welcome	Bare hyggelig	['barə 'hʏgeli]

Don't mention it!	Ikke noe å takke for!	['ikə 'nʊe ɔ takə fɔr]
It was nothing	Ingen årsak!	['iŋən 'oːʂak]
Excuse me! (fam.)	Unnskyld, …	['ʉnˌʂyl …]
Excuse me! (form.)	Unnskyld meg, …	['ʉnˌʂyl me …]
to excuse (forgive)	å unnskylde	[ɔ 'ʉnˌʂylə]
to apologize (vi)	å unnskylde seg	[ɔ 'ʉnˌʂylə sæj]
My apologies	Jeg ber om unnskyldning	[jæj ber ɔm 'ʉnˌʂyldniŋ]
I'm sorry!	Unnskyld!	['ʉnˌʂyl]
to forgive (vt)	å tilgi	[ɔ 'tilˌji]
It's okay! (that's all right)	Ikke noe problem	['ikə 'nʊe prʊ'blem]
please (adv)	vær så snill	['vær ʂɔ 'snil]
Don't forget!	Ikke glem!	['ikə 'glem]
Certainly!	Selvfølgelig!	[sɛl'følgəli]
Of course not!	Selvfølgelig ikke!	[sɛl'følgəli 'ikə]
Okay! (I agree)	OK! Enig!	[ɔ'kɛj], ['ɛni]
That's enough!	Det er nok!	[de ær 'nɔk]

3. Cardinal numbers. Part 1

0 zero	null	['nʉl]
1 one	en	['en]
2 two	to	['tʊ]
3 three	tre	['tre]
4 four	fire	['fire]
5 five	fem	['fɛm]
6 six	seks	['sɛks]
7 seven	sju	['ʂʉ]
8 eight	åtte	['ɔtə]
9 nine	ni	['ni]
10 ten	ti	['ti]
11 eleven	elleve	['ɛlvə]
12 twelve	tolv	['tɔl]
13 thirteen	tretten	['trɛtən]
14 fourteen	fjorten	['fjɔːʈən]
15 fifteen	femten	['fɛmtən]
16 sixteen	seksten	['sæjstən]
17 seventeen	sytten	['sʏtən]
18 eighteen	atten	['atən]
19 nineteen	nitten	['nitən]
20 twenty	tjue	['çʉe]
21 twenty-one	tjueen	['çʉe en]
22 twenty-two	tjueto	['çʉe tʊ]

23 twenty-three	tjuetre	['çʉe tre]
30 thirty	tretti	['trɛti]
31 thirty-one	trettien	['trɛti en]
32 thirty-two	trettito	['trɛti tʉ]
33 thirty-three	trettitre	['trɛti tre]
40 forty	førti	['fœ:ţi]
41 forty-one	førtien	['fœ:ţi en]
42 forty-two	førtito	['fœ:ţi tʉ]
43 forty-three	førtitre	['fœ:ţi tre]
50 fifty	femti	['fɛmti]
51 fifty-one	femtien	['fɛmti en]
52 fifty-two	femtito	['fɛmti tʉ]
53 fifty-three	femtitre	['fɛmti tre]
60 sixty	seksti	['sɛksti]
61 sixty-one	sekstien	['sɛksti en]
62 sixty-two	sekstito	['sɛksti tʉ]
63 sixty-three	sekstitre	['sɛksti tre]
70 seventy	sytti	['sʏti]
71 seventy-one	syttien	['sʏti en]
72 seventy-two	syttito	['sʏti tʉ]
73 seventy-three	syttitre	['sʏti tre]
80 eighty	åtti	['ɔti]
81 eighty-one	åttien	['ɔti en]
82 eighty-two	åttito	['ɔti tʉ]
83 eighty-three	åttitre	['ɔti tre]
90 ninety	nitti	['niti]
91 ninety-one	nittien	['niti en]
92 ninety-two	nittito	['niti tʉ]
93 ninety-three	nittitre	['niti tre]

4. Cardinal numbers. Part 2

100 one hundred	hundre	['hʉndrə]
200 two hundred	to hundre	['tʉ ˌhʉndrə]
300 three hundred	tre hundre	['tre ˌhʉndrə]
400 four hundred	fire hundre	['fire ˌhʉndrə]
500 five hundred	fem hundre	['fɛm ˌhʉndrə]
600 six hundred	seks hundre	['sɛks ˌhʉndrə]
700 seven hundred	syv hundre	['syv ˌhʉndrə]
800 eight hundred	åtte hundre	['ɔtə ˌhʉndrə]
900 nine hundred	ni hundre	['ni ˌhʉndrə]
1000 one thousand	tusen	['tʉsən]
2000 two thousand	to tusen	['tʉ ˌtʉsən]

3000 three thousand	**tre tusen**	['tre ˌtʉsən]
10000 ten thousand	**ti tusen**	['ti ˌtʉsən]
one hundred thousand	**hundre tusen**	['hʉndrə ˌtʉsən]
million	**million** (m)	[mi'ljun]
billion	**milliard** (m)	[mi'lja:d]

5. Numbers. Fractions

fraction	**brøk** (m)	['brøk]
one half	**en halv**	[en 'hal]
one third	**en tredjedel**	[en 'trɛdjəˌdel]
one quarter	**en fjerdedel**	[en 'fjærə del]
one eighth	**en åttendedel**	[en 'ɔtenəˌdel]
one tenth	**en tiendedel**	[en 'tienəˌdel]
two thirds	**to tredjedeler**	['tʉ 'trɛdjə delər]
three quarters	**tre fjerdedeler**	['tre 'fjærˌdelər]

6. Numbers. Basic operations

subtraction	**subtraksjon** (m)	[sʉbtrak'ʂun]
to subtract (vi, vt)	**å subtrahere**	[ɔ 'sʉbtraˌherə]
division	**divisjon** (m)	[divi'ʂun]
to divide (vt)	**å dividere**	[ɔ divi'derə]
addition	**addisjon** (m)	[adi'ʂun]
to add up (vt)	**å addere**	[ɔ a'derə]
to add (vi, vt)	**å addere**	[ɔ a'derə]
multiplication	**multiplikasjon** (m)	[mʉltiplika'ʂun]
to multiply (vt)	**å multiplisere**	[ɔ mʉltipli'serə]

7. Numbers. Miscellaneous

digit, figure	**siffer** (n)	['sifər]
number	**tall** (n)	['tal]
numeral	**tallord** (n)	['talˌu:r]
minus sign	**minus** (n)	['minʉs]
plus sign	**pluss** (n)	['plʉs]
formula	**formel** (m)	['fɔrməl]
calculation	**beregning** (m/f)	[be'rɛjniŋ]
to count (vi, vt)	**å telle**	[ɔ 'tɛle]
to count up	**å telle opp**	[ɔ 'tɛlə ɔpˀ]
to compare (vt)	**å sammenlikne**	[ɔ 'samənˌliknə]
How much?	**Hvor mye?**	[vʉr 'mye]
How many?	**Hvor mange?**	[vʉr 'maŋə]

sum, total	sum (m)	['sʉm]
result	resultat (n)	[resʉl'tɑt]
remainder	rest (m)	['rɛst]

a few (e.g., ~ years ago)	noen	['nʉən]
few (I have ~ friends)	få, ikke mange	['fɔ], ['ikə ˌmɑŋə]
a little (~ tired)	lite	['litə]
the rest	rest (m)	['rɛst]
one and a half	halvannen	[hɑl'ɑnən]
dozen	dusin (n)	[dʉ'sin]

in half (adv)	i 2 halvdeler	[i tʉ hɑl'delər]
equally (evenly)	jevnt	['jɛvnt]
half	halvdel (m)	['hɑldel]
time (three ~s)	gang (m)	['gɑŋ]

8. The most important verbs. Part 1

to advise (vt)	å råde	[ɔ 'roːdə]
to agree (say yes)	å samtykke	[ɔ 'sɑmˌtʏkə]
to answer (vi, vt)	å svare	[ɔ 'svɑrə]
to apologize (vi)	å unnskylde seg	[ɔ 'ʉnˌsʏlə sæj]
to arrive (vi)	å ankomme	[ɔ 'ɑnˌkɔmə]

to ask (~ oneself)	å spørre	[ɔ 'spørə]
to ask (~ sb to do sth)	å be	[ɔ 'be]
to be (vi)	å være	[ɔ 'værə]

to be afraid	å frykte	[ɔ 'frʏktə]
to be hungry	å være sulten	[ɔ 'værə 'sʉltən]
to be interested in ...	å interessere seg	[ɔ intəre'serə sæj]
to be needed	å være behøv	[ɔ 'værə bə'høv]
to be surprised	å bli forundret	[ɔ 'bli fɔ'rʉndrət]

to be thirsty	å være tørst	[ɔ 'værə 'tœşt]
to begin (vt)	å begynne	[ɔ be'jinə]
to belong to ...	å tilhøre ...	[ɔ 'tilˌhørə ...]
to boast (vi)	å prale	[ɔ 'prɑlə]
to break (split into pieces)	å bryte	[ɔ 'brytə]

to call (~ for help)	å tilkalle	[ɔ 'tilˌkɑlə]
can (v aux)	å kunne	[ɔ 'kʉnə]
to catch (vt)	å fange	[ɔ 'fɑŋə]
to change (vt)	å endre	[ɔ 'ɛndrə]
to choose (select)	å velge	[ɔ 'vɛlgə]

to come down (the stairs)	å gå ned	[ɔ 'gɔ ne]
to compare (vt)	å sammenlikne	[ɔ 'sɑmənˌliknə]
to complain (vi, vt)	å klage	[ɔ 'klɑgə]
to confuse (mix up)	å forveksle	[ɔ fɔr'vɛkşlə]

| to continue (vt) | å fortsette | [ɔ 'fɔrt,sɛtə] |
| to control (vt) | å kontrollere | [ɔ kʉntrɔ'lərə] |

to cook (dinner)	å lage	[ɔ 'lagə]
to cost (vt)	å koste	[ɔ 'kɔstə]
to count (add up)	å telle	[ɔ 'tɛlə]
to count on ...	å regne med ...	[ɔ 'rɛjnə mɛ ...]
to create (vt)	å opprette	[ɔ 'ɔp,rɛtə]
to cry (weep)	å gråte	[ɔ 'groːtə]

9. The most important verbs. Part 2

to deceive (vi, vt)	å fuske	[ɔ 'fʉskə]
to decorate (tree, street)	å pryde	[ɔ 'prydə]
to defend (a country, etc.)	å forsvare	[ɔ fɔ'şvarə]
to demand (request firmly)	å kreve	[ɔ 'krevə]
to dig (vt)	å grave	[ɔ 'gravə]

to discuss (vt)	å diskutere	[ɔ diskʉ'terə]
to do (vt)	å gjøre	[ɔ 'jørə]
to doubt (have doubts)	å tvile	[ɔ 'tvilə]
to drop (let fall)	å tappe	[ɔ 'tapə]
to enter (room, house, etc.)	å komme inn	[ɔ 'komə in]

to excuse (forgive)	å unnskylde	[ɔ 'ʉn,sylə]
to exist (vi)	å eksistere	[ɔ ɛksi'sterə]
to expect (foresee)	å forutse	[ɔ 'forʉt,sə]
to explain (vt)	å forklare	[ɔ for'klarə]
to fall (vi)	å falle	[ɔ 'falə]

to find (vt)	å finne	[ɔ 'finə]
to finish (vt)	å slutte	[ɔ 'şlʉtə]
to fly (vi)	å fly	[ɔ 'fly]
to follow ... (come after)	å følge etter ...	[ɔ 'følə 'ɛtər ...]
to forget (vi, vt)	å glemme	[ɔ 'glemə]

to forgive (vt)	å tilgi	[ɔ 'til,ji]
to give (vt)	å gi	[ɔ 'ji]
to give a hint	å gi et vink	[ɔ 'ji et 'vink]
to go (on foot)	å gå	[ɔ 'gɔ]

to go for a swim	å bade	[ɔ 'badə]
to go out (for dinner, etc.)	å gå ut	[ɔ 'gɔ ʉt]
to guess (the answer)	å gjette	[ɔ 'jɛtə]

to have (vt)	å ha	[ɔ 'ha]
to have breakfast	å spise frokost	[ɔ 'spisə ,frʊkɔst]
to have dinner	å spise middag	[ɔ 'spisə 'mi,da]
to have lunch	å spise lunsj	[ɔ 'spisə ,lʉnş]

to hear (vt)	å høre	[ɔ 'hørə]
to help (vt)	å hjelpe	[ɔ 'jɛlpə]
to hide (vt)	å gjemme	[ɔ 'jɛmə]
to hope (vi, vt)	å håpe	[ɔ 'hoːpə]
to hunt (vi, vt)	å jage	[ɔ 'jagə]
to hurry (vi)	å skynde seg	[ɔ 'ʂynə sæj]

10. The most important verbs. Part 3

to inform (vt)	å informere	[ɔ infɔr'merə]
to insist (vi, vt)	å insistere	[ɔ insi'sterə]
to insult (vt)	å fornærme	[ɔ fɔː'ŋærmə]
to invite (vt)	å innby, å invitere	[ɔ 'inby], [ɔ invi'terə]
to joke (vi)	å spøke	[ɔ 'spøkə]

to keep (vt)	å beholde	[ɔ be'hɔlə]
to keep silent	å tie	[ɔ 'tie]
to kill (vt)	å døde, å myrde	[ɔ 'dødə], [ɔ 'myːdə]
to know (sb)	å kjenne	[ɔ 'çɛnə]
to know (sth)	å vite	[ɔ 'vitə]
to laugh (vi)	å le, å skratte	[ɔ 'le], [ɔ 'skratə]

to liberate (city, etc.)	å befri	[ɔ be'fri]
to like (I like ...)	å like	[ɔ 'likə]
to look for ... (search)	å søke ...	[ɔ 'søkə ...]
to love (sb)	å elske	[ɔ 'ɛlskə]
to make a mistake	å gjøre feil	[ɔ 'jørə ˌfæjl]

to manage, to run	å styre, å lede	[ɔ 'styrə], [ɔ 'ledə]
to mean (signify)	å bety	[ɔ 'bety]
to mention (talk about)	å omtale, å nevne	[ɔ 'ɔmˌtalə], [ɔ 'nɛvnə]
to miss (school, etc.)	å skulke	[ɔ 'skʉlkə]
to notice (see)	å bemerke	[ɔ be'mærkə]

to object (vi, vt)	å innvende	[ɔ 'inˌvɛnə]
to observe (see)	å observere	[ɔ obsɛr'verə]
to open (vt)	å åpne	[ɔ 'ɔpnə]
to order (meal, etc.)	å bestille	[ɔ be'stilə]
to order (mil.)	å beordre	[ɔ be'ɔrdrə]
to own (possess)	å besidde, å eie	[ɔ bɛ'sidə], [ɔ 'æjə]

to participate (vi)	å delta	[ɔ 'dɛlta]
to pay (vi, vt)	å betale	[ɔ be'talə]
to permit (vt)	å tillate	[ɔ 'tiˌlatə]
to plan (vt)	å planlegge	[ɔ 'planˌlegə]
to play (children)	å leke	[ɔ 'lekə]

to pray (vi, vt)	å be	[ɔ 'be]
to prefer (vt)	å foretrekke	[ɔ 'fɔrəˌtrɛkə]
to promise (vt)	å love	[ɔ 'lɔvə]

to pronounce (vt)	å uttale	[ɔ 'ʉtˌtalə]
to propose (vt)	å foreslå	[ɔ 'forəˌslɔ]
to punish (vt)	å straffe	[ɔ 'strafə]

11. The most important verbs. Part 4

to read (vi, vt)	å lese	[ɔ 'lesə]
to recommend (vt)	å anbefale	[ɔ 'anbeˌfalə]
to refuse (vi, vt)	å vegre seg	[ɔ 'vɛgrə sæj]
to regret (be sorry)	å beklage	[ɔ be'klagə]
to rent (sth from sb)	å leie	[ɔ 'læjə]

to repeat (say again)	å gjenta	[ɔ 'jɛnta]
to reserve, to book	å reservere	[ɔ resɛr'verə]
to run (vi)	å løpe	[ɔ 'løpə]
to save (rescue)	å redde	[ɔ 'redə]
to say (~ thank you)	å si	[ɔ 'si]

to scold (vt)	å skjelle	[ɔ 'ʂɛ:lə]
to see (vt)	å se	[ɔ 'se]
to sell (vt)	å selge	[ɔ 'sɛlə]
to send (vt)	å sende	[ɔ 'sɛnə]
to shoot (vi)	å skyte	[ɔ 'ʂytə]

to shout (vi)	å skrike	[ɔ 'skrikə]
to show (vt)	å vise	[ɔ 'visə]
to sign (document)	å underskrive	[ɔ 'ʉnəˌskrivə]
to sit down (vi)	å sette seg	[ɔ 'sɛtə sæj]

to smile (vi)	å smile	[ɔ 'smilə]
to speak (vi, vt)	å tale	[ɔ 'talə]
to steal (money, etc.)	å stjele	[ɔ 'stjelə]
to stop (for pause, etc.)	å stoppe	[ɔ 'stɔpə]
to stop (please ~ calling me)	å slutte	[ɔ 'ʂlʉtə]

to study (vt)	å studere	[ɔ stʉ'derə]
to swim (vi)	å svømme	[ɔ 'svœmə]
to take (vt)	å ta	[ɔ 'ta]
to think (vi, vt)	å tenke	[ɔ 'tɛnkə]
to threaten (vt)	å true	[ɔ 'trʉə]

to touch (with hands)	å røre	[ɔ 'rørə]
to translate (vt)	å oversette	[ɔ 'ɔvəˌsɛtə]
to trust (vt)	å stole på	[ɔ 'stʉlə pɔ]
to try (attempt)	å prøve	[ɔ 'prøvə]
to turn (e.g., ~ left)	å svinge	[ɔ 'sviŋə]

| to underestimate (vt) | å undervurdere | [ɔ 'ʉnərvʉːˌderə] |
| to understand (vt) | å forstå | [ɔ fo'ʂtɔ] |

| to unite (vt) | å forene | [ɔ fɔ'renə] |
| to wait (vt) | å vente | [ɔ 'vɛntə] |

to want (wish, desire)	å ville	[ɔ 'vilə]
to warn (vt)	å varsle	[ɔ 'vaʂlə]
to work (vi)	å arbeide	[ɔ 'ar̩bæjdə]
to write (vt)	å skrive	[ɔ 'skrivə]
to write down	å skrive ned	[ɔ 'skrivə ne]

12. Colors

color	farge (m)	['fargə]
shade (tint)	nyanse (m)	[ny'ansə]
hue	fargetone (m)	['fargə.tʉnə]
rainbow	regnbue (m)	['ræjn̩bʉːə]

white (adj)	hvit	['vit]
black (adj)	svart	['svaːʈ]
gray (adj)	grå	['grɔ]

green (adj)	grønn	['grœn]
yellow (adj)	gul	['gʉl]
red (adj)	rød	['rø]

blue (adj)	blå	['blɔ]
light blue (adj)	lyseblå	['lysə.blɔ]
pink (adj)	rosa	['rɔsa]
orange (adj)	oransje	[ɔ'ranʂɛ]
violet (adj)	fiolett	[fiʊ'lət]
brown (adj)	brun	['brʉn]

| golden (adj) | gullgul | ['gʉl] |
| silvery (adj) | sølv- | ['søl-] |

beige (adj)	beige	['bɛːʂ]
cream (adj)	kremfarget	['krɛm.fargət]
turquoise (adj)	turkis	[tʉr'kis]
cherry red (adj)	kirsebærrød	['çiʂəbær̩rød]
lilac (adj)	lilla	['lila]
crimson (adj)	karminrød	['karmʊ'sin̩rød]

light (adj)	lys	['lys]
dark (adj)	mørk	['mœrk]
bright, vivid (adj)	klar	['klar]

colored (pencils)	farge-	['fargə-]
color (e.g., ~ film)	farge-	['fargə-]
black-and-white (adj)	svart-hvit	['svaːʈ vit]
plain (one-colored)	ensfarget	['ɛns.fargət]
multicolored (adj)	mangefarget	['maŋə.fargət]

13. Questions

Who?	Hvem?	['vɛm]
What?	Hva?	['va]
Where? (at, in)	Hvor?	['vʊr]
Where (to)?	Hvorhen?	['vʊrhen]
From where?	Hvorfra?	['vʊrfra]
When?	Når?	[nɔr]
Why? (What for?)	Hvorfor?	['vʊrfʊr]
Why? (~ are you crying?)	Hvorfor?	['vʊrfʊr]
What for?	Hvorfor?	['vʊrfʊr]
How? (in what way)	Hvordan?	['vʊ:dan]
What? (What kind of ...?)	Hvilken?	['vilkən]
Which?	Hvilken?	['vilkən]
To whom?	Til hvem?	[til 'vɛm]
About whom?	Om hvem?	[ɔm 'vɛm]
About what?	Om hva?	[ɔm 'va]
With whom?	Med hvem?	[me 'vɛm]
How many?	Hvor mange?	[vʊr 'maŋə]
How much?	Hvor mye?	[vʊr 'mye]
Whose?	Hvis?	['vis]

14. Function words. Adverbs. Part 1

Where? (at, in)	Hvor?	['vʊr]
here (adv)	her	['hɛr]
there (adv)	der	['dɛr]
somewhere (to be)	et sted	[et 'sted]
nowhere (not anywhere)	ingensteds	['iŋən,stɛts]
by (near, beside)	ved	['ve]
by the window	ved vinduet	[ve 'vindʉə]
Where (to)?	Hvorhen?	['vʊrhen]
here (e.g., come ~!)	hit	['hit]
there (e.g., to go ~)	dit	['dit]
from here (adv)	herfra	['hɛr,fra]
from there (adv)	derfra	['dɛr,fra]
close (adv)	nær	['nær]
far (adv)	langt	['laŋt]
near (e.g., ~ Paris)	nær	['nær]
nearby (adv)	i nærheten	[i 'nær,hetən]
not far (adv)	ikke langt	['ikə 'laŋt]

left (adj)	venstre	['vɛnstrə]
on the left	til venstre	[til 'vɛnstrə]
to the left	til venstre	[til 'vɛnstrə]

right (adj)	høyre	['højrə]
on the right	til høyre	[til 'højrə]
to the right	til høyre	[til 'højrə]

in front (adv)	foran	['fɔrɑn]
front (as adj)	fremre	['frɛmrə]
ahead (the kids ran ~)	fram	['frɑm]

behind (adv)	bakom	['bɑkɔm]
from behind	bakfra	['bɑk‚frɑ]
back (towards the rear)	tilbake	[til'bɑkə]

| middle | midt (m) | ['mit] |
| in the middle | i midten | [i 'mitən] |

at the side	fra siden	[frɑ 'sidən]
everywhere (adv)	overalt	[ɔvər'ɑlt]
around (in all directions)	rundt omkring	['rʉnt ɔm'kriŋ]

from inside	innefra	['inə‚frɑ]
somewhere (to go)	et sted	[et 'sted]
straight (directly)	rett, direkte	['rɛt], ['di'rɛktə]
back (e.g., come ~)	tilbake	[til'bɑkə]

| from anywhere | et eller annet steds fra | [et 'elər ‚ɑ:nt 'stɛts frɑ] |
| from somewhere | et eller annet steds fra | [et 'elər ‚ɑ:nt 'stɛts frɑ] |

firstly (adv)	for det første	[for de 'fœştə]
secondly (adv)	for det annet	[for de 'ɑ:nt]
thirdly (adv)	for det tredje	[for de 'trɛdje]

suddenly (adv)	plutselig	['plʉtseli]
at first (in the beginning)	i begynnelsen	[i be'jinəlsən]
for the first time	for første gang	[for 'fœştə ‚gɑŋ]
long before ...	lenge før ...	['leŋə 'før ...]
anew (over again)	på nytt	[pɔ 'nʏt]
for good (adv)	for godt	[for 'gɔt]

never (adv)	aldri	['ɑldri]
again (adv)	igjen	[i'jɛn]
now (adv)	nå	['nɔ]
often (adv)	ofte	['ɔftə]
then (adv)	da	['dɑ]
urgently (quickly)	omgående	['ɔm‚gɔ:nə]
usually (adv)	vanligvis	['vɑnli‚vis]

| by the way, ... | forresten, ... | [fɔ'rɛstən ...] |
| possible (that is ~) | mulig, kanskje | ['mʉli], ['kɑnşə] |

probably (adv)	sannsynligvis	[san'synli,vis]
maybe (adv)	kanskje	['kanʂə]
besides ...	dessuten, ...	[des'ʉtən ...]
that's why ...	derfor ...	['dɛrfɔr ...]
in spite of ...	på tross av ...	['pɔ 'trɔs ɑ: ...]
thanks to ...	takket være ...	['takət ,værə ...]

what (pron.)	hva	['va]
that (conj.)	at	[at]
something	noe	['nʉe]
anything (something)	noe	['nʉe]
nothing	ingenting	['iŋəntiŋ]

who (pron.)	hvem	['vɛm]
someone	noen	['nʉən]
somebody	noen	['nʉən]

nobody	ingen	['iŋən]
nowhere (a voyage to ~)	ingensteds	['iŋən,stɛts]
nobody's	ingens	['iŋəns]
somebody's	noens	['nʉəns]

so (I'm ~ glad)	så	['sɔ:]
also (as well)	også	['ɔsɔ]
too (as well)	også	['ɔsɔ]

15. Function words. Adverbs. Part 2

Why?	Hvorfor?	['vʊrfʊr]
for some reason	av en eller annen grunn	[ɑ: en elər 'anən ,grʉn]
because ...	fordi ...	[fɔ'di ...]
for some purpose	av en eller annen grunn	[ɑ: en elər 'anən ,grʉn]

and	og	['ɔ]
or	eller	['elər]
but	men	['men]
for (e.g., ~ me)	for, til	[fɔr], [til]

too (~ many people)	for, altfor	['fɔr], ['altfɔr]
only (exclusively)	bare	['barə]
exactly (adv)	presis, eksakt	[prɛ'sis], [ɛk'sakt]
about (more or less)	cirka	['sirka]

approximately (adv)	omtrent	[ɔm'trɛnt]
approximate (adj)	omtrentlig	[ɔm'trɛntli]
almost (adv)	nesten	['nɛstən]
the rest	rest (m)	['rɛst]

| the other (second) | den annen | [den 'anən] |
| other (different) | andre | ['andrə] |

each (adj)	hver	['vɛr]
any (no matter which)	hvilken som helst	['vilkən sɔm 'hɛlst]
many, much (a lot of)	mye	['mye]
many people	mange	['maŋə]
all (everyone)	alle	['alə]

in return for ...	til gjengjeld for ...	[til 'jɛnjɛl fɔr ...]
in exchange (adv)	istedenfor	[i'steden,fɔr]
by hand (made)	for hånd	[fɔr 'hɔn]
hardly (negative opinion)	neppe	['nepə]

probably (adv)	sannsynligvis	[san'synli,vis]
on purpose (intentionally)	med vilje	[me 'viljə]
by accident (adv)	tilfeldigvis	[til'fɛldivis]

very (adv)	meget	['megət]
for example (adv)	for eksempel	[fɔr ɛk'sɛmpəl]
between	mellom	['mɛlom]
among	blant	['blant]
so much (such a lot)	så mye	['sɔ: mye]
especially (adv)	særlig	['sæ:l̩i]

Basic concepts. Part 2

16. Weekdays

Monday	**mandag** (m)	['manˌda]
Tuesday	**tirsdag** (m)	['tiʂˌda]
Wednesday	**onsdag** (m)	['ʊnsˌda]
Thursday	**torsdag** (m)	['tɔʂˌda]
Friday	**fredag** (m)	['frɛˌda]
Saturday	**lørdag** (m)	['løɾˌda]
Sunday	**søndag** (m)	['sønˌda]
today (adv)	**i dag**	[i 'da]
tomorrow (adv)	**i morgen**	[i 'mɔ:ən]
the day after tomorrow	**i overmorgen**	[i 'ɔvərˌmɔ:ən]
yesterday (adv)	**i går**	[i 'gɔr]
the day before yesterday	**i forgårs**	[i 'fɔrˌgɔʂ]
day	**dag** (r)	['da]
working day	**arbeidsdag** (m)	['arbæjdsˌda]
public holiday	**festdag** (m)	['fɛstˌda]
day off	**fridag** (m)	['friˌda]
weekend	**ukeslutt** (m), **helg** (f)	['ʉkəˌslʉt], ['hɛlg]
all day long	**hele dagen**	['helə 'dagən]
the next day (adv)	**neste dag**	['nɛstə ˌda]
two days ago	**for to dager siden**	[for tʊ 'dagər ˌsidən]
the day before	**dagen før**	['dagən 'før]
daily (adj)	**daglig**	['dagli]
every day (adv)	**hver dag**	['vɛr da]
week	**uke** (m/f)	['ʉkə]
last week (adv)	**siste uke**	['sistə 'ʉkə]
next week (adv)	**i neste uke**	[i 'nɛstə 'ʉkə]
weekly (adj)	**ukentlig**	['ʉkəntli]
every week (adv)	**hver uke**	['vɛr 'ʉkə]
twice a week	**to ganger per uke**	['tʊ 'gaŋər pər 'ʉkə]
every Tuesday	**hver tirsdag**	['vɛr 'tiʂda]

17. Hours. Day and night

morning	**morgen** (m)	['mɔ:ən]
in the morning	**om morgenen**	[ɔm 'mɔ:enən]
noon, midday	**middag** (m)	['miˌda]

in the afternoon	om ettermiddagen	[ɔm 'ɛtər‚midagən]
evening	kveld (m)	['kvɛl]
in the evening	om kvelden	[ɔm 'kvɛlən]
night	natt (m/f)	['nat]
at night	om natta	[ɔm 'nata]
midnight	midnatt (m/f)	['mid‚nat]
second	sekund (m/n)	[se'kʉn]
minute	minutt (n)	[mi'nʉt]
hour	time (m)	['timə]
half an hour	halvtime (m)	['hal‚timə]
a quarter-hour	kvarter (n)	[kva:‚ter]
fifteen minutes	femten minutter	['fɛmtən mi'nʉtər]
24 hours	døgn (n)	['døjn]
sunrise	soloppgang (m)	['sʉlɔp‚gaŋ]
dawn	daggry (n)	['dag‚gry]
early morning	tidlig morgen (m)	['tili 'mɔ:ən]
sunset	solnedgang (m)	['sʉlned‚gaŋ]
early in the morning	tidlig om morgenen	['tili ɔm 'mɔ:enən]
this morning	i morges	[i 'mɔrəs]
tomorrow morning	i morgen tidlig	[i 'mɔ:ən 'tili]
this afternoon	i formiddag	[i 'fɔrmi‚da]
in the afternoon	om ettermiddagen	[ɔm 'ɛtər‚midagən]
tomorrow afternoon	i morgen ettermiddag	[i 'mɔ:ən 'ɛtər‚mida]
tonight (this evening)	i kveld	[i 'kvɛl]
tomorrow night	i morgen kveld	[i 'mɔ:ən ‚kvɛl]
at 3 o'clock sharp	presis klokka tre	[prɛ'sis 'klɔka tre]
about 4 o'clock	ved fire-tiden	[ve 'fire ‚tidən]
by 12 o'clock	innen klokken tolv	['inən 'klɔkən tɔl]
in 20 minutes	om tjue minutter	[ɔm 'çʉə mi'nʉtər]
in an hour	om en time	[ɔm en 'timə]
on time (adv)	i tide	[i 'tidə]
a quarter of …	kvart på …	['kva:ʈ pɔ …]
within an hour	innen en time	['inən en 'timə]
every 15 minutes	hvert kvarter	['vɛːʈ kva:'ʈer]
round the clock	døgnet rundt	['døjne ‚rʉnt]

18. Months. Seasons

January	januar (m)	['janʉ‚ar]
February	februar (m)	['febrʉ‚ar]
March	mars (m)	['maʂ]
April	april (m)	[a'pril]
May	mai (m)	['maj]
June	juni (m)	['jʉni]

July	juli (n)	['juli]
August	august (m)	[au'gʊst]
September	september (m)	[sep'tɛmber]
October	oktober (m)	[ɔk'tʊbər]
November	november (m)	[nʊ'vɛmbər]
December	desember (m)	[de'sɛmbər]
spring	vår (m)	['vɔːr]
in spring	om våren	[ɔm 'voːrɛn]
spring (as adj)	vår-, vårlig	['vɔːr-], ['vɔːli]
summer	sommer (m)	['sɔmər]
in summer	om sommeren	[ɔm 'sɔmerən]
summer (as adj)	sommer-	['sɔmər-]
fall	høst (m)	['høst]
in fall	om høsten	[ɔm 'høstən]
fall (as adj)	høst-, høstlig	['høst-], ['høstli]
winter	vinter (m)	['vintər]
in winter	om vinteren	[ɔm 'vinterən]
winter (as adj)	vinter-	['vintər-]
month	måned (m)	['moːnət]
this month	denne måneden	['dɛnə 'moːnedən]
next month	neste måned	['nɛstə 'mɔːnət]
last month	forrige måned	['fɔriə ˌmɔːnət]
a month ago	for en måned siden	[fɔr en 'mɔːnət ˌsidən]
in a month (a month later)	om en måned	[ɔm en 'mɔːnət]
in 2 months (2 months later)	om to måneder	[ɔm 'tʊ 'moːnedər]
the whole month	en hel måned	[en 'hel 'moːnət]
all month long	hele måned	['helə 'mɔːnət]
monthly (~ magazine)	månedlig	['moːnədl]
monthly (adv)	månedligt	['moːnedlət]
every month	hver måned	[ˌvɛr 'moːnət]
twice a month	to ganger per måned	['tʊ 'ɡɑŋər per 'moːnət]
year	år (r)	['ɔr]
this year	i år	[i 'oːr]
next year	neste år	['nɛstə ˌoːr]
last year	i fjor	[i 'fjɔr]
a year ago	for et år siden	[fɔr et 'oːr ˌsidən]
in a year	om et år	[ɔm et 'oːr]
in two years	om to år	[ɔm 'tʊ 'oːr]
the whole year	hele året	['helə 'oːrə]
all year long	hele året	['helə 'oːrə]
every year	hvert år	['vɛːt 'oːr]

annual (adj)	årlig	['oːḷi]
annually (adv)	årlig, hvert år	['oːḷi], ['vɛːt 'ɔr]
4 times a year	fire ganger per år	['fire 'gɑŋər per 'oːr]

date (e.g., today's ~)	dato (m)	['dɑtʊ]
date (e.g., ~ of birth)	dato (m)	['dɑtʊ]
calendar	kalender (m)	[kɑ'lendər]

half a year	halvår (n)	['hɑḷoːr]
six months	halvår (n)	['hɑḷoːr]
season (summer, etc.)	årstid (m/f)	['oːs̩tid]
century	århundre (n)	['ɔr̩hʉndrə]

19. Time. Miscellaneous

time	tid (m/f)	['tid]
moment	øyeblikk (n)	['øjə̩blik]
instant (n)	øyeblikk (n)	['øjə̩blik]
instant (adj)	øyeblikkelig	['øjə̩blikəli]
lapse (of time)	tidsavsnitt (n)	['tids̩ɑfsnit]
life	liv (n)	['liv]
eternity	evighet (m)	['ɛvi̩het]

epoch	epoke (m)	[ɛ'pʊkə]
era	æra (m)	['ærɑ]
cycle	syklus (m)	['syklʉs]
period	periode (m)	[pæri'ʉdə]
term (short-~)	sikt (m)	['sikt]

the future	framtid (m/f)	['frɑm̩tid]
future (as adj)	framtidig, fremtidig	['frɑm̩tidi], ['frɛm̩tidi]
next time	neste gang	['nɛstə ̩gɑŋ]
the past	fortid (m/f)	['foː̩tid]
past (recent)	forrige	['foriə]
last time	siste gang	['sistə ̩gɑŋ]

later (adv)	senere	['senerə]
after (prep.)	etterpå	['ɛtər̩po]
nowadays (adv)	for nærværende	[for 'nær̩værnə]
now (adv)	nå	['nɔ]
immediately (adv)	umiddelbart	['ʉmidəḷ̩bɑːt]
soon (adv)	snart	['snɑːt]
in advance (beforehand)	på forhånd	[po 'foːr̩hon]

a long time ago	for lenge siden	[for 'leŋə ̩sidən]
recently (adv)	nylig	['nyli]
destiny	skjebne (m)	['ʂɛbnə]
memories (childhood ~)	minner (n pl)	['minər]
archives	arkiv (n)	[ɑr'kiv]
during ...	under ...	['ʉnər ...]

long, a long time (adv)	lenge	['leŋə]
not long (adv)	ikke lenge	['ikə 'leŋə]
early (in the morning)	tidlig	['tili]
late (not early)	sent	['sɛnt]

forever (for good)	for alltid	[fɔr 'al̩ˌtid]
to start (begin)	å begynne	[ɔ be'jinə]
to postpone (vt)	å utsette	[ɔ 'ʉtˌsɛtə]

at the same time	samtidig	['samˌtidi]
permanently (adv)	alltid, stadig	['al̩ˌtid], ['stadi]
constant (noise, pain)	konstant	[kʉn'stant]
temporary (adj)	midlertidig, temporær	['midləˌtidi], ['tɛmpɔˌrær]
sometimes (adv)	av og til	['av ɔ ˌtil]
rarely (adv)	sjelden	['sɛlən]
often (adv)	ofte	['ɔftə]

20. Opposites

| rich (adj) | rik | ['rik] |
| poor (adj) | fattig | ['fati] |

| ill, sick (adj) | syk | ['syk] |
| well (not sick) | frisk | ['frisk] |

| big (adj) | stor | ['stʉr] |
| small (adj) | liten | ['litən] |

| quickly (adv) | fort | ['fʉːt] |
| slowly (adv) | langsomt | ['laŋsɔmt] |

| fast (adj) | hurtig | ['høːti] |
| slow (adj) | langsom | ['laŋsɔm] |

| glad (adj) | glad | ['gla] |
| sad (adj) | sørgmodig | [sør'mʉdiˈ] |

| together (adv) | sammen | ['samən] |
| separately (adv) | separat | [sepa'rat] |

| aloud (to read) | høyt | ['højt] |
| silently (to oneself) | for seg selv | [fɔr sæj 'sɛl] |

| tall (adj) | høy | ['høj] |
| low (adj) | lav | ['lav] |

| deep (adj) | dyp | ['dyp] |
| shallow (adj) | grunn | ['grʉn] |

| yes | ja | ['ja] |

no	nei	['næj]

| distant (in space) | fjern | ['fjæːn̩] |
| nearby (adj) | nær | ['nær] |

| far (adv) | langt | ['lɑŋt] |
| nearby (adv) | i nærheten | [i 'nær̩ˌhetən] |

| long (adj) | lang | ['lɑŋ] |
| short (adj) | kort | ['kuːt] |

| good (kindhearted) | god | ['gʊ] |
| evil (adj) | ond | ['ʊn] |

| married (adj) | gift | ['jift] |
| single (adj) | ugift | [ʉː'jift] |

| to forbid (vt) | å forby | [ɔ forˈby] |
| to permit (vt) | å tillate | [ɔ 'tiˌlɑtə] |

| end | slutt (m) | ['ʂlʉt] |
| beginning | begynnelse (m) | [be'jinəlsə] |

| left (adj) | venstre | ['vɛnstrə] |
| right (adj) | høyre | ['højrə] |

| first (adj) | første | ['fœʂtə] |
| last (adj) | sist | ['sist] |

| crime | forbrytelse (m) | [for'brytəlsə] |
| punishment | straff (m) | ['strɑf] |

| to order (vt) | å beordre | [ɔ be'ordrə] |
| to obey (vi, vt) | å underordne seg | [ɔ 'ʉnərˌordnə sæj] |

| straight (adj) | rett | ['rɛt] |
| curved (adj) | kroket | ['krɔkət] |

| paradise | paradis (n) | ['pɑrɑˌdis] |
| hell | helvete (n) | ['hɛlvetə] |

| to be born | å fødes | [ɔ 'fødə] |
| to die (vi) | å dø | [ɔ 'dø] |

| strong (adj) | sterk | ['stærk] |
| weak (adj) | svak | ['svɑk] |

| old (adj) | gammel | ['gɑməl] |
| young (adj) | ung | ['ʉŋ] |

| old (adj) | gammel | ['gɑməl] |
| new (adj) | ny | ['ny] |

hard (adj)	**hard**	['hɑr]
soft (adj)	**bløt**	['bløt]
warm (tepid)	**varm**	['vɑrm]
cold (adj)	**kald**	['kɑl]
fat (adj)	**tykk**	['tʏk]
thin (adj)	**tynn**	['tʏn]
narrow (adj)	**smal**	['smɑl]
wide (adj)	**bred**	['bre]
good (adj)	**bra**	['brɑ]
bad (adj)	**dårlig**	['doːli]
brave (adj)	**tapper**	['tɑpər]
cowardly (adj)	**feig**	['fæjg]

21. Lines and shapes

square	**kvadrat** (n)	[kvɑ'drɑt]
square (as adj)	**kvadratisk**	[kvɑ'drɑtisk]
circle	**sirkel** (m)	['sirkəl]
round (adj)	**rund**	['rʉn]
triangle	**trekart** (m)	['treˌkant]
triangular (adj)	**trekartet**	['treˌkantət]
oval	**oval** (m)	[ʊ'vɑl]
oval (as adj)	**oval**	[ʊ'vɑl]
rectangle	**rektangel** (n)	['rɛkˌtɑŋəl]
rectangular (adj)	**rettvinklet**	['rɛtˌvinklət]
pyramid	**pyramide** (m)	[pyrɑ'midə]
rhombus	**rombe** (m)	['rʊmbə]
trapezoid	**trapes** (m/n)	[trɑ'pes]
cube	**kube, terning** (m)	['kʉbə], ['tæːŋiŋ]
prism	**prisme** (n)	['prismə]
circumference	**omkrets** (m)	['ɔmˌkrɛts]
sphere	**sfære** (m)	['sfærə]
ball (solid sphere)	**kule** (m/f)	['kʉːlə]
diameter	**diameter** (m)	['diɑˌmetər]
radius	**radius** (m)	['rɑdiʉs]
perimeter (circle's ~)	**perimeter** (n)	[peri'metər]
center	**midtpunkt** (n)	['mitˌpʉnkt]
horizontal (adj)	**horisontal**	[hʉrisɔn'tɑl]
vertical (adj)	**loddrett, lodd-**	['lɔdˌrɛt], ['lɔd-]
parallel (n)	**parallell** (m)	[pɑrɑ'lel]
parallel (as adj)	**parallell**	[pɑrɑ'lel]

line	linje (m)	['linjə]
stroke	strek (m)	['strek]
straight line	rett linje (m/f)	['rɛt 'linjə]
curve (curved line)	kurve (m)	['kʉrvə]
thin (line, etc.)	tynn	['tʏn]
contour (outline)	kontur (m)	[kʊn'tʉr]

intersection	skjæringspunkt (n)	['særiŋs‚pʉnkt]
right angle	rett vinkel (m)	['rɛt 'vinkəl]
segment	segment (n)	[seg'mɛnt]
sector	sektor (m)	['sɛktʉr]
side (of triangle)	side (m/f)	['sidə]
angle	vinkel (m)	['vinkəl]

22. Units of measurement

weight	vekt (m)	['vɛkt]
length	lengde (m/f)	['leŋdə]
width	bredde (m)	['brɛdə]
height	høyde (m)	['højdə]
depth	dybde (m)	['dʏbdə]
volume	volum (n)	[vɔ'lʉm]
area	areal (n)	[‚arɛ'ɑl]

gram	gram (n)	['grɑm]
milligram	milligram (n)	['mili‚grɑm]
kilogram	kilogram (n)	['çilu‚grɑm]
ton	tonn (m/n)	['tɔn]
pound	pund (n)	['pʉn]
ounce	unse (m)	['ʉnsə]

meter	meter (m)	['metər]
millimeter	millimeter (m)	['mili‚metər]
centimeter	centimeter (m)	['sɛnti‚metər]
kilometer	kilometer (m)	['çilu‚metər]
mile	mil (m/f)	['mil]

inch	tomme (m)	['tɔmə]
foot	fot (m)	['fʊt]
yard	yard (m)	['jɑ:rd]

square meter	kvadratmeter (m)	[kvɑ'drɑt‚metər]
hectare	hektar (n)	['hɛktɑr]

liter	liter (m)	['litər]
degree	grad (m)	['grɑd]
volt	volt (m)	['vɔlt]
ampere	ampere (m)	[am'pɛr]
horsepower	hestekraft (m/f)	['hɛstə‚krɑft]
quantity	mengde (m)	['mɛŋdə]

a little bit of ...	få ...	['fɔ ...]
half	halvdel (m)	['haldel]
dozen	dusin (n)	[dʉ'sin]
piece (item)	stykke (n)	['stʏkə]

size	størrelse (m)	['stœrəlsɛ]
scale (map ~)	målestokk (m)	['moːlə‚stɔk]

minimal (adj)	minimal	[mini'mɑl]
the smallest (adj)	minste	['minstə]
medium (adj)	middel-	['midəl-]
maximal (adj)	maksimal	[mɑksi'mɑl]
the largest (adj)	største	['stœɛstə]

23. Containers

canning jar (glass ~)	glaskrukke (m/f)	['glɑs‚krʉkə]
can	boks (m)	['bɔks]
bucket	bøtte (m/f)	['bœtə]
barrel	tønne (m)	['tœnə]

wash basin (e.g., plastic ~)	vaskefat (n)	['vɑskə‚fɑː]
tank (100L water ~)	tank (m)	['tɑnk]
hip flask	lommelerke (m/f)	['lʉmə‚lærkə]
jerrycan	bensinkanne (m/f)	[bɛn'sin‚kɑnə]
tank (e.g., tank car)	tank (m)	['tɑnk]

mug	krus (n)	['krʉs]
cup (of coffee, etc.)	kopp (m)	['kɔp]
saucer	tefat (n)	['te‚fɑt]
glass (tumbler)	glass (n)	['glɑs]
wine glass	vinglass (n)	['vin‚glɑs]
stock pot (soup pot)	gryte (m/f)	['grytə]

bottle (~ of wine)	flaske (m)	['flɑskə]
neck (of the bottle, etc.)	flaskehals (m)	['flɑskə‚hɑls]

carafe (decanter)	karaffel (m)	[kɑ'rɑfəl]
pitcher	mugge (m/f)	['mʉgə]
vessel (container)	beholder (m)	[be'hɔlər]
pot (crock, stoneware ~)	pott, potte (m)	['pɔt], ['pɔtə]
vase	vase (m)	['vɑsə]

bottle (perfume ~)	flakong (m)	[flɑ'kɔŋ]
vial, small bottle	flaske (m/f)	['flɑskə]
tube (of toothpaste)	tube (m)	['tʉbə]

sack (bag)	sekk (m)	['sɛk]
bag (paper ~, plastic ~)	pose (m)	['pʉsə]
pack (of cigarettes, etc.)	pakke (m/f)	['pɑkə]

box (e.g., shoebox)	eske (m/f)	['ɛskə]
crate	kasse (m/f)	['kasə]
basket	kurv (m)	['kʉrv]

24. Materials

material	materiale (n)	[materi'alə]
wood (n)	tre (n)	['trɛ]
wood-, wooden (adj)	tre-, av tre	['trɛ-], [a: 'trɛ]
glass (n)	glass (n)	['glɑs]
glass (as adj)	glass-	['glɑs-]
stone (n)	stein (m)	['stæjn]
stone (as adj)	stein-	['stæjn-]
plastic (n)	plast (m)	['plɑst]
plastic (as adj)	plast-	['plɑst-]
rubber (n)	gummi (m)	['gʉmi]
rubber (as adj)	gummi-	['gʉmi-]
cloth, fabric (n)	tøy (n)	['tøj]
fabric (as adj)	tøy-	['tøj-]
paper (n)	papir (n)	[pa'pir]
paper (as adj)	papir-	[pa'pir-]
cardboard (n)	papp, kartong (m)	['pɑp], [ka:'ʈɔŋ]
cardboard (as adj)	papp-, kartong-	['pɑp-], [ka:'ʈɔŋ-]
polyethylene	polyetylen (n)	['pʉlyɛty,len]
cellophane	cellofan (m)	[sɛlu'fan]
linoleum	linoleum (m)	[li'nɔleum]
plywood	kryssfiner (m)	['krʏsfi,nɛr]
porcelain (n)	porselen (n)	[pɔʂə'len]
porcelain (as adj)	porselens-	[pɔʂə'lens-]
clay (n)	leir (n)	['læjr]
clay (as adj)	leir-	['læjr-]
ceramic (n)	keramikk (m)	[çera'mik]
ceramic (as adj)	keramisk	[çe'ramisk]

25. Metals

metal (n)	metall (n)	[me'tal]
metal (as adj)	metall-	[me'tal-]
alloy (n)	legering (m/f)	[le'geriŋ]

gold (n)	gull (n)	['gʉl]
gold, golden (adj)	av gull, gull-	[ɑ: 'gʉl], ['gʉl-]
silver (n)	sølv (n)	['søl]
silver (as adj)	sølv-, av sølv	['søl-], [ɑ: 'søl]
iron (n)	jern (n)	['jæ:ŋ]
iron-, made of iron (adj)	jern-	['jæ:ŋ-]
steel (n)	stål (n)	['stɔl]
steel (as adj)	stål-	['stɔl-]
copper (n)	kobber (n)	['kɔbər]
copper (as adj)	kobber-	['kɔbər-]
aluminum (n)	aluminium (n)	[ɑlu'minium]
aluminum (as adj)	aluminium-	[ɑlu'minium-]
bronze (n)	bronse (m)	['brɔnsə]
bronze (as adj)	bronse-	['brɔnsə-]
brass	messing (m)	['mɛsiŋ]
nickel	nikkel (m)	['nikəl]
platinum	platina (m/n)	['plɑtinɑ]
mercury	kvikksølv (n)	['kvik‚søl]
tin	tinn (n)	['tin]
lead	bly (n)	['bly]
zinc	sink (m/n)	['sink]

HUMAN BEING

Human being. The body

26. Humans. Basic concepts

human being	menneske (n)	['mɛnəskə]
man (adult male)	mann (m)	['man]
woman	kvinne (m/f)	['kvinə]
child	barn (n)	['bɑːɳ]
girl	jente (m/f)	['jɛntə]
boy	gutt (m)	['gʉt]
teenager	tenåring (m)	['tɛnoːriŋ]
old man	eldre mann (m)	['ɛldrə ˌman]
old woman	eldre kvinne (m/f)	['ɛldrə ˌkvinə]

27. Human anatomy

organism (body)	organisme (m)	[ɔrgɑ'nismə]
heart	hjerte (n)	['jæːʈə]
blood	blod (n)	['blʉ]
artery	arterie (m)	[ɑːˈʈeriə]
vein	vene (m)	['veːnə]
brain	hjerne (m)	['jæːɳə]
nerve	nerve (m)	['nærvə]
nerves	nerver (m pl)	['nærvər]
vertebra	ryggvirvel (m)	['ryɡˌvirvəl]
spine (backbone)	ryggrad (m)	['ryɡˌrɑd]
stomach (organ)	magesekk (m)	['mɑɡəˌsɛk]
intestines, bowels	innvoller, tarmer (m pl)	['inˌvɔlər], ['tɑrmər]
intestine (e.g., large ~)	tarm (m)	['tɑrm]
liver	lever (m)	['levər]
kidney	nyre (m/n)	['nyrə]
bone	bein (n)	['bæjn]
skeleton	skjelett (n)	[ʂe'let]
rib	ribbein (n)	['ribˌbæjn]
skull	hodeskalle (m)	['hʉdəˌskɑlə]
muscle	muskel (m)	['mʉskəl]
biceps	biceps (m)	['bisɛps]

triceps	triceps (m)	['trisɛps]
tendon	sene (m/f)	['seːnə]
joint	ledd (n)	['led]
lungs	lunger (m pl)	['lʉŋər]
genitals	kjønnsorganer (n pl)	['çœnsˌɔrˈgɔnər]
skin	hud (m/f)	['hʉd]

28. Head

head	hode (n)	['hʉdə]
face	ansikt (n)	['ansikt]
nose	nese (m/f)	['nese]
mouth	munn (m)	['mʉn]

eye	øye (r.)	['øjə]
eyes	øyne (n pl)	['øjnə]
pupil	pupill (m)	[pʉ'pil]
eyebrow	øyenbryn (n)	['øjənˌbryn]
eyelash	øyenvipp (m)	['øjənˌvip]
eyelid	øyelokk (m)	['øjəˌlɔk]

tongue	tunge (m/f)	['tʉŋə]
tooth	tann (m/f)	['tan]
lips	lepper (m/f pl)	['lepər]
cheekbones	kinnbein (n pl)	['çinˌbæjn]
gum	tannkjøtt (n)	['tanˌçœt]
palate	gane (m)	['gɑnə]

nostrils	nesebor (n pl)	['nesəˌbʉr]
chin	hake (m/f)	['hɑkə]
jaw	kjeve (m)	['çɛvə]
cheek	kinn (n)	['çin]

forehead	panne (m/f)	['panə]
temple	tinning (m)	['tiniŋ]
ear	øre (n)	['ørə]
back of the head	bakhode (n)	['bakˌhʉdə]
neck	hals (m)	['hals]
throat	strupe, hals (m)	['strʉpə], ['hals]

hair	hår (n pl)	['hɔr]
hairstyle	frisyre (m)	[fri'syrə]
haircut	hårfasong (m)	['hoːrfaˌsɔŋ]
wig	parykk (m)	pa'rʏk]

mustache	mustasje (m)	[mʉ'stɑʂə]
beard	skjegg (n)	['ʂɛg]
to have (a beard, etc.)	å ha	[ɔ 'ha]
braid	flette (m/f)	['fletə]
sideburns	bakkenbarter (pl)	['bakənˌbaːțər]

red-haired (adj)	rødhåret	['rø‚ho:rət]
gray (hair)	grå	['grɔ]
bald (adj)	skallet	['skalət]
bald patch	skallet flekk (m)	['skalət ‚flek]

| ponytail | hestehale (m) | ['hɛstə‚halə] |
| bangs | pannelugg (m) | ['panə‚lʉg] |

29. Human body

hand	hånd (m/f)	['hɔn]
arm	arm (m)	['arm]
finger	finger (m)	['fiŋər]
toe	tå (m/f)	['tɔ]
thumb	tommel (m)	['tɔməl]
little finger	lillefinger (m)	['lilə‚fiŋər]
nail	negl (m)	['nɛjl]

fist	knyttneve (m)	['knʏt‚nevə]
palm	håndflate (m/f)	['hɔn‚flatə]
wrist	håndledd (n)	['hɔn‚led]
forearm	underarm (m)	['ʉnər‚arm]
elbow	albue (m)	['al‚bʉə]
shoulder	skulder (m)	['skʉldər]

leg	bein (n)	['bæjn]
foot	fot (m)	['fʊt]
knee	kne (n)	['knɛ]
calf (part of leg)	legg (m)	['leg]
hip	hofte (m)	['hoftə]
heel	hæl (m)	['hæl]

body	kropp (m)	['krɔp]
stomach	mage (m)	['magə]
chest	bryst (n)	['brʏst]
breast	bryst (n)	['brʏst]
flank	side (m/f)	['sidə]
back	rygg (m)	['rʏg]
lower back	korsrygg (m)	['kɔ:ʂ‚rʏg]
waist	liv (n), midje (m/f)	['liv], ['midjə]

navel (belly button)	navle (m)	['navlə]
buttocks	rumpeballer (m pl)	['rʉmpə‚balər]
bottom	bak (m)	['bak]

beauty mark	føflekk (m)	['fø‚flek]
birthmark (café au lait spot)	fødselsmerke (n)	['føtsəls‚mærke]
tattoo	tatovering (m/f)	[tatʉ'vɛriŋ]
scar	arr (n)	['ar]

Clothing & Accessories

30. Outerwear. Coats

clothes	klær (n)	['klær]
outerwear	yttertøy (n)	['ytə̩tøj]
winter clothing	vinterklær (n pl)	['vintər‚klær]
coat (overcoat)	frakk (m), kåpe (m/f)	['frɑk], ['ko:pə]
fur coat	pels (m), pelskåpe (m/f)	['pɛls], ['pɛls‚ko:pə]
fur jacket	pelsjakke (m/f)	['pɛls‚jakə]
down coat	dunjakke (m/f)	['dʉn‚jakə]
jacket (e.g., leather ~)	jakke (m/f)	['jakə]
raincoat (trenchcoat, etc.)	regnfrakk (m)	['ræjn‚frɑk]
waterproof (adj)	vanntett	['vɑn‚tɛt]

31. Men's & women's clothing

shirt (button shirt)	skjorte (m/f)	['sœ:tə]
pants	bukse (m)	['bʉksə]
jeans	jeans (m)	['dʒins]
suit jacket	dressjakke (m/f)	['drɛs‚jakə]
suit	dress (m)	['drɛs]
dress (frock)	kjole (m)	['çulə]
skirt	skjørt (n)	['sø:t]
blouse	bluse (m)	['blʉsə]
knitted jacket (cardigan, etc.)	strikket trøye (m/f)	['strikə 'trøjə]
jacket (of woman's suit)	blazer (m)	['blæsər]
T-shirt	T-skjorte (m/f)	['te‚sœ:tə]
shorts (short trousers)	shorts (m)	['sɔ:ts]
tracksuit	treningsdrakt (m/f)	['treniŋs‚drɑkt]
bathrobe	badekåpe (m/f)	['bɑdə‚ko:pə]
pajamas	pyjamas (m)	[py'sɑmɑs]
sweater	sweater (m)	['svɛtər]
pullover	pullover (m)	[pʉ'lɔvər]
vest	vest (m)	['vɛst]
tailcoat	livkjole (m)	['liv‚çulə]
tuxedo	smoking (m)	['smɔkiŋ]

uniform	uniform (m)	[ʉni'fɔrm]
workwear	arbeidsklær (n pl)	['ɑrbæjds̩klær]
overalls	kjeledress, overall (m)	['çelə̩drɛs], ['ɔvɛr̩ɔl]
coat (e.g., doctor's smock)	kittel (m)	['çitəl]

32. Clothing. Underwear

underwear	undertøy (n)	['ʉnə̩tøj]
boxers, briefs	underbukse (m/f)	['ʉnər̩bʉksə]
panties	truse (m/f)	['trʉsə]
undershirt (A-shirt)	undertrøye (m/f)	['ʉnə̩trøjə]
socks	sokker (m pl)	['sɔkər]
nightgown	nattkjole (m)	['nat̩çulə]
bra	behå (m)	['be̩hɔ]
knee highs (knee-high socks)	knestrømper (m/f pl)	['knɛ̩strømpər]
pantyhose	strømpebukse (m/f)	['strømpə̩bʉksə]
stockings (thigh highs)	strømper (m/f pl)	['strømpər]
bathing suit	badedrakt (m/f)	['badə̩drakt]

33. Headwear

hat	hatt (m)	['hat]
fedora	hatt (m)	['hat]
baseball cap	baseball cap (m)	['bɛjsbɔl kɛp]
flatcap	sikspens (m)	['sikspens]
beret	alpelue, baskerlue (m/f)	['alpə̩lʉə], ['baskə̩lʉə]
hood	hette (m/f)	['hɛtə]
panama hat	panamahatt (m)	['panamɑ̩hat]
knit cap (knitted hat)	strikket lue (m/f)	['strikə̩lʉə]
headscarf	skaut (n)	['skaʊt]
women's hat	hatt (m)	['hat]
hard hat	hjelm (m)	['jɛlm]
garrison cap	båtlue (m/f)	['bot̩lʉə]
helmet	hjelm (m)	['jɛlm]
derby	bowlerhatt, skalk (m)	['bouler̩hat], ['skalk]
top hat	flosshatt (m)	['flɔs̩hat]

34. Footwear

footwear	skotøy (n)	['skʊtøj]
shoes (men's shoes)	skor (m pl)	['skʊr]

shoes (women's shoes)	pumps (m pl)	['pʉmps]
boots (e.g., cowboy ~)	støvler (m pl)	['støvlər]
slippers	tøfler (m pl)	['tøflər]

tennis shoes (e.g., Nike ~)	tennissko (m pl)	['tɛnis,skʉ]
sneakers	canvas sko (m pl)	['kɑnvɑs ,skʉ]
(e.g., Converse ~)		
sandals	sandaler (m pl)	[sɑn'dɑlər]

cobbler (shoe repairer)	skomaker (m)	['skʉ,mɑkər]
heel	hæl (m)	['hæl]
pair (of shoes)	par (r)	['pɑr]

shoestring	skolisse (m/f)	['skʉ,lisə]
to lace (vt)	å snøre	[ɔ 'snørə]
shoehorn	skohorn (n)	['skʉ,hʉːn̩]
shoe polish	skokrem (m)	['skʉ,krɛm]

35. Textile. Fabrics

cotton (n)	bomull (m/f)	['bʉ,mʉl]
cotton (as adj)	bomulls-	['bʉ,mʉls-]
flax (n)	lin (r)	['lin]
flax (as adj)	lin-	['lin-]

silk (n)	silke (m)	['silkə]
silk (as adj)	silke-	['silkə-]
wool (n)	ull (m f)	['ʉl]
wool (as adj)	ull-, av ull	['ʉl-], ['ɑː ʉl]

velvet	fløyel (m)	['fløjəl]
suede	semsket skinn (n)	['sɛmsket ,ʂin]
corduroy	kordfløyel (m/n)	['kɔːd̪,fløjəl]

nylon (n)	nylon (n)	['ny,lon]
nylon (as adj)	nylon-	['ny,lon-]
polyester (n)	polyester (m)	[pʉly'ɛstər]
polyester (as adj)	polyester-	[pʉly'ɛstər-]

leather (n)	lær, skinn (n)	['lær], ['ʂin]
leather (as adj)	lær-, av lær	['lær-], ['ɑː lær]
fur (n)	pels (m)	['pɛls]
fur (e.g., ~ coat)	pels-	['pɛls-]

36. Personal accessories

| gloves | hansker (m pl) | ['hɑnskər] |
| mittens | votter (m pl) | ['vɔtər] |

scarf (muffler)	skjerf (n)	['ṣærf]
glasses (eyeglasses)	briller (m pl)	['brilər]
frame (eyeglass ~)	innfatning (m/f)	['in‚fatniŋ]
umbrella	paraply (m)	[para'ply]
walking stick	stokk (m)	['stɔk]
hairbrush	hårbørste (m)	['hɔr‚bœṣtə]
fan	vifte (m/f)	['viftə]

tie (necktie)	slips (n)	['slips]
bow tie	sløyfe (m/f)	['ṣløjfə]
suspenders	bukseseler (m pl)	['bʉksə'selər]
handkerchief	lommetørkle (n)	['lʊmə‚tœrklə]

comb	kam (m)	['kam]
barrette	hårspenne (m/f/n)	['hɔ:r‚spɛnə]
hairpin	hårnål (m/f)	['hɔ:r‚nol]
buckle	spenne (m/f/n)	['spɛnə]

| belt | belte (m) | ['bɛltə] |
| shoulder strap | skulderreim, rem (m/f) | ['skʉldə‚ræjm], ['rem] |

bag (handbag)	veske (m/f)	['vɛskə]
purse	håndveske (m/f)	['hɔn‚vɛskə]
backpack	ryggsekk (m)	['ryg‚sɛk]

37. Clothing. Miscellaneous

fashion	mote (m)	['mʊtə]
in vogue (adj)	moteriktig	['mʊtə‚rikti]
fashion designer	moteskaper (m)	['mʊtə‚skapər]

collar	krage (m)	['kragə]
pocket	lomme (m/f)	['lʊmə]
pocket (as adj)	lomme-	['lʊmə-]
sleeve	erme (n)	['ærmə]
hanging loop	hempe (m)	['hɛmpə]
fly (on trousers)	gylf, buksesmekk (m)	['gylf], ['bʉksə‚smɛk]

zipper (fastener)	glidelås (m/n)	['glidə‚lɔs]
fastener	hekte (m/f), knepping (m)	['hɛktə], ['knɛpiŋ]
button	knapp (m)	['knap]
buttonhole	klapphull (n)	['klap‚hʉl]
to come off (ab. button)	å falle av	[ɔ 'falə a:]

to sew (vi, vt)	å sy	[ɔ 'sy]
to embroider (vi, vt)	å brodere	[ɔ brʊ'derə]
embroidery	broderi (n)	[brʊde'ri]
sewing needle	synål (m/f)	['sy‚nol]
thread	tråd (m)	['trɔ]
seam	søm (m)	['søm]

to get dirty (vi)	å skitne seg til	[ɔ 'ʂitnə sæj til]
stain (mark, spot)	flekk (m)	['flek]
to crease, crumple (vi)	å bli skrukkete	[ɔ 'bli 'skrʉketə]
to tear, to rip (vt)	å rive	[ɔ 'rivə]
clothes moth	møll (m/n)	['møl]

38. Personal care. Cosmetics

toothpaste	tannpasta (m)	['tɑn,pɑstɑ]
toothbrush	tannbørste (m)	['tɑn,bœʂtə]
to brush one's teeth	å pusse tennene	[ɔ 'pʉsə 'tɛnənə]
razor	høve (m)	['høvəl]
shaving cream	barberkrem (m)	[bɑr'bɛr,krɛm]
to shave (vi)	å barbere seg	[ɔ bɑr'berə sæj]
soap	såpe (m/f)	['soːpə]
shampoo	sjampo (m)	['ʂɑm,pʉ]
scissors	saks (m/f)	['sɑks]
nail file	neglefil (m/f)	['nɛjlə,fil]
nail clippers	negleklipper (m)	['nɛjlə,klipər]
tweezers	pinsett (m)	[pin'sɛt]
cosmetics	kosmetikk (m)	[kʉsme'tik]
face mask	ansiktsmaske (m/f)	['ɑnsikts,mɑskə]
manicure	manikyr (m)	[mɑni'kyr]
to have a manicure	å få manikyr	[ɔ 'fɔ mɑni'kyr]
pedicure	pedikyr (m)	[pedi'kyr]
make-up bag	sminkeveske (m/f)	['sminkə,vɛskə]
face powder	pudder (n)	['pʉdər]
powder compact	pudderdåse (m)	['pʉdər,doːsə]
blusher	rouge (m)	['ruːʂ]
perfume (bottled)	parfyme (m)	[pɑr'fymə]
toilet water (lotion)	eau de toilette (m)	['ɔː də twɑ'let]
lotion	lotion (m)	['loʉʂɛn]
cologne	eau de cologne (m)	['ɔː də kɔ'lɔn]
eyeshadow	øyeskygge (m)	['øjə,sygə]
eyeliner	eyeliner (m)	['ɑːj,lɑjnər]
mascara	maskara (m)	[mɑ'skɑrɑ]
lipstick	leppestift (m)	['lepə,stift]
nail polish, enamel	neglelakk (m)	['nɛjlə,lɑk]
hair spray	hårlakk (m)	['hoːr,lɑk]
deodorant	deodorant (m)	[deudʉ'rɑnt]
cream	krem (m)	['krɛm]
face cream	ansiktskrem (m)	['ɑnsikts,krɛm]

hand cream	håndkrem (m)	['hɔn‚krɛm]
anti-wrinkle cream	antirynkekrem (m)	[anti'rʏnkə‚krɛm]
day cream	dagkrem (m)	['dɑg‚krɛm]
night cream	nattkrem (m)	['nɑt‚krɛm]
day (as adj)	dag-	['dɑg-]
night (as adj)	natt-	['nɑt-]

tampon	tampong (m)	[tɑm'pɔŋ]
toilet paper (toilet roll)	toalettpapir (n)	[tʊɑ'let pɑ'pir]
hair dryer	hårføner (m)	['hoːr‚føner]

39. Jewelry

jewelry	smykker (n pl)	['smʏkər]
precious (e.g., ~ stone)	edel-	['ɛdəl-]
hallmark stamp	stempel (n)	['stɛmpəl]

ring	ring (m)	['riŋ]
wedding ring	giftering (m)	['jiftə‚riŋ]
bracelet	armbånd (n)	['ɑrm‚bɔn]

earrings	øreringer (m pl)	['ørə‚riŋər]
necklace (~ of pearls)	halssmykke (n)	['hɑls‚smʏkə]
crown	krone (m/f)	['krʊnə]
bead necklace	perlekjede (m/n)	['pærlə‚çɛːdə]

diamond	diamant (m)	[diɑ'mɑnt]
emerald	smaragd (m)	[smɑ'rɑgd]
ruby	rubin (m)	[rʉ'bin]
sapphire	safir (m)	[sɑ'fir]
pearl	perler (m pl)	['pærlər]
amber	rav (n)	['rɑv]

40. Watches. Clocks

watch (wristwatch)	armbåndsur (n)	['ɑrmbɔns‚ʉr]
dial	urskive (m/f)	['ʉː‚sivə]
hand (of clock, watch)	viser (m)	['visər]
metal watch band	armbånd (n)	['ɑrm‚bɔn]
watch strap	rem (m/f)	['rem]

battery	batteri (n)	[bɑtɛ'ri]
to be dead (battery)	å bli utladet	[ɔ 'bli 'ʉt‚lɑdət]
to change a battery	å skifte batteriene	[ɔ 'ʂiftə bɑtɛ'rienə]
to run fast	å gå for fort	[ɔ 'gɔ fɔ 'fɔːʈ]
to run slow	å gå for sakte	[ɔ 'gɔ fɔ 'sɑktə]
wall clock	veggur (n)	['vɛg‚ʉr]
hourglass	timeglass (n)	['timə‚glɑs]

sundial	**solur** (n)	['soˌlʉr]
alarm clock	**vekkerklokka** (m/f)	['vɛkərˌklɔkɑ]
watchmaker	**urmaker** (m)	['ʉrˌmɑkər]
to repair (vt)	**å reparere**	[ɔ repɑ'reˑə]

Food. Nutricion

41. Food

meat	kjøtt (n)	['çœt]
chicken	høne (m/f)	['hønə]
Rock Cornish hen (poussin)	kylling (m)	['çyliŋ]
duck	and (m/f)	['an]
goose	gås (m/f)	['gɔs]
game	vilt (n)	['vilt]
turkey	kalkun (m)	[kɑl'kʉn]
pork	svinekjøtt (n)	['svinə‚çœt]
veal	kalvekjøtt (n)	['kɑlvə‚çœt]
lamb	fårekjøtt (n)	['fo:rə‚çœt]
beef	oksekjøtt (n)	['ɔksə‚çœt]
rabbit	kanin (m)	[kɑ'nin]
sausage (bologna, pepperoni, etc.)	pølse (m/f)	['pølsə]
vienna sausage (frankfurter)	wienerpølse (m/f)	['vinər‚pølsə]
bacon	bacon (n)	['bɛjkən]
ham	skinke (m)	['ʂinkə]
gammon	skinke (m)	['ʂinkə]
pâté	pate, paté (m)	[pɑ'te]
liver	lever (m)	['levər]
hamburger (ground beef)	kjøttfarse (m)	['çœt‚fɑrʂə]
tongue	tunge (m/f)	['tʉŋə]
egg	egg (n)	['ɛg]
eggs	egg (n pl)	['ɛg]
egg white	eggehvite (m)	['ɛgə‚vitə]
egg yolk	plomme (m/f)	['plʊmə]
fish	fisk (m)	['fisk]
seafood	sjømat (m)	['ʂø‚mɑt]
crustaceans	krepsdyr (n pl)	['krɛps‚dyr]
caviar	kaviar (m)	['kɑvi‚ɑr]
crab	krabbe (m)	['krɑbə]
shrimp	reke (m/f)	['rekə]
oyster	østers (m)	['østəʂ]
spiny lobster	langust (m)	[lɑŋ'gʉst]

octopus	**blekksprut** (m)	['blek,sprʉt]
squid	**blekksprut** (m)	['blek,sprʉt]
sturgeon	**stør** (m)	['stør]
salmon	**laks** (m)	['lɑks]
halibut	**kveite** (m/f)	['kvæejtə]
cod	**torsk** (m)	['tɔʂk]
mackerel	**makrell** (m)	[mɑ'krɛl]
tuna	**tunfisk** (m)	['tʉn,fisk]
eel	**ål** (m)	['ɔl]
trout	**ørret** (m)	['øret]
sardine	**sarcin** (m)	[sɑ:'din]
pike	**gjedde** (m/f)	['jɛdə]
herring	**sild** (m/f)	['sil]
bread	**brød** (n)	['brø]
cheese	**ost** (m)	['ʊst]
sugar	**sukker** (n)	['sʉkər]
salt	**salt** (n)	['sɑlt]
rice	**ris** (n)	['ris]
pasta (macaroni)	**pasta, makaroni** (m)	['pɑstɑ], [mɑkɑ'rʉni]
noodles	**nudler** (m pl)	['nʉdlər]
butter	**smør** (n)	['smør]
vegetable oil	**vegetabilsk olje** (m)	[vegetɑ'bilsk ,ɔljə]
sunflower oil	**solsikkeolje** (m)	['sʊlsikə,ɔljə]
margarine	**margarin** (m)	[mɑrgɑ'rin]
olives	**olivener** (m pl)	[ʊ'livenər]
olive oil	**olivenolje** (m)	[ʊ'livən,ɔljə]
milk	**melk** (m/f)	['mɛlk]
condensed milk	**kondensert melk** (m/f)	[kʊndən'se:ʈ ,mɛlk]
yogurt	**jogurt** (m)	['jɔgʉ:t]
sour cream	**rømme, syrnet fløte** (m)	['rœmə], ['sy:ɳet 'fløtə]
cream (of milk)	**fløte** (m)	['fløtə]
mayonnaise	**majones** (m)	[mɑjɔ'nɛs]
buttercream	**krem** (m)	['krɛm]
cereal grains (wheat, etc.)	**gryn** (n)	['gryn]
flour	**mel** (n)	['mel]
canned food	**hermetikk** (m)	[hɛrme'tik]
cornflakes	**cornflakes** (m)	['kɔ:ɳ,flejks]
honey	**honning** (m)	['hɔniŋ]
jam	**syltetøy** (n)	['syltə,tøj]
chewing gum	**tyggegummi** (m)	['tygə,gʉmi]

42. Drinks

water	vann (n)	['van]
drinking water	drikkevann (n)	['drikə‚van]
mineral water	mineralvann (n)	[minə'ral‚van]

still (adj)	uten kullsyre	['ʉtən kʉl'syrə]
carbonated (adj)	kullsyret	[kʉl'syrət]
sparkling (adj)	med kullsyre	[me kʉl'syrə]
ice	is (m)	['is]
with ice	med is	[me 'is]

non-alcoholic (adj)	alkoholfri	['alkʉhʉl‚fri]
soft drink	alkoholfri drikk (m)	['alkʉhʉl‚fri drik]
refreshing drink	leskedrikk (m)	['leskə‚drik]
lemonade	limonade (m)	[limɔ'nadə]

liquors	rusdrikker (m pl)	['rʉs‚drikər]
wine	vin (m)	['vin]
white wine	hvitvin (m)	['vit‚vin]
red wine	rødvin (m)	['rø‚vin]

liqueur	likør (m)	[li'kør]
champagne	champagne (m)	[ʂam'panjə]
vermouth	vermut (m)	['værmʉt]

whiskey	whisky (m)	['viski]
vodka	vodka (m)	['vɔdka]
gin	gin (m)	['dʒin]
cognac	konjakk (m)	['kʉnjak]
rum	rom (m)	['rʉm]

coffee	kaffe (m)	['kafə]
black coffee	svart kaffe (m)	['svɑːʈ 'kafə]
coffee with milk	kaffe (m) med melk	['kafə me 'mɛlk]
cappuccino	cappuccino (m)	[kapʉ'tʃinɔ]
instant coffee	pulverkaffe (m)	['pʉlvər‚kafə]

milk	melk (m/f)	['mɛlk]
cocktail	cocktail (m)	['kɔk‚tɛjl]
milkshake	milkshake (m)	['milk‚ʂɛjk]

juice	jus, juice (m)	['dʒʉs]
tomato juice	tomatjuice (m)	[tʉ'mat‚dʒʉs]
orange juice	appelsinjuice (m)	[apel'sin‚dʒʉs]
freshly squeezed juice	nypresset juice (m)	['ny‚prɛsə 'dʒʉs]

beer	øl (m/n)	['øl]
light beer	lettøl (n)	['let‚øl]
dark beer	mørkt øl (n)	['mœrkt‚øl]
tea	te (m)	['te]

| black tea | svart te (m) | ['svɑːt ˌte] |
| green tea | grønn te (m) | ['grœn ˌte] |

43. Vegetables

| vegetables | grønnsaker (m pl) | ['grœn ˌsɑkər] |
| greens | grønnsaker (m pl) | ['grœn ˌsɑkər] |

tomato	tomat (m)	[tʊ'mɑt]
cucumber	agurk (m)	[ɑ'gʉrk]
carrot	gulrot (m/f)	['gʉlˌrʊt]
potato	potet (m/f)	[pʊ'tet]
onion	løk (m)	['løk]
garlic	hvitløk (m)	['vitˌløk]

cabbage	kål (m)	['kɔl]
cauliflower	blomkål (m)	['blɔmˌkɔl]
Brussels sprouts	rosenkål (m)	['rʉsənˌkɔl]
broccoli	brokkoli (m)	['brɔkɔli]

beetroot	rødbete (m/f)	['røˌbetə]
eggplant	aubergine (m)	[ɔbɛr'sin]
zucchini	squash (m)	['skvɔs]
pumpkin	gresskar (n)	['grɛskɑr]
turnip	nepe (m/f)	['nepə]

parsley	persille (m/f)	[pæ'silə]
dill	dill (m)	['dil]
lettuce	salat (m)	[sɑ'lɑt]
celery	selleri (m/n)	[sɛleˌri]
asparagus	asparges (m)	[ɑ'spɑrʂəs]
spinach	spinat (m)	[spi'nɑt]

pea	erter (m pl)	['æːˌtər]
beans	bønner (m/f pl)	['bœnər]
corn (maize)	mais (m)	['mɑis]
kidney bean	bønne (m/f)	['bœnə]

bell pepper	pepper (m)	['pɛpər]
radish	reddik (m)	['rɛdik]
artichoke	artisjokk (m)	[ˌɑːʈi'ʂɔk]

44. Fruits. Nuts

fruit	frukt (m/f)	['frʉkt]
apple	eple (n)	['ɛplə]
pear	pære (m/f)	['pærə]
lemon	sitron (m)	[si'trʊn]

| orange | appelsin (m) | [apel'sin] |
| strawberry (garden ~) | jordbær (n) | ['ju:r.bær] |

mandarin	mandarin (m)	[manda'rin]
plum	plomme (m/f)	['plʊmə]
peach	fersken (m)	['fæʂkən]
apricot	aprikos (m)	[apri'kʊs]
raspberry	bringebær (n)	['briŋə.bær]
pineapple	ananas (m)	['ananas]

banana	banan (m)	[ba'nan]
watermelon	vannmelon (m)	['vanme.lʊn]
grape	drue (m)	['druə]
sour cherry	kirsebær (n)	['çiʂə.bær]
sweet cherry	morell (m)	[mʊ'rɛl]
melon	melon (m)	[me'lun]

grapefruit	grapefrukt (m/f)	['grɛjp.frʉkt]
avocado	avokado (m)	[avo'kadɔ]
papaya	papaya (m)	[pa'paja]
mango	mango (m)	['maŋu]
pomegranate	granateple (n)	[gra'nat.ɛplə]

redcurrant	rips (m)	['rips]
blackcurrant	solbær (n)	['sʊl.bær]
gooseberry	stikkelsbær (n)	['stikəls.bær]
bilberry	blåbær (n)	['blɔ.bær]
blackberry	bjørnebær (m)	['bjœ:nə.bær]

raisin	rosin (m)	[rʊ'sin]
fig	fiken (m)	['fikən]
date	daddel (m)	['dadəl]

peanut	jordnøtt (m)	['ju:r.nœt]
almond	mandel (m)	['mandəl]
walnut	valnøtt (m/f)	['val.nœt]
hazelnut	hasselnøtt (m/f)	['hasəl.nœt]
coconut	kokosnøtt (m/f)	['kʊkʊs.nœt]
pistachios	pistasier (m pl)	[pi'staʂiər]

45. Bread. Candy

bakers' confectionery (pastry)	bakevarer (m/f pl)	['bakə.varər]
bread	brød (n)	['brø]
cookies	kjeks (m)	['çɛks]

chocolate (n)	sjokolade (m)	[ʂʊkʊ'ladə]
chocolate (as adj)	sjokolade-	[ʂʊkʊ'ladə-]
candy (wrapped)	sukkertøy (n), karamell (m)	['sʉkə:tøj], [kara'mɛl]

cake (e.g., cupcake)	**kake** (m/f)	['kɑkə]
cake (e.g., birthday ~)	**bløtkake** (m/f)	['bløt̩ˌkɑkə]
pie (e.g., apple ~)	**pai** (m)	['pɑj]
filling (for cake, pie)	**fyll** (m/n)	['fʏl]
jam (whole fruit jam)	**syltetøy** (n)	['sʏltəˌtøj]
marmalade	**marmelade** (m)	[mɑrmeˈlɑdə]
waffles	**vaffel** (m)	['vɑfəl]
ice-cream	**iskrem** (m)	['iskrɛm]
pudding	**pudding** (m)	['pʉdiŋ]

46. Cooked dishes

course, dish	**rett** (m)	['rɛt]
cuisine	**kjøkken** (n)	['çœkən]
recipe	**oppskrift** (m)	['ɔpˌskrift]
portion	**porsjon** (m)	[pɔ'ʂʉn]
salad	**salat** (m)	[sɑ'lɑt]
soup	**suppe** (m/f)	['sʉpə]
clear soup (broth)	**buljong** (m)	[bu'ljɔŋ]
sandwich (bread)	**smørbrød** (n)	['smørˌbrɛ]
fried eggs	**speilegg** (n)	['spæjlˌɛg]
hamburger (beefburger)	**hamburger** (m)	['hɑmbʉrçər]
beefsteak	**biff** (m)	['bif]
side dish	**tilbehør** (n)	['tilbəˌhør]
spaghetti	**spagetti** (m)	[spɑ'gɛti]
mashed potatoes	**potetmos** (m)	[pʉ'tetˌmʉs]
pizza	**pizza** (m)	['pitsɑ]
porridge (oatmeal, etc.)	**grøt** (m)	['grøt]
omelet	**omelett** (m)	[ɔmə'let]
boiled (e.g., ~ beef)	**kokt**	['kʉkt]
smoked (adj)	**røkt**	['røkt]
fried (adj)	**stekt**	['stɛkt]
dried (adj)	**tørket**	['tœrkət]
frozen (adj)	**frossen, dypfryst**	['frɔsən], ['dypˌfrʏst]
pickled (adj)	**syltet**	['sʏltət]
sweet (sugary)	**søt**	['søt]
salty (adj)	**salt**	['sɑlt]
cold (adj)	**kald**	['kɑl]
hot (adj)	**het, varm**	['het], ['vɑrm]
bitter (adj)	**bitter**	['bitər]
tasty (adj)	**lekker**	['lekər]
to cook in boiling water	**å koke**	[ɔ 'kʉkə]

to cook (dinner)	å lage	[ɔ 'lagə]
to fry (vt)	å steke	[ɔ 'stekə]
to heat up (food)	å varme opp	[ɔ 'varmə ɔp]
to salt (vt)	å salte	[ɔ 'saltə]
to pepper (vt)	å pepre	[ɔ 'pɛprə]
to grate (vt)	å rive	[ɔ 'rivə]
peel (n)	skall (n)	['skal]
to peel (vt)	å skrelle	[ɔ 'skrɛlə]

47. Spices

salt	salt (n)	['salt]
salty (adj)	salt	['salt]
to salt (vt)	å salte	[ɔ 'saltə]
black pepper	svart pepper (m)	['svaːt 'pɛpər]
red pepper (milled ~)	rød pepper (m)	['rø 'pɛpər]
mustard	sennep (m)	['sɛnəp]
horseradish	pepperrot (m/f)	['pɛpər,rʊt]
condiment	krydder (n)	['krʏdər]
spice	krydder (n)	['krʏdər]
sauce	saus (m)	['saʊs]
vinegar	eddik (m)	['ɛdik]
anise	anis (m)	['anis]
basil	basilik (m)	[basi'lik]
cloves	nellik (m)	['nɛlik]
ginger	ingefær (m)	['iŋə,fær]
coriander	koriander (m)	[kʊri'andər]
cinnamon	kanel (m)	[ka'nel]
sesame	sesam (m)	['sesam]
bay leaf	laurbærblad (n)	['laʊrbær,bla]
paprika	paprika (m)	['paprika]
caraway	karve, kummin (m)	['karvə], ['kʉmin]
saffron	safran (m)	[sa'fran]

48. Meals

food	mat (m)	['mat]
to eat (vi, vt)	å spise	[ɔ 'spisə]
breakfast	frokost (m)	['frʊkɔst]
to have breakfast	å spise frokost	[ɔ 'spisə ,frʊkɔst]
lunch	lunsj, lunch (m)	['lʉnʂ]
to have lunch	å spise lunsj	[ɔ 'spisə ,lʉnʂ]

dinner	middag (m)	['mi̯da]
to have dinner	å spise middag	[ɔ 'spisə 'mi̯da]
appetite	appetitt (m)	[ape'tit]
Enjoy your meal!	God appetitt!	['gʊ ape'tit]
to open (~ a bottle)	å åpne	[ɔ 'ɔpnə]
to spill (liquid)	å spille	[ɔ 'spilə]
to spill out (vi)	å bli spilt	[ɔ 'bli 'spilt]
to boil (vi)	å koke	[ɔ 'kʊkə]
to boil (vt)	å koke	[ɔ 'kʊkə]
boiled (~ water)	kokt	['kʊkt]
to chill, cool down (vt)	å svalne	[ɔ 'svalnə]
to chill (vi)	å avkjøles	[ɔ 'av̩çœləs]
taste, flavor	smak (m)	['smak]
aftertaste	bismak (m)	['bismak]
to slim down (lose weight)	å være på diet	[ɔ 'værə pɔ di'et]
diet	diett (m)	[di'et]
vitamin	vitamin (n)	[vita'min]
calorie	kalori (m)	[kalʊ'ri]
vegetarian (n)	vegetarianer (m)	[vegetari'anər]
vegetarian (adj)	vegetarisk	[vege'tarisk]
fats (nutrient)	fett (n)	['fɛt]
proteins	proteiner (n pl)	[prote'inər]
carbohydrates	kullhydrater (n pl)	['kʉlhy̩dratər]
slice (of lemon, ham)	skive (m/f)	['ʂivə]
piece (of cake, pie)	stykke (n)	['stʏkə]
crumb (of bread, cake, etc.)	smule (m)	['smʉlə]

49. Table setting

spoon	skje (m)	['ʂe]
knife	kniv (m)	['kniv]
fork	gaffel (m)	['gafəl]
cup (e.g., coffee ~)	kopp (m)	['kɔp]
plate (dinner ~)	tallerken (m)	[ta'lærkən]
saucer	tefat (n)	['te̩fat]
napkin (on table)	serviett (m)	[sɛrvi'ɛt]
toothpick	tannpirker (m)	['tɑn̩pirkər]

50. Restaurant

| restaurant | restaurant (m) | [rɛstʊ'ran] |
| coffee house | kafé, kaffebar (m) | [ka'fe], ['kɔfə̩bar] |

pub, bar	**bar** (m)	['bɑr]
tearoom	**tesalong** (m)	['tesɑˌlɔŋ]
waiter	**servitør** (m)	['særvi'tør]
waitress	**servitrise** (m/f)	[særvi'trisə]
bartender	**bartender** (m)	['bɑːˌtɛndər]
menu	**meny** (m)	[me'ny]
wine list	**vinkart** (n)	['vinˌkɑːt]
to book a table	**å reservere bord**	[ɔ resɛr'verə 'bʊr]
course, dish	**rett** (m)	['rɛt]
to order (meal)	**å bestille**	[ɔ be'stilə]
to make an order	**å bestille**	[ɔ be'stilə]
aperitif	**aperitiff** (m)	[ɑperi'tif]
appetizer	**forrett** (m)	['fɔrɛt]
dessert	**dessert** (m)	[de'sɛːr]
check	**regning** (m/f)	['rɛjniŋ]
to pay the check	**å betale regningen**	[ɔ be'tɑlə 'rɛjniŋən]
to give change	**å gi tilbake veksel**	[ɔ ji til'bɑkə 'vɛksəl]
tip	**driks** (m)	['driks]

Family, relatives and friends

51. Personal information. Forms

name (first name)	**navn** (n)	['navn]
surname (last name)	**etternavn** (n)	['ɛtəˌnavn]
date of birth	**fødselsdato** (m)	['føtsəlsˌdatʊ]
place of birth	**fødested** (n)	['fødəˌsted]
nationality	**nasjonalitet** (m)	[naʂʊnɑli'tet]
place of residence	**bosted** (n)	['bʊˌsted]
country	**land** (r)	['lan]
profession (occupation)	**yrke** (r), **profesjon** (m)	['yrkə], [prʊfe'ʂʊn]
gender, sex	**kjønn** (n)	['çœn]
height	**høyde** (m)	['højdə]
weight	**vekt** (m)	['vɛkt]

52. Family members. Relatives

mother	**mor** (m/f)	['mʊr]
father	**far** (m	['fɑr]
son	**sønn** (m)	['sœn]
daughter	**datter** (m/f)	['datər]
younger daughter	**yngste datter** (m/f)	['yŋstə 'datər]
younger son	**yngste sønn** (m)	['yŋstə 'sœn]
eldest daughter	**eldste datter** (m/f)	['ɛlstə 'datər]
eldest son	**eldste sønn** (m)	['ɛlstə 'sœn]
brother	**bror** (m)	['brʊr]
elder brother	**eldre bror** (m)	['ɛldrə ˌbrʊr]
younger brother	**lillebror** (m)	['liləˌbrʊr]
sister	**søster** (m/f)	['søstər]
elder sister	**eldre søster** (m/f)	['ɛldrə ˌsøstər]
younger sister	**lillesøster** (m/f)	['liləˌsøster]
cousin (masc.)	**fetter** (m/f)	['fɛtər]
cousin (fem.)	**kusine** (m)	[kʉ'sinə]
mom, mommy	**mamma** (m)	['mama]
dad, daddy	**pappa** (m)	['papa]
parents	**foreldre** (pl)	[for'ɛldrə]
child	**barn** (r)	['bɑːn]
children	**barn** (r pl)	['bɑːn]

grandmother	bestemor (m)	['bɛstə‚mʊr]
grandfather	bestefar (m)	['bɛstə‚far]
grandson	barnebarn (n)	['bɑ:ŋə‚bɑ:ŋ]
granddaughter	barnebarn (n)	['bɑ:ŋə‚bɑ:ŋ]
grandchildren	barnebarn (n pl)	['bɑ:ŋə‚bɑ:ŋ]

uncle	onkel (m)	['ʊnkəl]
aunt	tante (m/f)	['tɑntə]
nephew	nevø (m)	[ne'vø]
niece	niese (m/f)	[ni'esə]

mother-in-law (wife's mother)	svigermor (m/f)	['sviɡər‚mʊr]
father-in-law (husband's father)	svigerfar (m)	['sviɡər‚far]
son-in-law (daughter's husband)	svigersønn (m)	['sviɡər‚sœn]
stepmother	stemor (m/f)	['ste‚mʊr]
stepfather	stefar (m)	['ste‚far]
infant	brystbarn (n)	['brʏst‚bɑ:ŋ]
baby (infant)	spedbarn (n)	['spe‚bɑ:ŋ]
little boy, kid	lite barn (n)	['litə 'bɑ:ŋ]

wife	kone (m/f)	['kʊnə]
husband	mann (m)	['mɑn]
spouse (husband)	ektemann (m)	['ɛktə‚mɑn]
spouse (wife)	hustru (m)	['hʉstrʉ]

married (masc.)	gift	['jift]
married (fem.)	gift	['jift]
single (unmarried)	ugift	[ʉ:'jift]
bachelor	ungkar (m)	['ʉŋ‚kɑr]
divorced (masc.)	fraskilt	['frɑ‚silt]
widow	enke (m)	['ɛnkə]
widower	enkemann (m)	['ɛnkə‚mɑn]

relative	slektning (m)	['ʂlektniŋ]
close relative	nær slektning (m)	['nær 'slektniŋ]
distant relative	fjern slektning (m)	['fjæ:ŋ 'slektniŋ]
relatives	slektninger (m pl)	['ʂlektniŋər]

orphan (boy or girl)	foreldreløst barn (n)	[fɔr'ɛldrəløst ‚bɑ:ŋ]
guardian (of a minor)	formynder (m)	['fɔr‚mʏnər]
to adopt (a boy)	å adoptere	[ɔ adɔp'terə]
to adopt (a girl)	å adoptere	[ɔ adɔp'terə]

53. Friends. Coworkers

| friend (masc.) | venn (m) | ['vɛn] |
| friend (fem.) | venninne (m/f) | [vɛ'ninə] |

friendship	**vennskap** (n)	['vɛnˌskɑp]
to be friends	**å være venner**	[ɔ 'værə 'vɛnər]
buddy (masc.)	**venn** (m)	['vɛn]
buddy (fem.)	**venninne** (m/f)	[vɛ'ninə]
partner	**partner** (m)	['pɑːʈnər]
chief (boss)	**sjef** (m)	['ʂɛf]
superior (n)	**overordnet** (m)	['ɔvərˌordnet]
owner, proprietor	**eier** (m)	['æjər]
subordinate (n)	**underordnet** (m)	['ʉnərˌordˌet]
colleague	**kollega** (m)	[kʊ'legɑ]
acquaintance (person)	**bekjent** (m)	[be'çɛnt]
fellow traveler	**medpassasjer** (m)	['meˌpɑsɑ'ʂɛr]
classmate	**klassekamerat** (m)	['klɑsəˌkamə'rɑːt]
neighbor (masc.)	**nabo** (m)	['nɑbʊ]
neighbor (fem.)	**nabo** (m)	['nɑbʊ]
neighbors	**naboer** (m pl)	['nɑbʊər]

54. Man. Woman

woman	**kvinne** (m/f)	['kvinə]
girl (young woman)	**jente** (m/f)	['jɛntə]
bride	**brud** (m/f)	['brʉd]
beautiful (adj)	**vakker**	['vɑkər]
tall (adj)	**høy**	['høj]
slender (adj)	**slank**	['ʂlɑnk]
short (adj)	**liten av vekst**	['litən ɑ: 'vɛkst]
blonde (n)	**blondine** (m)	[blɔn'dinə]
brunette (n)	**brunette** (m)	[brʉ'nɛtə]
ladies' (adj)	**dame-**	['damə-]
virgin (girl)	**jomfru** (m/f)	['ʉmfrʉ]
pregnant (adj)	**gravid**	[grɑ'vid]
man (adult male)	**mann** (m)	['mɑn]
blond (n)	**blond mann** (m)	['blɔn ˌmɑn]
brunet (n)	**mørkhåret mann** (m)	['mœrkˌhɔːret mɑn]
tall (adj)	**høy**	['høj]
short (adj)	**liten av vekst**	['litən ɑ: 'vɛkst]
rude (rough)	**grov**	['grɔv]
stocky (adj)	**undersetsig**	['ʉnəˌsɛtsi]
robust (adj)	**robust**	[rʊ'bʉst]
strong (adj)	**sterk**	['stærk]
strength	**kraft, styrke** (m)	['krɑft], ['sːyrkə]

stout, fat (adj)	**tykk**	['tʏk]
swarthy (adj)	**mørkhudet**	['mœrkˌhʉdət]
slender (well-built)	**slank**	['ʂlɑnk]
elegant (adj)	**elegant**	[ɛle'gɑnt]

55. Age

age	**alder** (m)	['ɑldər]
youth (young age)	**ungdom** (m)	['ʉŋˌdɔm]
young (adj)	**ung**	['ʉŋ]
younger (adj)	**yngre**	['ʏŋrə]
older (adj)	**eldre**	['ɛldrə]
young man	**unge mann** (m)	['ʉŋə ˌmɑn]
teenager	**tenåring** (m)	['tɛnoːriŋ]
guy, fellow	**kar** (m)	['kɑr]
old man	**gammel mann** (m)	['gɑməl ˌmɑn]
old woman	**gammel kvinne** (m/f)	['gɑməl ˌkvinə]
adult (adj)	**voksen**	['vɔksən]
middle-aged (adj)	**middelaldrende**	['midəlˌɑldrɛnə]
elderly (adj)	**eldre**	['ɛldrə]
old (adj)	**gammel**	['gɑməl]
retirement	**pensjon** (m)	[pɑn'ʂʉn]
to retire (from job)	**å gå av med pensjon**	[ɔ 'go ɑː me pɑn'ʂʉn]
retiree	**pensjonist** (m)	[pɑnʂu'nist]

56. Children

child	**barn** (n)	['bɑːɳ]
children	**barn** (n pl)	['bɑːɳ]
twins	**tvillinger** (m pl)	['tviliŋər]
cradle	**vogge** (m/f)	['vɔgə]
rattle	**rangle** (m/f)	['rɑŋlə]
diaper	**bleie** (m/f)	['blæjə]
pacifier	**smokk** (m)	['smʊk]
baby carriage	**barnevogn** (m/f)	['bɑːɳəˌvɔŋn]
kindergarten	**barnehage** (m)	['bɑːɳəˌhɑgə]
babysitter	**babysitter** (m)	['bɛbyˌsitər]
childhood	**barndom** (m)	['bɑːɳˌdɔm]
doll	**dukke** (m/f)	['dʉkə]
toy	**leketøy** (n)	['lekəˌtøj]

construction set (toy)	**byggesett** (n)	['bʏɡəˌsɛt]
well-bred (adj)	**veloppdragen**	['vel.ɔpˈdraɡən]
ill-bred (adj)	**uoppdragen**	[ʉopˈdraɡən]
spoiled (adj)	**bortskjemt**	['bʊːtʃɛmt]

to be naughty	**å være stygg**	[ɔ 'væːrə 'stʏɡ]
mischievous (adj)	**skøyeraktig**	['skøjəˌraktɪ]
mischievousness	**skøyeraktighet** (m)	['skøjəˌraktihet]
mischievous child	**skøyer** (m)	['skøjər]

obedient (adj)	**lydig**	['lʏdi]
disobedient (adj)	**ulydig**	[ʉ'lʏdi]

docile (adj)	**føyelig**	['føjli]
clever (smart)	**klok**	['klʊk]
child prodigy	**vidunderbarn** (n)	['vidˌʉndəˑˌbɑːn]

57. Married couples. Family life

to kiss (vt)	**å kysse**	[ɔ 'çʏsə]
to kiss (vi)	**å kysse hverandre**	[ɔ 'çʏsə ˌverandrə]
family (n)	**familie** (m)	[fɑ'miliə]
family (as adj)	**familie-**	[fɑ'miliə-]
couple	**par** n)	['pɑr]
marriage (state)	**ekteskap** (n)	['ɛktəˌskɑp]
hearth (home)	**hjemmets arne** (m)	['jɛmets 'ɑːŋə]
dynasty	**dynasti** (n)	[dinɑs'ti]

date	**stevnemøte** (n)	['stɛvnəˌmøtə]
kiss	**kyss** (n)	['çʏs]

love (for sb)	**kjærlighet** (m)	['çæːliˌheˑt]
to love (sb)	**å elske**	[ɔ 'ɛlskə]
beloved	**elskling**	['ɛlsklɪŋ]

tenderness	**ømhet** (m)	['ømˌhet]
tender (affectionate)	**øm**	['øm]
faithfulness	**troskap** (m)	['trʊˌskɑp]
faithful (adj)	**trofast**	['trʊfɑst]
care (attention)	**omsorg** (m)	['ɔmˌsɔrg]
caring (~ father)	**omsorgsfull**	['ɔmˌsɔrgsfʉl]

newlyweds	**nygifte** (n)	['nyˌjiftə]
honeymoon	**hvetebrødsdager** (m pl)	['vetɛbrøs dɑɡər]
to get married (ab. woman)	**å gifte seg**	[ɔ 'jiftə sæj]
to get married (ab. man)	**å gifte seg**	[ɔ 'jiftə sæj]

wedding	**bryllup** (n)	['brʏlʉp]
golden wedding	**gullbryllup** (n)	['ɡʉlˌbrʏlʉp]

anniversary	årsdag (m)	['oːʂˌdɑ]
lover (masc.)	elsker (m)	['ɛlskər]
mistress (lover)	elskerinne (m/f)	['ɛlskəˌrinə]
adultery	utroskap (m)	['ʉˌtroskɑp]
to cheat on ... (commit adultery)	å være utro	[ɔ 'væːrə 'ʉˌtrʊ]
jealous (adj)	sjalu	[ʂɑ'lʉː]
to be jealous	å være sjalu	[ɔ 'væːrə ʂɑ'lʉː]
divorce	skilsmisse (m)	['ʂilsˌmisə]
to divorce (vi)	å skille seg	[ɔ 'ʂilə sæj]
to quarrel (vi)	å krangle	[ɔ 'krɑŋlə]
to be reconciled (after an argument)	å forsone seg	[ɔ fɔ'ʂʊnə sæj]
together (adv)	sammen	['sɑmən]
sex	sex (m)	['sɛks]
happiness	lykke (m/f)	['lʏkə]
happy (adj)	lykkelig	['lʏkəli]
misfortune (accident)	ulykke (m/f)	['ʉˌlʏkə]
unhappy (adj)	ulykkelig	['ʉˌlʏkəli]

Character. Feelings. Emotions

58. Feelings. Emotions

feeling (emotion)	følelse (m)	['føləlsə]
feelings	følelser (m pl)	['føləlsər]
to feel (vt)	å kjenne	[ɔ 'çɛnə]

hunger	sult (т)	['sʉlt]
to be hungry	å være sulten	[ɔ 'værə 'sʉltən]
thirst	tørst (n)	['tœʂt]
to be thirsty	å være tørst	[ɔ 'værə 'tœʂt]
sleepiness	søvnighet (m)	['sœvni̩het]
to feel sleepy	å være søvnig	[ɔ 'værə 'sœvni]

tiredness	tretthet (m)	['trɛt̩het]
tired (adj)	trett	['trɛt]
to get tired	å bli trett	[ɔ 'bli 'trɛt]

mood (humor)	humør (n)	[hʉ'mør]
boredom	kjedsomhet (m/f)	['çɛdsom̩het]
to be bored	å kjede seg	[ɔ 'çedə sæj]
seclusion	avsondrethet (m/f)	['afsondrɛt̩het]
to seclude oneself	å isolere seg	[ɔ isʉ'lerə sæj]

to worry (make anxious)	å bekymre, å uroe	[ɔ be'çymrə], [ɔ 'ʉːrʉə]
to be worried	å bekymre seg	[ɔ be'çymrə sæj]
worrying (n)	bekymring (m/f)	[be'çymriŋ]
anxiety	uro (n/f)	['ʉrʉ]
preoccupied (adj)	bekymret	[be'çymrət]
to be nervous	å være nervøs	[ɔ 'værə nær'vøs]
to panic (vi)	å få panikk	[ɔ 'fɔ pɑ'nik]

| hope | håp (n | ['hɔp] |
| to hope (vi, vt) | å håpe | [ɔ 'hoːpə] |

certainty	sikkerhet (m/f)	['sikər̩het]
certain, sure (adj)	sikker	['sikər]
uncertainty	usikkerhet (m)	['ʉsikər̩het]
uncertain (adj)	usikker	['ʉ̩sikər]

drunk (adj)	beruset, full	[be'rʉsət], ['fʉl]
sober (adj)	edru	['ɛdrʉ]
weak (adj)	svak	['svɑk]
happy (adj)	lykkelig	['lʏkəli]
to scare (vt)	å skremme	[ɔ 'skrɛmə]

| fury (madness) | raseri (n) | [rɑsɛ'ri] |
| rage (fury) | raseri (n) | [rɑsɛ'ri] |

depression	depresjon (m)	[dɛpre'ʂʊn]
discomfort (unease)	ubehag (n)	['ʉbe‚hɑg]
comfort	komfort (m)	[kʊm'fɔːr]
to regret (be sorry)	å beklage	[ɔ be'klɑgə]
regret	beklagelse (m)	[be'klɑgəlsə]
bad luck	uhell (n)	['ʉ‚hɛl]
sadness	sorg (m/f)	['sɔr]

shame (remorse)	skam (m/f)	['skɑm]
gladness	glede (m/f)	['gledə]
enthusiasm, zeal	entusiasme (m)	[ɛntʉsi'ɑsmə]
enthusiast	entusiast (m)	[ɛntʉsi'ɑst]
to show enthusiasm	å vise entusiasme	[ɔ 'visə ɛntʉsi'ɑsmə]

59. Character. Personality

character	karakter (m)	[kɑrɑk'ter]
character flaw	karakterbrist (m/f)	[kɑrɑk'ter‚brist]
mind	sinn (n)	['sin]
reason	forstand (m)	[fɔ'ʂtɑn]

conscience	samvittighet (m)	[sɑm'viti‚het]
habit (custom)	vane (m)	['vɑnə]
ability (talent)	evne (m/f)	['ɛvnə]
can (e.g., ~ swim)	å kunne	[ɔ 'kʉnə]

patient (adj)	tålmodig	[tɔl'mʊdi]
impatient (adj)	utålmodig	['ʉtɔl‚mʊdi]
curious (inquisitive)	nysgjerrig	['nʏ‚ʂæri]
curiosity	nysgjerrighet (m)	['nʏ‚ʂæri‚het]

modesty	beskjedenhet (m)	[be'ʂeden‚het]
modest (adj)	beskjeden	[be'ʂedən]
immodest (adj)	ubeskjeden	['ʉbe‚ʂedən]

laziness	lathet (m)	['lɑt‚het]
lazy (adj)	doven	['dʊvən]
lazy person (masc.)	dovendyr (n)	['dʊvən‚dyr]

cunning (n)	list (m/f)	['list]
cunning (as adj)	listig	['listi]
distrust	mistro (m/f)	['mis‚trɔ]
distrustful (adj)	mistroende	['mis‚trʉenə]

generosity	gavmildhet (m)	['gɑvmil‚het]
generous (adj)	generøs	[ʂenə'røs]
talented (adj)	talentfull	[tɑ'lent‚fʉl]

talent	talent (n)	[tɑ'lent]
courageous (adj)	modig	['mʊdi]
courage	mot (n)	['mʊt]
honest (adj)	ærlig	['æːli]
honesty	ærlighet (m)	['æːliˌhet]

careful (cautious)	forsiktig	[fɔ'şikti]
brave (courageous)	modig	['mʊdi]
serious (adj)	alvorlig	[al'voːli]
strict (severe, stern)	streng	['strɛŋ]

decisive (adj)	besluttsom	[be'şlʉtˌsɔm]
indecisive (adj)	ubesluttsom	[ʉbe'şlʉtˌsɔm]
shy, timid (adj)	forsagt	['fɔˌşakt]
shyness, timidity	forsagthet (m)	['fɔşaktˌhet]

confidence (trust)	tillit (n)	['tilit]
to believe (trust)	å tro	[ɔ 'trʊ]
trusting (credulous)	tillitsfull	['tilitsˌfʉl]

sincerely (adv)	oppriktig	[ɔp'rikti]
sincere (adj)	oppriktig	[ɔp'rikti]
sincerity	oppriktighet (m)	[ɔp'riktiˌhet]
open (person)	åpen	['ɔpən]

calm (adj)	stille	['stilə]
frank (sincere)	oppriktig	[ɔp'rikti]
naïve (adj)	naiv	[nɑ'iv]
absent-minded (adj)	forstrødd	['fʉˌstrød]
funny (odd)	morsom	['mʊşɔm]

greed	grådighet (m)	['groːdiˌheː]
greedy (adj)	grådig	['groːdi]
stingy (adj)	gjerrig	['jæri]
evil (adj)	ond	['ʊn]
stubborn (adj)	hårdnakket	['hoːrˌnakɛt]
unpleasant (adj)	ubehagelig	[ʉbe'hagɛli]

selfish person (masc.)	egoist (m)	[ɛgʊ'ist]
selfish (adj)	egoistisk	[ɛgʊ'istisk]
coward	feiging (m)	['fæjgiŋ]
cowardly (adj)	feig	['fæjg]

60. Sleep. Dreams

to sleep (vi)	å sove	[ɔ 'sove]
sleep, sleeping	søvn (m)	['sœvn]
dream	drøm (m)	['drøm]
to dream (in sleep)	å drømme	[ɔ 'drœmə]
sleepy (adj)	søvnig	['sœvni]

bed	seng (m/f)	['sɛŋ]
mattress	madrass (m)	[ma'dras]
blanket (comforter)	dyne (m/f)	['dynə]
pillow	pute (m/f)	['pʉtə]
sheet	laken (n)	['lɑkən]

insomnia	søvnløshet (m)	['sœvnløs͵het]
sleepless (adj)	søvnløs	['sœvn͵løs]
sleeping pill	sovetablett (n)	['sɔve͵tab'let]
to take a sleeping pill	å ta en sovetablett	[ɔ 'tɑ en 'sɔve͵tab'let]

to feel sleepy	å være søvnig	[ɔ 'værə 'sœvni]
to yawn (vi)	å gjespe	[ɔ 'jɛspə]
to go to bed	å gå til sengs	[ɔ 'gɔ til 'sɛŋs]
to make up the bed	å re opp sengen	[ɔ 're ɔp 'sɛŋən]
to fall asleep	å falle i søvn	[ɔ 'falə i 'sœvn]

nightmare	mareritt (n)	['mɑrə͵rit]
snore, snoring	snork (m)	['snɔrk]
to snore (vi)	å snorke	[ɔ 'snɔrkə]

alarm clock	vekkerklokka (m/f)	['vɛkər͵klɔka]
to wake (vt)	å vekke	[ɔ 'vɛkə]
to wake up	å våkne	[ɔ 'vɔknə]
to get up (vi)	å stå opp	[ɔ 'stɔ: ɔp]
to wash up (wash face)	å vaske seg	[ɔ 'vaskə sæj]

61. Humour. Laughter. Gladness

humor (wit, fun)	humor (m/n)	['hʉmʊr]
sense of humor	sans (m) for humor	['sans fɔr 'hʉmʊr]
to enjoy oneself	å more seg	[ɔ 'mʊrə sæj]
cheerful (merry)	glad, munter	['glɑ], ['mʉntər]
merriment (gaiety)	munterhet (m)	['mʉntər͵het]

smile	smil (m/n)	['smil]
to smile (vi)	å smile	[ɔ 'smilə]
to start laughing	å begynne å skratte	[ɔ be'jinə ɔ 'skratə]
to laugh (vi)	å le, å skratte	[ɔ 'le], [ɔ 'skratə]
laugh, laughter	latter (m), skratt (m/n)	['latər], ['skrat]

anecdote	anekdote (m)	[anek'dɔtə]
funny (anecdote, etc.)	morsom	['mʉʂɔm]
funny (odd)	morsom	['mʉʂɔm]

to joke (vi)	å spøke	[ɔ 'spøkə]
joke (verbal)	skjemt, spøk (m)	['ʂɛmt], ['spøk]
joy (emotion)	glede (m/f)	['gledə]
to rejoice (vi)	å glede seg	[ɔ 'gledə sæj]
joyful (adj)	glad	['glɑ]

62. Discussion, conversation. Part 1

communication	kommunikasjon (m)	[kʊmʉnikə'ʂʊn]
to communicate	å kommunisere	[ɔ kʊmʉni serə]
conversation	samtale (m)	['sam tɑlə]
dialog	dialog (m)	[diɑ'lɔg]
discussion (discourse)	diskusjon (m)	[diskʉ'ʂʊn]
dispute (debate)	debatt (m)	[de'bɑt]
to dispute	å diskutere	[ɔ diskʉ'terə]
interlocutor	samtalepartner (m)	['sam tɑlə 'pɑːʈnər]
topic (theme)	emne (n)	['ɛmnə]
point of view	synspunkt (n)	['sʏns pʉnt]
opinion (point of view)	mening (m/f)	['menin]
speech (talk)	tale (m)	['tɑlə]
discussion (of report, etc.)	diskusjon (m)	[diskʉ'ʂʊn]
to discuss (vt)	å drøfte, å diskutere	[ɔ 'drœftə], [ɔ diskʉ'terə]
talk (conversation)	samtale (m)	['sam tɑlə]
to talk (to chat)	å snakke, å samtale	[ɔ 'snɑkə], [ɔ 'sam tɑlə]
meeting	møte (n)	['møtə]
to meet (vi, vt)	å møtes	[ɔ 'møtəs]
proverb	ordspråk (n)	['uːr sprɔk]
saying	ordstev (n)	['uːr stev]
riddle (poser)	gåte (m)	['goːtə]
to pose a riddle	å utgjøre en gåte	[ɔ ʉt'jørə en 'goːtə]
password	passord (n)	['pɑs uːr]
secret	hemmelighet (m/f)	['hɛməli het]
oath (vow)	ed (ɪr)	['ɛd]
to swear (an oath)	å sverge	[ɔ 'sværgə]
promise	løfte (n), loven (m)	['lœftə], ['lovən]
to promise (vt)	å love	[ɔ 'lovə]
advice (counsel)	råd (ɪ)	['rɔd]
to advise (vt)	å råde	[ɔ 'roːdə]
to follow one's advice	å følge råd	[ɔ 'følə 'roːd]
to listen to ... (obey)	å adlyde	[ɔ 'ɑd lydə]
news	nyhet (m)	['nyhet]
sensation (news)	sensasjon (m)	[sɛnsɑ'ʂʊn]
information (data)	opplysninger (m/f pl)	['ɔp lʏsninər]
conclusion (decision)	slutning (m)	['slʉtnin]
voice	røst (m/f), stemme (m)	['røst], ['stɛmə]
compliment	kompliment (m)	[kʊmpli'mɑn]
kind (nice)	elskverdig	[ɛlsk'værdɪ]
word	ord (ɪ)	['uːr]
phrase	frase (m)	['frɑsə]

answer	svar (n)	['svɑr]
truth	sannhet (m)	['sɑnˌhet]
lie	løgn (m/f)	['løjn]

thought	tanke (m)	['tɑnkə]
idea (inspiration)	ide (m)	[i'de]
fantasy	fantasi (m)	[fɑntɑ'si]

63. Discussion, conversation. Part 2

respected (adj)	respektert	[rɛspɛk'tɛːt]
to respect (vt)	å respektere	[ɔ rɛspɛk'terə]
respect	respekt (m)	[rɛ'spɛkt]
Dear ... (letter)	Kjære ...	['çærə ...]

to introduce (sb to sb)	å introdusere	[ɔ introdʉ'serə]
to make acquaintance	å stifte bekjentskap med ...	[ɔ 'stiftə be'çɛnˌskɑp me ...]
intention	hensikt (m)	['hɛnˌsikt]
to intend (have in mind)	å ha til hensikt	[ɔ 'hɑ til 'hɛnˌsikt]
wish	ønske (n)	['ønskə]
to wish (~ good luck)	å ønske	[ɔ 'ønskə]

surprise (astonishment)	overraskelse (m/f)	['ɔvəˌrɑskəlsə]
to surprise (amaze)	å forundre	[ɔ fɔ'rʉndrə]
to be surprised	å bli forundret	[ɔ 'bli fɔ'rʉndrət]

to give (vt)	å gi	[ɔ 'ji]
to take (get hold of)	å ta	[ɔ 'tɑ]
to give back	å gi tilbake	[ɔ 'ji til'bɑkə]
to return (give back)	å returnere	[ɔ retʉr'nerə]

to apologize (vi)	å unnskylde seg	[ɔ 'ʉnˌsylə sæj]
apology	unnskyldning (m/f)	['ʉnˌsyldniŋ]
to forgive (vt)	å tilgi	[ɔ 'tilˌji]

to talk (speak)	å tale	[ɔ 'tɑlə]
to listen (vi)	å lye, å lytte	[ɔ 'lyə], [ɔ 'lʏtə]
to hear out	å høre på	[ɔ 'hørə pɔ]
to understand (vt)	å forstå	[ɔ fɔ'ʂtɔ]

to show (to display)	å vise	[ɔ 'visə]
to look at ...	å se på ...	[ɔ 'se pɔ ...]
to call (yell for sb)	å kalle	[ɔ 'kɑlə]
to distract (disturb)	å distrahere	[ɔ distrɑ'erə]
to disturb (vt)	å forstyrre	[ɔ fɔ'ʂtʏrə]
to pass (to hand sth)	å rekke	[ɔ 'rɛkə]

| demand (request) | begjæring (m/f) | [be'jæriŋ] |
| to request (ask) | å be, å bede | [ɔ 'be], [ɔ 'bedə] |

demand (firm request)	krav (r)	['krɑv]
to demand (request firmly)	å kreve	[ɔ 'krevə]
to tease (call names)	å erte	[ɔ 'ɛːʈə]
to mock (make fun of)	å håne	[ɔ 'hoːnə]
mockery, derision	hån (m)	['hɔn]
nickname	kallenavn, tilnavn (n)	['kalə,nɑvn], ['til,nɑvn]
insinuation	insinuasjon (m)	[insinʉɑ'ʂʊn]
to insinuate (imply)	å insinuere	[ɔ insinʉ'erə]
to mean (vt)	å bety	[ɔ 'bety]
description	beskrivelse (m)	[be'skrivəlsə]
to describe (vt)	å beskrive	[ɔ be'skrivɛ]
praise (compliments)	ros (n)	['rʊs]
to praise (vt)	å rose, å berømme	[ɔ 'rʊsə], [ɔ be'rœmə]
disappointment	skuffelse (m)	['skʉfəlsə]
to disappoint (vt)	å skuffe	[ɔ 'skʉfə]
to be disappointed	å bli skuffet	[ɔ 'bli 'skʉfət]
supposition	antagelse (m)	[an'tɑgəlsə]
to suppose (assume)	å anta, å formode	[ɔ 'an,tɑ], [ɔ for'mʊdə]
warning (caution)	advarsel (m)	['ɑd,vɑsəl]
to warn (vt)	å advare	[ɔ 'ɑd,vɑrə]

64. Discussion, conversation. Part 3

to talk into (convince)	å overtale	[ɔ 'ove,tɑlə]
to calm down (vt)	å berolige	[ɔ be'rʊliə]
silence (~ is golden)	taushet (m)	['taʊs,het]
to be silent (not speaking)	å tie	[ɔ 'tie]
to whisper (vi, vt)	å hviske	[ɔ 'viskə]
whisper	hvisking (m/f)	['viskiŋ]
frankly, sincerely (adv)	oppriktig	[ɔp'rikti]
in my opinion ...	etter min mening ...	['ɛtər min 'meniŋ ...]
detail (of the story)	detalj (m)	[de'talj]
detailed (adj)	detaljert	[deta'ljeːʈ]
in detail (adv)	i detaljer	[i de'taljer]
hint, clue	vink (n)	['vink]
to give a hint	å gi et vink	[ɔ 'ji et 'vink]
look (glance)	blikk (n)	['blik]
to have a look	å kaste et blikk	[ɔ 'kastə et 'blik]
fixed (look)	stiv	['stiv]
to blink (vi)	å blinke	[ɔ 'blinkə]

| to wink (vi) | å blinke | [ɔ 'blinkə] |
| to nod (in assent) | å nikke | [ɔ 'nikə] |

sigh	sukk (n)	['sʉk]
to sigh (vi)	å sukke	[ɔ 'sʉkə]
to shudder (vi)	å gyse	[ɔ 'jisə]
gesture	gest (m)	['gɛst]
to touch (one's arm, etc.)	å røre	[ɔ 'rørə]
to seize	å gripe	[ɔ 'gripə]
(e.g., ~ by the arm)		
to tap (on the shoulder)	å klappe	[ɔ 'klɑpə]

Look out!	Pass på!	['pɑs 'pɔ]
Really?	Virkelig?	['virkəli]
Are you sure?	Er du sikker?	[ɛr dʉ 'sikər]
Good luck!	Lykke til!	['lʏkə til]
I see!	Jeg forstår!	['jæ fɔ'ʂtoːr]
What a pity!	Det var synd!	[de vɑr 'sʏn]

65. Agreement. Refusal

consent	samtykke (n)	['sɑmˌtʏkə]
to consent (vi)	å samtykke	[ɔ 'sɑmˌtʏkə]
approval	godkjennelse (m)	['gʉˌçɛnəlsə]
to approve (vt)	å godkjenne	[ɔ 'gʉˌçɛnə]
refusal	avslag (n)	['ɑfˌslɑg]
to refuse (vi, vt)	å vegre seg	[ɔ 'vɛgrə sæj]

Great!	Det er fint!	['de ær 'fint]
All right!	Godt!	['gɔt]
Okay! (I agree)	OK! Enig!	[ɔ'kɛj], ['ɛni]

forbidden (adj)	forbudt	[fɔr'bʉt]
it's forbidden	det er forbudt	[de ær fɔr'bʉt]
it's impossible	det er umulig	[de ær ʉ'mʉli]
incorrect (adj)	uriktig, ikke riktig	['ʉˌrikti], ['ikə ˌrikti]

to reject (~ a demand)	å avslå	[ɔ 'ɑfˌslɔ]
to support (cause, idea)	å støtte	[ɔ 'stœtə]
to accept (~ an apology)	å akseptere	[ɔ ɑksɛp'terə]

to confirm (vt)	å bekrefte	[ɔ be'krɛftə]
confirmation	bekreftelse (m)	[be'krɛftəlsə]
permission	tillatelse (m)	['tiˌlɑtəlsə]
to permit (vt)	å tillate	[ɔ 'tiˌlɑtə]
decision	beslutning (m)	[be'ʂlʉtniŋ]
to say nothing	å tie	[ɔ 'tie]
(hold one's tongue)		
condition (term)	betingelse (m)	[be'tiŋəlsə]
excuse (pretext)	foregivende (n)	['fɔrəˌjivnə]

| praise (compliments) | ros (m) | ['rʊs] |
| to praise (vt) | å rose, å berømme | [ɔ 'rʊsə], [ɔ be'rœmə] |

66. Success. Good luck. Failure

success	suksess (m)	[sʉk'sɛ]
successfully (adv)	med suksess	[me sʉk'sɛ]
successful (adj)	vellykket	['vel‚lʏkət]

luck (good luck)	hell (n), lykke (m/f)	['hɛl], ['lʏkə]
Good luck!	Lykke til!	['lʏkə til]
lucky (e.g., ~ day)	heldig, lykkelig	['hɛldi], ['lʏkəli]
lucky (fortunate)	heldig	['hɛldi]

failure	mis ykkelse, fiasko (m)	['mis‚lʏkəlsə], [fi'ɑskʊ]
misfortune	uhell (n), utur (m)	['ʉˌhɛl], ['ʉˌtʉr]
bad luck	uhell (n)	['ʉˌhɛl]
unsuccessful (adj)	mis ykket	['mis‚lʏkət]
catastrophe	katastrofe (m)	[kɑtɑ'strofə]

pride	stolthet (m)	['stɔlt‚het]
proud (adj)	stolt	['stɔlt]
to be proud	å være stolt	[ɔ 'værə 'stɔlt]

winner	seierherre (m)	['sæjərˌhɛrə]
to win (vi)	å seire, å vinne	[ɔ 'sæjrə], [ɔ 'vinə]
to lose (not win)	å tape	[ɔ 'tɑpə]
try	forsøk (n)	['fɔ'søk]
to try (vi)	å prøve, å forsøke	[ɔ 'prøvə], [ɔ fɔ'søkə]
chance (opportunity)	sjanse (m)	['ʂɑnsə]

67. Quarrels. Negative emotions

shout (scream)	skrik (n)	['skrik]
to shout (vi)	å skrike	[ɔ 'skrikə]
to start to cry out	å begynne å skrike	[ɔ be'jinə ɔ 'skrikə]

quarrel	krangel (m)	['krɑŋəl]
to quarrel (vi)	å krangle	[ɔ 'krɑŋlə]
fight (squabble)	skandale (m)	[skɑn'dɑlə]
to make a scene	å gjøre skandale	[ɔ 'jørə skɑn'dɑlə]
conflict	konflikt (m)	[kʊn'flikt]
misunderstanding	misforståelse (m)	[misfɔ'ʂtɔəlsə]

insult	forrærmelse (m)	[fɔː'nærməlsə]
to insult (vt)	å fornærme	[ɔ fɔː'nærmə]
insulted (adj)	forrærmet	[fɔː'nærmət]
resentment	forrærmelse (m)	[fɔː'nærməlsə]

to offend (vt)	å fornærme	[ɔ fɔːˈɳærmə]
to take offense	å bli fornærmet	[ɔ ˈbli fɔːˈɳærmət]
indignation	forargelse (m)	[fɔˈrɑrgəlsə]
to be indignant	å bli indignert	[ɔ ˈbli indiˈgnɛːt]
complaint	klage (m)	[ˈklɑgə]
to complain (vi, vt)	å klage	[ɔ ˈklɑgə]
apology	unnskyldning (m/f)	[ˈʉnˌsyldniŋ]
to apologize (vi)	å unnskylde seg	[ɔ ˈʉnˌsylə sæj]
to beg pardon	å be om forlatelse	[ɔ ˈbe ɔm fɔːˈlɑtəlsə]
criticism	kritikk (m)	[kriˈtik]
to criticize (vt)	å kritisere	[ɔ kritiˈserə]
accusation	anklagelse (m)	[ˈɑnˌklɑgəlsə]
to accuse (vt)	å anklage	[ɔ ˈɑnˌklɑgə]
revenge	hevn (m)	[ˈhɛvn]
to avenge (get revenge)	å hevne	[ɔ ˈhɛvnə]
to pay back	å hevne	[ɔ ˈhɛvnə]
disdain	forakt (m)	[fɔˈrɑkt]
to despise (vt)	å forakte	[ɔ fɔˈrɑktə]
hatred, hate	hat (n)	[ˈhɑt]
to hate (vt)	å hate	[ɔ ˈhɑtə]
nervous (adj)	nervøs	[nærˈvøs]
to be nervous	å være nervøs	[ɔ ˈværə nærˈvøs]
angry (mad)	vred, sint	[ˈvred], [ˈsint]
to make angry	å gjøre sint	[ɔ ˈjørə ˌsint]
humiliation	ydmykelse (m)	[ˈydˌmykəlsə]
to humiliate (vt)	å ydmyke	[ɔ ˈydˌmykə]
to humiliate oneself	å ydmyke seg	[ɔ ˈydˌmykə sæj]
shock	sjokk (n)	[ˈʂɔk]
to shock (vt)	å sjokkere	[ɔ ʂɔˈkerə]
trouble (e.g., serious ~)	knipe (m/f)	[ˈknipə]
unpleasant (adj)	ubehagelig	[ʉbeˈhɑgeli]
fear (dread)	redsel, frykt (m)	[ˈrɛtsəl], [ˈfrʏkt]
terrible (storm, heat)	fryktelig	[ˈfrʏkteli]
scary (e.g., ~ story)	uhyggelig, skremmende	[ˈʉhygəli], [ˈskrɛmənə]
horror	redsel (m)	[ˈrɛtsəl]
awful (crime, news)	forferdelig	[fɔrˈfærdəli]
to begin to tremble	å begynne å ryste	[ɔ beˈjinə ɔ ˈrystə]
to cry (weep)	å gråte	[ɔ ˈgroːtə]
to start crying	å begynne å gråte	[ɔ beˈjinə ɔ ˈgroːtə]
tear	tåre (m/f)	[ˈtoːrə]
fault	skyld (m/f)	[ˈʂyl]

guilt (feeling)	**skyldfølelse** (m)	['şyl̩ˌfølɛlsə]
dishonor (disgrace)	**skam, vanære** (m/f)	['skam], ['ˌʋanærə]
protest	**protest** (m)	[prʊ'tɛst]
stress	**stress** (m/n)	['strɛs]
to disturb (vt)	**å forstyrre**	[ɔ fo'ştʏrə]
to be furious	**å være sint**	[ɔ 'værə ˌsint]
mad, angry (adj)	**vred, sint**	['ʋred], ['sint]
to end (~ a relationship)	**å avbryte**	[ɔ 'ɑʋˌbrytə]
to swear (at sb)	**å sverge**	[ɔ 'sværgə]
to scare (become afraid)	**å bli skremt**	[ɔ 'bli 'skrɛmt]
to hit (strike with hand)	**å slå**	[ɔ 'şlɔ]
to fight (street fight, etc.)	**å slåss**	[ɔ 'şlɔs]
to settle (a conflict)	**å løse**	[ɔ 'løsə]
discontented (adj)	**misfornøyd, utilfreds**	['misˌfɔ:'ŋøjd], ['ʉtilˌfrɛds]
furious (adj)	**rasende**	['rɑsenə]
It's not good!	**Det er ikke bra!**	[de ær ikə 'brɑ]
It's bad!	**Det er dårlig!**	[de ær 'do:ļi]

Medicine

68. Diseases

sickness	sykdom (m)	['sʏk̩dɔm]
to be sick	å være syk	[ɔ 'væɾə 'syk]
health	helse (m/f)	['hɛlsə]
runny nose (coryza)	snue (m)	['snʉə]
tonsillitis	angina (m)	[an'gina]
cold (illness)	forkjølelse (m)	[fɔr'çœləlsə]
to catch a cold	å forkjøle seg	[ɔ fɔr'çœlə sæj]
bronchitis	bronkitt (m)	[brɔn'kit]
pneumonia	lungebetennelse (m)	['lʉŋə be'tɛnəlsə]
flu, influenza	influensa (m)	[inflʉ'ɛnsa]
nearsighted (adj)	nærsynt	['næ̩sʏnt]
farsighted (adj)	langsynt	['laŋsʏnt]
strabismus (crossed eyes)	skjeløydhet (m)	['ʂɛløjd̩het]
cross-eyed (adj)	skjeløyd	['ʂɛl̩øjd]
cataract	grå stær, katarakt (m)	['grɔ ̩stær], [kata'rakt]
glaucoma	glaukom (n)	[glau'kɔm]
stroke	hjerneslag (n)	['jæːɳə̩slag]
heart attack	infarkt (n)	[in'farkt]
myocardial infarction	myokardieinfarkt (n)	['miɔ'kardiə in'farkt]
paralysis	paralyse, lammelse (m)	['para'lyse], ['laməlsə]
to paralyze (vt)	å lamme	[ɔ 'lamə]
allergy	allergi (m)	[alæ:'gi]
asthma	astma (m)	['astma]
diabetes	diabetes (m)	[dia'betəs]
toothache	tannpine (m/f)	['tan̩pinə]
caries	karies (m)	['karies]
diarrhea	diaré (m)	[dia'rɛ]
constipation	forstoppelse (m)	[fɔ'ʂtɔpəlsə]
stomach upset	magebesvær (m)	['magə̩be'svær]
food poisoning	matforgiftning (m/f)	['mat̩fɔr'jiftniŋ]
to get food poisoning	å få matforgiftning	[ɔ 'fɔ mat̩fɔr'jiftniŋ]
arthritis	artritt (m)	[a:t̩'rit]
rickets	rakitt (m)	[ra'kit]
rheumatism	revmatisme (m)	[revma'tismə]

atherosclerosis	arteriosklerose (m)	[aː'teriʊskleˌrʊsə]
gastritis	magekatarr, gastritt (m)	['magəkaˌtar], [ˌga'strit]
appendicitis	appendisitt (m)	[apɛndi'sit]
cholecystitis	galleblærebetennelse (m)	['galəˌblærə be'tɛnəlse]
ulcer	magesår (n)	['magəˌsɔr]

measles	meslinger (m pl)	['mɛsˌliŋər]
rubella (German measles)	røde hunder (m pl)	['rødə 'hʉnər]
jaundice	gulsott (m/f)	['gʉlˌsʊt]
hepatitis	hepatitt (m)	[hepa'tit]

schizophrenia	schizofreni (m)	[ʂisʊfre'ni]
rabies (hydrophobia)	rabies (m)	['rabiəs]
neurosis	nevrose (m)	[nev'rʊsə]
concussion	hjernerystelse (m)	['jæːŋəˌrʏstəlsə]

cancer	kreft, cancer (m)	['krɛft], ['kansər]
sclerosis	sklerose (m)	[skle'rʊsə]
multiple sclerosis	multippel sklerose (m)	[mʉl'tipəl sklε'rʊsə]

alcoholism	alkoholisme (m)	[alkʊhʊ'lisnə]
alcoholic (n)	alkoholiker (m)	[alkʊ'hʊlikɛr]
syphilis	syfilis (m)	['syfilis]
AIDS	AIDS, aids (m)	['ɛjds]

tumor	svulst, tumor (m)	['svʉlst], [tʉ'mʊr]
malignant (adj)	ondartet, malign	['ʊnˌɑːʈət], [ma'lign]
benign (adj)	godartet	['gʊˌɑːʈət]

fever	feber (m)	['febər]
malaria	malaria (m)	[ma'laria]
gangrene	koldbrann (m)	['kɔlbran]
seasickness	sjøsyke (m)	['søˌsykə]
epilepsy	epilepsi (m)	[ɛpilep'si]

epidemic	epidemi (m)	[ɛpide'mi]
typhus	tyfus (m)	['tyfʉs]
tuberculosis	tuberkulose (m)	[tubærkʉ'lɔsə]
cholera	kolera (m)	['kʊlera]
plague (bubonic ~)	pest (m)	['pɛst]

69. Symptoms. Treatments. Part 1

symptom	symptom (n)	[sʏmp'tʊm]
temperature	temperatur (m)	[tɛmpəra'tʉr]
high temperature (fever)	høy temperatur (m)	['høj tɛmpəra'tʉr]
pulse	puls (m)	['pʉls]

| dizziness (vertigo) | svimmelhet (m) | ['sviməlˌhet] |
| hot (adj) | varm | ['varm] |

shivering	skjelving (m/f)	['ʂɛlviŋ]
pale (e.g., ~ face)	blek	['blek]

cough	hoste (m)	['hʊstə]
to cough (vi)	å hoste	[ɔ 'hʊstə]
to sneeze (vi)	å nyse	[ɔ 'nysə]
faint	besvimelse (m)	[bɛ'svimәlsə]
to faint (vi)	å besvime	[ɔ be'svimə]

bruise (hématome)	blåmerke (n)	['blɔˌmærkə]
bump (lump)	bule (m)	['bʉlə]
to bang (bump)	å slå seg	[ɔ 'ʂlɔ sæj]
contusion (bruise)	blåmerke (n)	['blɔˌmærkə]
to get a bruise	å slå seg	[ɔ 'ʂlɔ sæj]

to limp (vi)	å halte	[ɔ 'haltə]
dislocation	forvridning (m)	[fɔr'vridniŋ]
to dislocate (vt)	å forvri	[ɔ fɔr'vri]
fracture	brudd (n), fraktur (m)	['brʉd], [frɑk'tʉr]
to have a fracture	å få brudd	[ɔ 'fɔ 'brʉd]

cut (e.g., paper ~)	skjæresår (n)	['ʂæːrəˌsɔr]
to cut oneself	å skjære seg	[ɔ 'ʂæːrə sæj]
bleeding	blødning (m/f)	['blødniŋ]

burn (injury)	brannsår (n)	['brɑnˌsɔr]
to get burned	å brenne seg	[ɔ 'brɛnə sæj]

to prick (vt)	å stikke	[ɔ 'stikə]
to prick oneself	å stikke seg	[ɔ 'stikə sæj]
to injure (vt)	å skade	[ɔ 'skadə]
injury	skade (n)	['skadə]
wound	sår (n)	['sɔr]
trauma	traume (m)	['trɑʊmə]

to be delirious	å snakke i villelse	[ɔ 'snɑkə i 'vilәlsə]
to stutter (vi)	å stamme	[ɔ 'stɑmə]
sunstroke	solstikk (n)	['sʊlˌstik]

70. Symptoms. Treatments. Part 2

pain, ache	smerte (m)	['smæːtə]
splinter (in foot, etc.)	flis (m/f)	['flis]

sweat (perspiration)	svette (m)	['svɛtə]
to sweat (perspire)	å svette	[ɔ 'svɛtə]
vomiting	oppkast (n)	['ɔpˌkast]
convulsions	kramper (m pl)	['krɑmpər]
pregnant (adj)	gravid	[grɑ'vid]
to be born	å fødes	[ɔ 'fødə]

delivery, labor	fødsel (m)	['føtsəl]
to deliver (~ a baby)	å føde	[ɔ 'fødə]
abortion	abort (m)	[a'bɔːt]

breathing, respiration	åndedrett (n)	['ɔndə,drɛː]
in-breath (inhalation)	innånding (m/f)	['in,ɔniŋ]
out-breath (exhalation)	utånding (m/f)	['ʉt,ɔndiŋ]
to exhale (breathe out)	å puste ut	[ɔ 'pʉstə ʉt]
to inhale (vi)	å ånde inn	[ɔ 'ɔndə ,in]

disabled person	handikappet person (m)	['handi,kaɔət pæ'ʂʉn]
cripple	krøpling (m)	['krøpliŋ]
drug addict	narkoman (m)	[narkʉ'mcn]

deaf (adj)	døv	['døv]
mute (adj)	stum	['stʉm]
deaf mute (adj)	døvstum	['døf,stʉm]

mad, insane (adj)	gal	['gal]
madman (demented person)	gal mann (m)	['gal ,man]
madwoman	gal kvinne (m/f)	['gal ,kvinə]
to go insane	å bli sinnssyk	[ɔ 'bli 'sin,syk]

gene	gen (m)	['gen]
immunity	immunitet (m)	[imʉni'tet]
hereditary (adj)	arvelig	['arvəli]
congenital (adj)	medfødt	['meː,føt]

virus	virus (m)	['virʉs]
microbe	mikrobe (m)	[mi'krʉbə]
bacterium	bakterie (m)	[bak'teriə]
infection	infeksjon (m)	[infɛk'ʂʉn]

71. Symptoms. Treatments. Part 3

| hospital | sykehus (n) | ['sykə,hʉs] |
| patient | pasient (m) | [pasi'ɛnt] |

diagnosis	diagnose (m)	[dia'gnʉsə]
cure	kur (m)	['kʉr]
medical treatment	behandling (m/f)	[be'handl ŋ]
to get treatment	å bli behandlet	[ɔ 'bli be'handlət]
to treat (~ a patient)	å behandle	[ɔ be'handlə]
to nurse (look after)	å skjøtte	[ɔ 'ʂøtə]
care (nursing ~)	sykepleie (m/f)	['sykə,plæjə]

operation, surgery	operasjon (m)	[ɔpəra'ʂʉn]
to bandage (head, limb)	å forbinde	[ɔ for'binə]
bandaging	forbinding (m)	[for'biniŋ]

vaccination	**vaksinering** (m/f)	[vaksi'neriŋ]
to vaccinate (vt)	**å vaksinere**	[ɔ vaksi'nerə]
injection, shot	**injeksjon** (m), **sprøyte** (m/f)	[injɛk'ʂʊn], ['sprøjtə]
to give an injection	**å gi en sprøyte**	[ɔ 'ji en 'sprøjtə]

attack	**anfall** (n)	['an,fal]
amputation	**amputasjon** (m)	[ampʉta'ʂʊn]
to amputate (vt)	**å amputere**	[ɔ ampʉ'terə]
coma	**koma** (m)	['kʊma]
to be in a coma	**å ligge i koma**	[ɔ 'ligə i 'kʊma]
intensive care	**intensivavdeling** (m/f)	['inten,siv 'av,deliŋ]

to recover (~ from flu)	**å bli frisk**	[ɔ 'bli 'frisk]
condition (patient's ~)	**tilstand** (m)	['til,stan]
consciousness	**bevissthet** (m)	[be'vist,het]
memory (faculty)	**minne** (n), **hukommelse** (m)	['minə], [hʉ'kɔmǝlsə]

to pull out (tooth)	**å trekke ut**	[ɔ 'trɛkə ʉt]
filling	**fylling** (m/f)	['fʏliŋ]
to fill (a tooth)	**å plombere**	[ɔ plʊm'berə]

hypnosis	**hypnose** (m)	[hʏp'nʊsə]
to hypnotize (vt)	**å hypnotisere**	[ɔ hʏpnʊti'serə]

72. Doctors

doctor	**lege** (m)	['legə]
nurse	**sykepleierske** (m/f)	['sykə,plæjeʂkə]
personal doctor	**personlig lege** (m)	[pæ'ʂʊnli 'legə]

dentist	**tannlege** (m)	['tan,legə]
eye doctor	**øyelege** (m)	['øjə,legə]
internist	**terapeut** (m)	[tera'pɛut]
surgeon	**kirurg** (m)	[çi'rʉrg]

psychiatrist	**psykiater** (m)	[syki'atər]
pediatrician	**barnelege** (m)	['baːṇə,legə]
psychologist	**psykolog** (m)	[sykʊ'lɔg]
gynecologist	**gynekolog** (m)	[gynekʊ'lɔg]
cardiologist	**kardiolog** (m)	[kaːɖiʊ'lɔg]

73. Medicine. Drugs. Accessories

medicine, drug	**medisin** (m)	[medi'sin]
remedy	**middel** (n)	['midəl]
to prescribe (vt)	**å ordinere**	[ɔ ɔrdi'nerə]
prescription	**resept** (m)	[re'sɛpt]

tablet, pill	**tablett** (m)	[tab'let]
ointment	**salve** (m/f)	['salvə]
ampule	**ampulle** (m)	[am'pʉlə]
mixture	**mikstur** (m)	[miks'tʉr]
syrup	**sirup** (m)	['sirʉp]
pill	**pille** (m/f)	['pilə]
powder	**pulver** (n)	['pʉlvər]
gauze bandage	**gasbind** (n)	['gas,bin]
cotton wool	**vatt** (m/n)	['vat]
iodine	**jod** (m/n)	['ʉd]
Band-Aid	**plaster** (n)	['plastər]
eyedropper	**pipette** (m)	[pi'pɛtə]
thermometer	**termometer** (n)	[tɛrmʊ'metər]
syringe	**sprøyte** (m/f)	['sprøjtə]
wheelchair	**rullestol** (m)	['rʉlə,stʊl]
crutches	**krykker** (m/f pl)	['krʏkər]
painkiller	**smertestillende middel** (n)	['smæːțə,stilenə 'midəl]
laxative	**laksativ** (n)	[laksa'tiv]
spirits (ethanol)	**sprit** (m)	['sprit]
medicinal herbs	**legeurter** (m/f pl)	['legə,ʉːțər]
herbal (~ tea)	**urte-**	['ʉːțə-]

74. Smoking. Tobacco products

tobacco	**tobakk** (m)	[tʊ'bak]
cigarette	**sigarett** (m)	[siga'rɛt]
cigar	**sigar** (m)	[si'gar]
pipe	**pipe** (m/f)	['pipə]
pack (of cigarettes)	**pakke** (m/f)	['pakə]
matches	**fyrstikker** (m/f pl)	['fy,stikər]
matchbox	**fyrstikkeske** (m)	['fyștik,ɛskə]
lighter	**tenner** (m)	['tɛnər]
ashtray	**askebeger** (n)	['askə,begər]
cigarette case	**sigarettetui** (n)	[siga'rɛt ɛtʉ'i]
cigarette holder	**munnstykke** (n)	['mʉn,stʏkə]
filter (cigarette tip)	**filter** (n)	['filtər]
to smoke (vi, vt)	**å røyke**	[ɔ 'røjkə]
to light a cigarette	**å tenne en sigarett**	[ɔ 'tɛnə en siga'rɛt]
smoking	**røyking, røkning** (m)	['røjkiŋ], ['røkniŋ]
smoker	**røyker** (m)	['røjkər]
stub, butt (of cigarette)	**stump** (m)	['stʉmp]
smoke, fumes	**røyk** (m)	['røjk]
ash	**aske** (m/f)	['askə]

HUMAN HABITAT

City

75. City. Life in the city

city, town	**by** (m)	['by]
capital city	**hovedstad** (m)	['hʊvəd‚stɑd]
village	**landsby** (m)	['lɑns‚by]
city map	**bykart** (n)	['by‚kɑːt]
downtown	**sentrum** (n)	['sɛntrum]
suburb	**forstad** (m)	['fɔ‚stɑd]
suburban (adj)	**forstads-**	['fɔ‚stɑds-]
outskirts	**utkant** (m)	['ʉt‚kɑnt]
environs (suburbs)	**omegner** (m pl)	['ɔm‚æjnər]
city block	**kvarter** (n)	[kvɑːʈer]
residential block (area)	**boligkvarter** (n)	['bʊli‚kvɑːʈer]
traffic	**trafikk** (m)	[trɑ'fik]
traffic lights	**trafikklys** (n)	[trɑ'fik‚lys]
public transportation	**offentlig transport** (m)	['ɔfentli trɑns'pɔːʈ]
intersection	**veikryss** (n)	['væjkrʏs]
crosswalk	**fotgjengerovergang** (m)	['fʊtjɛŋər 'ɔvər‚gɑŋ]
pedestrian underpass	**undergang** (m)	['ʉnər‚gɑŋ]
to cross (~ the street)	**å gå over**	[ɔ 'gɔ 'ɔvər]
pedestrian	**fotgjenger** (m)	['fʊtjɛŋər]
sidewalk	**fortau** (n)	['fɔːʈaʊ]
bridge	**bro** (m/f)	['brʊ]
embankment (river walk)	**kai** (m/f)	['kɑj]
fountain	**fontene** (m)	['fʊntnə]
allée (garden walkway)	**allé** (m)	[ɑ'leː]
park	**park** (m)	['pɑrk]
boulevard	**bulevard** (m)	[bule'vɑr]
square	**torg** (n)	['tɔr]
avenue (wide street)	**aveny** (m)	[ave'ny]
street	**gate** (m/f)	['gɑtə]
side street	**sidegate** (m/f)	['sidə‚gɑtə]
dead end	**blindgate** (m/f)	['blin‚gɑtə]
house	**hus** (n)	['hʉs]
building	**bygning** (m/f)	['bʏgniŋ]

skyscraper	skyskraper (m)	['ʂyˌskrɑpər]
facade	fasade (m)	[fɑ'sɑdə]
roof	tak (n)	['tɑk]
window	vindu (n)	['vindʉ]
arch	bue (n)	['bʉːə]
column	søyle (m)	['søjlə]
corner	hjørne (n)	['jœːŋə]

store window	utstillingsvindu (n)	['ʉtˌstiliŋs 'vindʉ]
signboard (store sign, etc.)	skilt (n)	['ʂilt]
poster	plakat (m)	[plɑ'kɑt]
advertising poster	reklameplakat (m)	[rɛ'klɑməˌplɑ'kɑt]
billboard	reklametavle (m/f)	[rɛ'klɑməˌtɑvlə]

garbage, trash	søppel (m/f/n), avfall (n)	['sœpəl], ['ɑvˌfɑl]
trashcan (public ~)	søppelkasse (m/f)	['sœpəlˌkɑsə]
to litter (vi)	å kaste søppel	[ɔ 'kɑstə 'sœpəl]
garbage dump	søppelfylling (m/f), deponi (n)	['sœpəlˌfyliŋ], [ˌdepo'ni]

phone booth	telefonboks (m)	[tele'fʉnˌbɔks]
lamppost	lyktestolpe (m)	['lʏktəˌstɔlpə]
bench (park ~)	benk (m)	['bɛŋk]

police officer	politi (m)	[pʊli'ti]
police	politi (n)	[pʊli'ti]
beggar	tigger (m)	['tigər]
homeless (n)	hjemløs	['jɛmˌløs]

76. Urban institutions

store	forretning, butikk (m)	[fo'rɛtniŋ], [bʉ'tik]
drugstore, pharmacy	apotek (n)	[ɑpʊ'tek]
eyeglass store	optikk (m)	[ɔp'tik]
shopping mall	kjøpesenter (n)	['çœpəˌsɛntər]
supermarket	supermarked (n)	['sʉpəˌmɑrˠet]

bakery	bakeri (n)	[bake'ri]
baker	baker (m)	['bakər]
pastry shop	konditori (n)	[kʊndito'ri]
grocery store	matbutikk (m)	['mɑtbʉˌtik]
butcher shop	slakterbutikk (m)	['ʂlaktəbʉˌtik]

| produce store | grønnsaksbutikk (m) | ['grœnˌsaks bʉ'tik] |
| market | marked (n) | ['mɑrkəd] |

coffee house	kafé, kaffebar (m)	[kɑ'fe], ['kɑfəˌbɑr]
restaurant	restaurant (m)	[rɛstʉ'rɑŋ]
pub, bar	pub (m)	['pʉb]
pizzeria	pizzeria (m)	[pitsə'riɑ]

hair salon	frisørsalong (m)	[fri'sør sɑˌlɔŋ]
post office	post (m)	['pɔst]
dry cleaners	renseri (n)	[rɛnse'ri]
photo studio	fotostudio (n)	['fotoˌstʉdiɔ]
shoe store	skobutikk (m)	['skʊˌbʉ'tik]
bookstore	bokhandel (m)	['bʊkˌhandəl]
sporting goods store	idrettsbutikk (m)	['idrɛts bʉ'tik]
clothes repair shop	reparasjon (m) av klær	[repɑrɑ'ʂʊn ɑː ˌklær]
formal wear rental	leie (m/f) av klær	['læjə ɑː ˌklær]
video rental store	filmutleie (m/f)	['filmˌʉt'læje]
circus	sirkus (m/n)	['sirkʉs]
zoo	zoo, dyrepark (m)	['sʊː], [dyrə'pɑrk]
movie theater	kino (m)	['çinʊ]
museum	museum (n)	[mʉ'seum]
library	bibliotek (n)	[bibliʊ'tek]
theater	teater (n)	[te'ɑtər]
opera (opera house)	opera (m)	['ʊperɑ]
nightclub	nattklubb (m)	['natˌklʉb]
casino	kasino (n)	[kɑ'sinʊ]
mosque	moské (m)	[mʊ'ske]
synagogue	synagoge (m)	[synɑ'gʊgə]
cathedral	katedral (m)	[kate'drɑl]
temple	tempel (n)	['tɛmpəl]
church	kirke (m/f)	['çirkə]
college	institutt (n)	[insti'tʉt]
university	universitet (n)	[ʉnivæʂi'tet]
school	skole (m/f)	['skʊlə]
prefecture	prefektur (n)	[prɛfɛk'tʉr]
city hall	rådhus (n)	['rɔdˌhʉs]
hotel	hotell (n)	[hʊ'tɛl]
bank	bank (m)	['bɑnk]
embassy	ambassade (m)	[ɑmbɑ'sɑdə]
travel agency	reisebyrå (n)	['ræjsə byˌrɔ]
information office	opplysningskontor (n)	[ɔp'lʏsniŋs kʊn'tʊr]
currency exchange	vekslingskontor (n)	['vɛkʂliŋs kʊn'tʊr]
subway	tunnelbane, T-bane (m)	['tʉnəlˌbɑnə], ['tɛːˌbɑnə]
hospital	sykehus (n)	['sykəˌhʉs]
gas station	bensinstasjon (m)	[bɛn'sinˌstɑ'ʂʊn]
parking lot	parkeringsplass (m)	[pɑr'keriŋsˌplɑs]

77. Urban transportation

bus	**buss** (m)	['bʉs]
streetcar	**trikk** (m)	['trik]
trolley bus	**trolleybuss** (m)	['trɔli,bʉs]
route (of bus, etc.)	**rute** (m/f)	['rʉtə]
number (e.g., bus ~)	**nummer** (n)	['nʉmər]
to go by ...	**å kjøre med ...**	[ɔ 'çœːrə me ...]
to get on (~ the bus)	**å gå på ...**	[ɔ 'gɔ pɔ ...]
to get off ...	**å gå av ...**	[ɔ 'gɔ aː ...]
stop (e.g., bus ~)	**holdeplass** (m)	['hɔlə,plas]
next stop	**neste holdeplass** (m)	['nɛstə 'hɔlə,plas]
terminus	**endestasjon** (m)	['ɛnə,sta'ʂʉn]
schedule	**rutetabell** (m)	['rʉtə,ta'bɛl]
to wait (vt)	**å vente**	[ɔ 'vɛntə]
ticket	**billett** (m)	[bi'let]
fare	**billettpris** (m)	[bi'let,pris]
cashier (ticket seller)	**kassærer** (m)	[ka'serər]
ticket inspection	**billettkontroll** (m)	[bi'let kʉn,trɔl]
ticket inspector	**billett inspektør** (m)	[bi'let inspɛk'tør]
to be late (for ...)	**å komme for sent**	[ɔ 'kɔmə fɔ'ʂɛnt]
to miss (~ the train, etc.)	**å komme for sent til ...**	[ɔ 'kɔmə fɔ'ʂɛnt til ...]
to be in a hurry	**å skynde seg**	[ɔ 'ʂynə sæj]
taxi, cab	**drosje** (m/f), **taxi** (m)	['drɔʂɛ], ['taksi]
taxi driver	**taxisjåfør** (m)	['taksi ʂɔ'før]
by taxi	**med taxi**	[me 'taksi]
taxi stand	**taxiholdeplass** (m)	['taksi 'hɔ ə,plas]
to call a taxi	**å taxi bestellen**	[ɔ 'taksi be'stɛlən]
to take a taxi	**å ta taxi**	[ɔ 'ta ,taksi]
traffic	**trafikk** (m)	[tra'fik]
traffic jam	**trafikkork** (m)	[tra'fik,kɔrk]
rush hour	**rushtid** (m/f)	['rʉʂ,tid]
to park (vi)	**å parkere**	[ɔ par'kerə]
to park (vt)	**å parkere**	[ɔ par'kerə]
parking lot	**parkeringsplass** (m)	[par'keriŋs,plas]
subway	**tunnelbane, T-bane** (m)	['tʉnəl,baːnə], ['tɛː,banə]
station	**stasjon** (m)	[sta'ʂʉn]
to take the subway	**å kjøre med T-bane**	[ɔ 'çøːrə me 'tɛː,banə]
train	**tog** (n)	['tɔg]
train station	**togstasjon** (m)	['tɔg,sta'ʂʉn]

78. Sightseeing

monument	monument (n)	[mɔnʉ'mɛnt]
fortress	festning (m/f)	['fɛstniŋ]
palace	palass (n)	[pɑ'lɑs]
castle	borg (m)	['bɔrg]
tower	tårn (n)	['tɔːɳ]
mausoleum	mausoleum (n)	[maʉsʉ'leum]
architecture	arkitektur (m)	[ɑrkitɛk'tʉr]
medieval (adj)	middelalderlig	['midəl‚ɑldɛːⁱ]
ancient (adj)	gammel	['gɑməl]
national (adj)	nasjonal	[nɑʂʉ'nɑl]
famous (monument, etc.)	kjent	['çɛnt]
tourist	turist (m)	[tʉ'rist]
guide (person)	guide (m)	['gɑjd]
excursion, sightseeing tour	utflukt (m/f)	['ʉt‚flʉkt]
to show (vt)	å vise	[ɔ 'visə]
to tell (vt)	å fortelle	[ɔ fɔ:'ʈɛlə]
to find (vt)	å finne	[ɔ 'finə]
to get lost (lose one's way)	å gå seg bort	[ɔ 'gɔ sæj 'bʊːʈ]
map (e.g., subway ~)	kart, linjekart (n)	['kɑːʈ], ['linjə'kɑːʈ]
map (e.g., city ~)	kart (n)	['kɑːʈ]
souvenir, gift	suvenir (m)	[sʉve'nir]
gift shop	suvenirbutikk (m)	[sʉve'nir bʉ'tik]
to take pictures	å fotografere	[ɔ fotɔgrɑ'ferə]
to have one's picture taken	å bli fotografert	[ɔ 'bli fotɔgrɑ'fɛːʈ]

79. Shopping

to buy (purchase)	å kjøpe	[ɔ 'çœːpə]
purchase	innkjøp (n)	['in‚çœp]
to go shopping	å gå shopping	[ɔ 'gɔ ‚ʂɔpiŋ]
shopping	shopping (m)	['ʂɔpiŋ]
to be open (ab. store)	å være åpen	[ɔ 'værə 'ɔpən]
to be closed	å være stengt	[ɔ 'værə 'stɛŋt]
footwear, shoes	skotøy (n)	['skʊtøj]
clothes, clothing	klær (n)	['klær]
cosmetics	kosmetikk (m)	[kʊsme'tik]
food products	matvarer (m/f pl)	['mɑt‚vɑrər]
gift, present	gave (m/f)	['gɑvə]
salesman	forselger (m)	[fɔ'ʂɛlər]
saleswoman	forselger (m)	[fɔ'ʂɛlər]

check out, cash desk	kasse (m/f)	['kɑsə]
mirror	speil (n)	['spæjl]
counter (store ~)	disk (m)	['disk]
fitting room	prøverom (n)	['prøvə,rʊm]

to try on	å prøve	[ɔ 'prøvə]
to fit (ab. dress, etc.)	å passe	[ɔ 'pɑsə]
to like (I like …)	å like	[ɔ 'likə]

price	pris (m)	['pris]
price tag	prislapp (m)	['pris,lɑp]
to cost (vt)	å koste	[ɔ 'kɔstə]
How much?	Hvor mye?	[vʊr 'mye]
discount	rabatt (m)	[rɑ'bɑt]

inexpensive (adj)	billig	['bili]
cheap (adj)	billig	['bili]
expensive (adj)	dyr	['dyr]
It's expensive	Det er dyrt	[de ær 'dy:t]

rental (n)	utleie (m/f)	['ʉt,læje]
to rent (~ a tuxedo)	å leie	[ɔ 'læjə]
credit (trade credit)	kreditt (m)	[krɛ'dit]
on credit (adv)	på kreditt	[pɔ krɛ'dit]

80. Money

money	penger (m pl)	['pɛŋər]
currency exchange	veksling (m/f)	['vɛksliŋ]
exchange rate	kurs (m)	['kʉs]
ATM	minibank (m)	['mini,bɑnk]
coin	mynt (m)	['mynt]

| dollar | dollar (m) | ['dɔlɑr] |
| euro | euro (m) | ['ɛʉrʉ] |

lira	lira (m)	['lire]
Deutschmark	mark (m/f)	['mɑrk]
franc	franc (m)	['frɑn]
pound sterling	pund sterling (m)	['pʉn stɛː'liŋ]
yen	yen (m)	['jɛn]

debt	skyld (m/f), gjeld (m)	['ʂyl], ['jɛl]
debtor	skyldner (m)	['ʂylnər]
to lend (money)	å låne ut	[ɔ 'lo:nə ʉt]
to borrow (vi, vt)	å låne	[ɔ 'lo:nə]

bank	bank (m)	['bɑnk]
account	konto (m)	['kɔntʉ]
to deposit (vt)	å sette inn	[ɔ 'sɛtə in]

| to deposit into the account | å sette inn på kontoen | [ɔ 'sɛtə in pɔ 'kɔntʊən] |
| to withdraw (vt) | å ta ut fra kontoen | [ɔ 'tɑ ʉt frɑ 'kɔntʊən] |

credit card	kredittkort (n)	[krɛ'dit̪ˌkɔːt̪]
cash	kontanter (m pl)	[kʊn'tɑntər]
check	sjekk (m)	['ʂɛk]
to write a check	å skrive en sjekk	[ɔ 'skrivə en 'ʂɛk]
checkbook	sjekkbok (m/f)	['ʂɛkˌbʊk]

wallet	lommebok (m)	['lʊməˌbʊk]
change purse	pung (m)	['pʉŋ]
safe	safe, seif (m)	['sɛjf]

heir	arving (m)	['ɑrviŋ]
inheritance	arv (m)	['ɑrv]
fortune (wealth)	formue (m)	['fɔrˌmʉə]

lease	leie (m)	['læje]
rent (money)	husleie (m/f)	['hʉsˌlæje]
to rent (sth from sb)	å leie	[ɔ 'læjə]

price	pris (m)	['pris]
cost	kostnad (m)	['kɔstnɑd]
sum	sum (m)	['sʉm]

to spend (vt)	å bruke	[ɔ 'brʉkə]
expenses	utgifter (m/f pl)	['ʉtˌjiftər]
to economize (vi, vt)	å spare	[ɔ 'spɑrə]
economical	sparsom	['spɑʂɔm]

to pay (vi, vt)	å betale	[ɔ be'tɑlə]
payment	betaling (m/f)	[be'tɑliŋ]
change (give the ~)	vekslepenger (pl)	['vɛkʂləˌpɛŋər]

tax	skatt (m)	['skɑt]
fine	bot (m/f)	['bʊt]
to fine (vt)	å bøtelegge	[ɔ 'bøtəˌlegə]

81. Post. Postal service

post office	post (m)	['pɔst]
mail (letters, etc.)	post (m)	['pɔst]
mailman	postbud (n)	['pɔstˌbʉd]
opening hours	åpningstider (m/f pl)	['ɔpniŋsˌtidər]

letter	brev (n)	['brev]
registered letter	rekommandert brev (n)	[rekʊmɑn'dɛːt̪ ˌbrev]
postcard	postkort (n)	['pɔstˌkɔːt̪]
telegram	telegram (n)	[tele'grɑm]
package (parcel)	postpakke (m/f)	['pɔstˌpɑkə]

money transfer	**pengeoverføring** (m/f)	['pɛŋə 'ɔvərˌføriŋ]
to receive (vt)	**å motta**	[ɔ 'mɔta]
to send (vt)	**å sende**	[ɔ 'sɛnə]
sending	**avsending** (m)	['afˌsɛniŋ]
address	**adresse** (m)	[ɑ'drɛsə]
ZIP code	**postnummer** (n)	['pɔstˌnʉmər]
sender	**avsender** (m)	['afˌsɛnər]
receiver	**mottaker** (m)	['mɔtˌtakər]
name (first name)	**fornavn** (n)	['fɔrˌnavn]
surname (last name)	**etternavn** (n)	['ɛtəˌnavn]
postage rate	**tariff** (m)	[ta'rif]
standard (adj)	**vanlig**	['vanli]
economical (adj)	**økonomisk**	[økʉ'nɔmisk]
weight	**vekt** (m)	['vɛkt]
to weigh (~ letters)	**å veie**	[ɔ 'væjə]
envelope	**konvolutt** (m)	[kʉnvʉ'lʉt]
postage stamp	**frimerke** (n)	['friˌmærkə]
to stamp an envelope	**å sette på frimerke**	[ɔ 'sɛtə pɔ 'friˌmærkə]

Dwelling. House. Home

82. House. Dwelling

house	**hus** (n)	['hʉs]
at home (adv)	**hjemme**	['jɛmə]
yard	**gård** (m)	['gɔːr]
fence (iron ~)	**gjerde** (n)	['jærə]
brick (n)	**tegl** (n), **murstein** (m)	['tæjl], ['mʉˌstæjn]
brick (as adj)	**tegl-**	['tæjl-]
stone (n)	**stein** (m)	['stæjn]
stone (as adj)	**stein-**	['stæjn-]
concrete (n)	**betong** (m)	[be'toŋ]
concrete (as adj)	**betong-**	[be'toŋ-]
new (new-built)	**ny**	['ny]
old (adj)	**gammel**	['gaməl]
decrepit (house)	**falleferdig**	['faləˌfæːɖi]
modern (adj)	**moderne**	[mʉ'dɛːnə]
multistory (adj)	**fleretasjes-**	['flerɛˌtaʂɛs-]
tall (~ building)	**høy**	['høj]
floor, story	**etasje** (m)	[ɛ'taʂə]
single-story (adj)	**enetasjes**	['ɛnɛˌtaʂɛs]
1st floor	**første etasje** (m)	['fœʂtə ɛ'taʂə]
top floor	**øverste etasje** (m)	['øvəʂtə ɛ'taʂə]
roof	**tak** (n)	['tak]
chimney	**skorstein** (m/f)	['skɔˌstæjn]
roof tiles	**takstein** (m)	['takˌstæjn]
tiled (adj)	**taksteins-**	['takˌstæjns-]
attic (storage place)	**loft** (n)	['lɔft]
window	**vindu** (n)	['vindʉ]
glass	**glass** (n)	['glas]
window ledge	**vinduskarm** (m)	['vindʉsˌkarm]
shutters	**vinduslemmer** (m pl)	['vindʉsˌlemər]
wall	**mur, vegg** (m)	['mʉr], ['vɛg]
balcony	**balkong** (m)	[bal'kɔŋ]
downspout	**nedløpsrør** (n)	['nedløpsˌrør]
upstairs (to be ~)	**oppe**	['ɔpə]
to go upstairs	**å gå ovenpå**	[ɔ 'gɔ 'ɔvənˌpɔ]
to come down (the stairs)	**å gå ned**	[ɔ 'gɔ ne]
to move (to new premises)	**å flytte**	[ɔ 'flʏtə]

83. House. Entrance. Lift

entrance	inngang (m)	['in,gɑŋ]
stairs (stairway)	trapp (m/f)	['trɑp]
steps	trinn (n pl)	['trin]
banister	gelender (n)	[ge'lendər]
lobby (hotel ~)	hall, lobby (m)	['hɑl], ['lɔbi]
mailbox	postkasse (m/f)	['pɔst,kɑsə]
garbage can	søppelkasse (m/f)	['sœpəl,kɑsə]
trash chute	søppelsjakt (m/f)	['sœpəl,sɑkt]
elevator	heis (m)	['hæjs]
freight elevator	lasteheis (m)	['lɑstə'hæjs]
elevator cage	heiskorg (m/f)	['hæjs,kɔrg]
to take the elevator	å ta heisen	[ɔ 'tɑ ,hæjsən]
apartment	leilighet (m/f)	['læjli,het]
residents (~ of a building)	beboere (m pl)	[be'buerə]
neighbor (masc.)	nabo (m)	['nɑbʉ]
neighbor (fem.)	nabo (m)	['nɑbʉ]
neighbors	naboer (m pl)	['nɑbʉər]

84. House. Doors. Locks

door	dør (m/f)	['dœr]
gate (vehicle ~)	grind (m/f), port (m)	['griŋ], ['pɔːt]
handle, doorknob	dørhåndtak (n)	['dœr,hɔnːɑk]
to unlock (unbolt)	å låse opp	[ɔ 'lɔːsə ɔɔ]
to open (vt)	å åpne	[ɔ 'ɔpnə]
to close (vt)	å lukke	[ɔ 'lʉkə]
key	nøkkel (m)	['nøkəl]
bunch (of keys)	knippe (n)	['knipə]
to creak (door, etc.)	å knirke	[ɔ 'knirkə]
creak	knirk (m/n)	['knirk]
hinge (door ~)	hengsel (m/n)	['hɛŋsel]
doormat	dørmatte (m/f)	['dœr,mɑtə]
door lock	dørlås (m/n)	['dœr,lɔs]
keyhole	nøkkelhull (n)	['nøkəl,hʉl]
crossbar (sliding bar)	slå (m/f)	['ʂlɔ]
door latch	slå (m/f)	['ʂlɔ]
padlock	hengelås (m/n)	['hɛŋe,lɔs]
to ring (~ the door bell)	å ringe	[ɔ 'riŋə]
ringing (sound)	ringing (m/f)	['riŋiŋ]
doorbell	ringeklokke (m/f)	['riŋə,klɔkə]
doorbell button	ringeklokke knapp (m)	['riŋə,klɔkə 'knɑp]

knock (at the door)	**kakking** (m/f)	['kɑkiŋ]
to knock (vi)	**å kakke**	[ɔ 'kɑkə]
code	**kode** (m)	['kʊdə]
combination lock	**kodelås** (m/n)	['kʊdə,lɔs]
intercom	**dørtelefon** (m)	['dœr,tele'fʊn]
number (on the door)	**nummer** (n)	['nʉmər]
doorplate	**dørskilt** (n)	['dœ,ʂilt]
peephole	**kikhull** (n)	['çik,hʉl]

85. Country house

village	**landsby** (m)	['lɑns,by]
vegetable garden	**kjøkkenhage** (m)	['çœkən,hagə]
fence	**gjerde** (n)	['jærə]
picket fence	**stakitt** (m/n)	[stɑ'kit]
wicket gate	**port, stakittport** (m)	['pɔːt], [stɑ'kit,pɔːt]
granary	**kornlåve** (m)	['kʊːn,loːvə]
root cellar	**jordkjeller** (m)	['juːr,çɛlər]
shed (garden ~)	**skur, skjul** (n)	['skʉr], ['ʂʉl]
well (water)	**brønn** (m)	['brœn]
stove (wood-fired ~)	**ovn** (m)	['ɔvn]
to stoke the stove	**å fyre**	[ɔ 'fyrə]
firewood	**ved** (m)	['ve]
log (firewood)	**vedstykke** (n), **vedskie** (f)	['vɛd,stʏkə], ['vɛ,ʂiə]
veranda	**veranda** (m)	[væ'randɑ]
deck (terrace)	**terrasse** (m)	[tɛ'rasə]
stoop (front steps)	**yttertrapp** (m/f)	['ytə,trɑp]
swing (hanging seat)	**gynge** (m/f)	['jiŋə]

86. Castle. Palace

castle	**borg** (m)	['bɔrg]
palace	**palass** (n)	[pɑ'las]
fortress	**festning** (m/f)	['fɛstniŋ]
wall (round castle)	**mur** (m)	['mʉr]
tower	**tårn** (n)	['tɔːɳ]
keep, donjon	**kjernetårn** (n)	['çæːɳə'tɔːɳ]
portcullis	**fallgitter** (n)	['fal,gitər]
underground passage	**underjordisk gang** (m)	['ʉnərju:rdisk 'gɑŋ]
moat	**vollgrav** (m/f)	['vɔl,grɑv]
chain	**kjede** (m)	['çɛ:də]
arrow loop	**skyteskår** (n)	['ʂytə,skɔr]

magnificent (adj)	**praktfull**	['prɑkt.fʉl]
majestic (adj)	**majestetisk**	[mɑje'stɛtisk]
impregnable (adj)	**uinntakelig**	[ʉən'takəli]
medieval (adj)	**middelalderlig**	['midəl.ɑldɛ:li]

87. Apartment

apartment	**leilighet** (m/f)	['læjli.het]
room	**rom** (n)	['rʊm]
bedroom	**soverom** (n)	['sɔvə.rʊm]
dining room	**spisestue** (m/f)	['spisə.stʉə]
living room	**dagligstue** (m/f)	['dɑgli.stʉə]
study (home office)	**arbeidsrom** (n)	['ɑrbæjds.rʊm]
entry room	**entré** (m)	[ɑn'trɛ:]
bathroom (room with a bath or shower)	**bad baderom** (n)	['bɑd], ['bɑdə.rʊm]
half bath	**toalett, WC** (n)	[tʊɑ'let], [vɛ'sɛ]
ceiling	**tak** (n)	['tɑk]
floor	**gulv** (n)	['gʉlv]
corner	**hjørne** (n)	['jœ:ŋə]

88. Apartment. Cleaning

to clean (vi, vt)	**å rydde**	[ɔ 'rʏdə]
to put away (to stow)	**å stue unna**	[ɔ 'stʉə 'ʉnɑ]
dust	**støv** (n)	['støv]
dusty (adj)	**støvet**	['støvət]
to dust (vt)	**å tørke støv**	[ɔ 'tœrkə 'støv]
vacuum cleaner	**støvsuger** (m)	['støf.sʉgər]
to vacuum (vt)	**å støvsuge**	[ɔ 'støf.sʉgə]
to sweep (vi, vt)	**å sope, å feie**	[ɔ 'sopə], ɔ 'fæjə]
sweepings	**søppel** (m/f/n)	['sœpəl]
order	**orden** (m)	['ɔrdən]
disorder, mess	**uorden** (m)	['ʉ:ɔrdən]
mop	**mopp** (m)	['mɔp]
dust cloth	**klut** (m)	['klʉt]
short broom	**feiekost** (m)	['fæjə.kʊs:]
dustpan	**feiebrett** (n)	['fæjə.brɛt]

89. Furniture. Interior

furniture	**møbler** (n pl)	['møblər]
table	**bord** (n)	['bʊr]

chair	**stol** (m)	['stʊl]
bed	**seng** (m/f)	['sɛŋ]
couch, sofa	**sofa** (m)	['sʊfɑ]
armchair	**lenestol** (m)	['lenəˌstʊl]
bookcase	**bokskap** (n)	['bʊkˌskɑp]
shelf	**hylle** (m/f)	['hʏlə]
wardrobe	**klesskap** (n)	['kleˌskɑp]
coat rack (wall-mounted ~)	**knaggbrett** (n)	['knɑgˌbrɛt]
coat stand	**stumtjener** (m)	['stʉmˌtjenər]
bureau, dresser	**kommode** (m)	[kʊ'mʊdə]
coffee table	**kaffebord** (n)	['kɑfəˌbʊr]
mirror	**speil** (n)	['spæjl]
carpet	**teppe** (n)	['tɛpə]
rug, small carpet	**lite teppe** (n)	['litə 'tɛpə]
fireplace	**peis** (m), **ildsted** (n)	['pæjs], ['ilsted]
candle	**lys** (n)	['lys]
candlestick	**lysestake** (m)	['lysəˌstɑkə]
drapes	**gardiner** (m/f pl)	[gɑ:'dinər]
wallpaper	**tapet** (n)	[tɑ'pet]
blinds (jalousie)	**persienne** (m)	[pæʂi'enə]
table lamp	**bordlampe** (m/f)	['bʊrˌlɑmpə]
wall lamp (sconce)	**vegglampe** (m/f)	['vɛgˌlɑmpə]
floor lamp	**gulvlampe** (m/f)	['gʉlvˌlɑmpə]
chandelier	**lysekrone** (m/f)	['lysəˌkrʊnə]
leg (of chair, table)	**bein** (n)	['bæjn]
armrest	**armlene** (n)	['ɑrmˌlenə]
back (backrest)	**rygg** (m)	['rʏg]
drawer	**skuff** (m)	['skʉf]

90. Bedding

bedclothes	**sengetøy** (n)	['sɛŋəˌtøj]
pillow	**pute** (m/f)	['pʉtə]
pillowcase	**putevar, putetrekk** (n)	['pʉtəˌvɑr], ['pʉtəˌtrɛk]
duvet, comforter	**dyne** (m/f)	['dynə]
sheet	**laken** (n)	['lɑkən]
bedspread	**sengeteppe** (n)	['sɛŋəˌtɛpə]

91. Kitchen

kitchen	**kjøkken** (n)	['çœkən]
gas	**gass** (m)	['gɑs]

| gas stove (range) | gasskomfyr (m) | ['gɑs kɔmˌfyr] |
| electric stove | elektrisk komfyr (m) | [ɛ'lektrisk kɔmˌfyr] |

| oven | bakeovn (m) | ['bɑkəˌɔvn] |
| microwave oven | mikrobølgeovn (m) | ['mikrʊˌbølgə'ɔvn] |

refrigerator	kjøleskap (n)	['çœləˌskɑp]
freezer	fryser (m)	['frysər]
dishwasher	oppvaskmaskin (m)	['ɔpvɑsk mɑˌʂin]

meat grinder	kjøttkvern (m/f)	['çœtˌkvɛːŋ]
juicer	juicepresse (m/f)	['dʒʉsˌprɛsə]
toaster	brødrister (m)	['brøˌristər]
mixer	mikser (m)	['miksər]

coffee machine	kaffetrakter (m)	['kɑfəˌtrɑktər]
coffee pot	kaffekanne (m/f)	['kɑfəˌkɑnə]
coffee grinder	kaffekvern (m/f)	['kɑfəˌkvɛːŋ]

kettle	tekjele (m)	['teˌçelə]
teapot	tekanne (m/f)	['teˌkɑnə]
lid	lokk (n)	['lɔk]
tea strainer	tesil (m)	['teˌsil]

spoon	skje (m)	['ʂe]
teaspoon	teskje (m)	['teˌʂe]
soup spoon	spiseskje (m)	['spisəˌʂɛ]
fork	gaffel (m)	['gɑfəl]
knife	kniv (m)	['kniv]

tableware (dishes)	servise (n)	[sær'visə]
plate (dinner ~)	tallerken (m)	[tɑ'lærkən]
saucer	tefat (n)	['teˌfɑt]

shot glass	shotglass (n)	['ʂɔtˌglɑs]
glass (tumbler)	glass (n)	['glɑs]
cup	kopp (m)	['kɔp]

sugar bowl	sukkerskål (m/f)	['sʉkərˌskɔl]
salt shaker	saltbøsse (m/f)	['sɑltˌbøsə]
pepper shaker	pepperbøsse (m/f)	['pɛpərˌbøsə]
butter dish	smørkopp (m)	['smœrˌkɔp]

stock pot (soup pot)	gryte (m/f)	['grytə]
frying pan (skillet)	steikepanne (m/f)	['stæjkəˌpɑnə]
ladle	sleiv (m/f)	['ʂlæjv]

| colander | dørslag (n) | ['dœʂlɑg] |
| tray (serving ~) | brett (n) | ['brɛt] |

| bottle | flaske (m) | ['flɑskə] |
| jar (glass) | glasskrukke (m/f) | ['glɑsˌkrʉkə] |

can	**boks** (m)	['bɔks]
bottle opener	**flaskeåpner** (m)	['flaskə‚ɔpnər]
can opener	**konservåpner** (m)	['kʉnsəv‚ɔpnər]
corkscrew	**korketrekker** (m)	['kɔrkə‚trɛkər]
filter	**filter** (n)	['filtər]
to filter (vt)	**å filtrere**	[ɔ fil'trerə]

trash, garbage (food waste, etc.)	**søppel** (m/f/n)	['sœpəl]
trash can (kitchen ~)	**søppelbøtte** (m/f)	['sœpəl‚bœtə]

92. Bathroom

bathroom	**bad, baderom** (n)	['bɑd], ['bɑdə‚rʉm]
water	**vann** (n)	['vɑn]
faucet	**kran** (m/f)	['krɑn]
hot water	**varmt vann** (n)	['vɑrmt ‚vɑn]
cold water	**kaldt vann** (n)	['kɑlt vɑn]

toothpaste	**tannpasta** (m)	['tɑn‚pɑstɑ]
to brush one's teeth	**å pusse tennene**	[ɔ 'pʉsə 'tɛnənə]
toothbrush	**tannbørste** (m)	['tɑn‚bœʂtə]

to shave (vi)	**å barbere seg**	[ɔ bɑr'berə sæj]
shaving foam	**barberskum** (n)	[bɑr'bɛ‚skʉm]
razor	**høvel** (m)	['høvəl]

to wash (one's hands, etc.)	**å vaske**	[ɔ 'vɑskə]
to take a bath	**å vaske seg**	[ɔ 'vɑskə sæj]

shower	**dusj** (m)	['dʉʂ]
to take a shower	**å ta en dusj**	[ɔ 'tɑ en 'dʉʂ]

bathtub	**badekar** (n)	['bɑdə‚kɑr]
toilet (toilet bowl)	**toalettstol** (m)	[tʊɑ'let‚stʊl]
sink (washbasin)	**vaskeservant** (m)	['vɑskə‚sɛr'vɑnt]

soap	**såpe** (m/f)	['so:pə]
soap dish	**såpeskål** (m/f)	['so:pə‚skɔl]

sponge	**svamp** (m)	['svɑmp]
shampoo	**sjampo** (m)	['ʂɑm‚pʊ]

towel	**håndkle** (n)	['hɔn‚kle]
bathrobe	**badekåpe** (m/f)	['bɑdə‚ko:pə]

laundry (process)	**vask** (m)	['vɑsk]
washing machine	**vaskemaskin** (m)	['vɑskə mɑ‚ʂin]
to do the laundry	**å vaske tøy**	[ɔ 'vɑskə 'tøj]
laundry detergent	**vaskepulver** (n)	['vɑskə‚pʉlvər]

93. Household appliances

TV set	TV (n), TV-apparat (n)	['tɛvɛ], ['tɛvɛ apa'rat]
tape recorder	båndopptaker (m)	['bɔn‚ɔptakər]
VCR (video recorder)	video (m)	['videʊ]
radio	radio (m)	['radiʊ]
player (CD, MP3, etc.)	spiler (m)	['spilər]

video projector	videoprojektor (m)	['videʊ prɔ'jɛktɔr]
home movie theater	hjemmekino (m)	['jɛmə‚çinʊ]
DVD player	DVD-spiller (m)	[deve'de ‚spilər]
amplifier	forsterker (m)	[fɔ'stærkər]
video game console	spilkonsoll (m)	['spil kʊn'sɔl]

video camera	videokamera (n)	['videʊ ‚kamera]
camera (photo)	kamera (n)	['kamera]
digital camera	digitalkamera (n)	[digi'tal ‚kamera]

vacuum cleaner	støvsuger (m)	['støf‚sʉgər]
iron (e.g., steam ~)	strykejern (n)	['strykə‚jæːɳ]
ironing board	strykebrett (n)	['strykə‚brɛt]

telephone	telefon (m)	[tele'fʊn]
cell phone	mobiltelefon (m)	[mʊ'bil tele'fʊn]
typewriter	skrivemaskin (m)	['skrivə ma‚ʂin]
sewing machine	symaskin (m)	['siːma‚ʂin]

microphone	mikrofon (m)	[mikrʊ'fʊn]
headphones	hodetelefoner (n pl)	['hɔdətelə‚fʊnər]
remote control (TV)	fjernkontroll (m)	['fjæːɳ kʊn'trɔl]

CD, compact disc	CD-rom (m)	['sɛdɛ‚rʊm]
cassette, tape	kassett (m)	[ka'sɛt]
vinyl record	plate, skive (m/f)	['platə], ['ʂivə]

94. Repairs. Renovation

renovations	renovering (m/f)	[renʊ'veriŋ]
to renovate (vt)	å renovere	[ɔ renʊ'verə]
to repair, to fix (vt)	å reparere	[ɔ repɑ'rerə]
to put in order	å bringe orden	[ɔ 'briŋə 'ɔrdən]
to redo (do again)	å gjøre om	[ɔ 'jørə ɔm]

paint	maling (m/f)	['maliŋ]
to paint (~ a wall)	å male	[ɔ 'malə]
house painter	maler (m)	['malər]
paintbrush	pensel (m)	['pɛnsəl]
whitewash	kalkmaling (m/f)	['kalk‚maliŋ]
to whitewash (vt)	å hvitmale	[ɔ 'vit‚malə]

wallpaper	tapet (n)	[ta'pet]
to wallpaper (vt)	å tapetsere	[ɔ tapet'serə]
varnish	ferniss (m)	['fæːˌn̩is]
to varnish (vt)	å lakkere	[ɔ la'kerə]

95. Plumbing

water	vann (n)	['van]
hot water	varmt vann (n)	['varmt ˌvan]
cold water	kaldt vann (n)	['kalt van]
faucet	kran (m/f)	['kran]

drop (of water)	dråpe (m)	['droːpə]
to drip (vi)	å dryppe	[ɔ 'drʏpə]
to leak (ab. pipe)	å lekke	[ɔ 'lekə]
leak (pipe ~)	lekk (m)	['lek]
puddle	pøl, pytt (m)	['pøl], ['pʏt]

pipe	rør (n)	['rør]
valve (e.g., ball ~)	ventil (m)	[vɛn'til]
to be clogged up	å bli tilstoppet	[ɔ 'bli til'stɔpət]

tools	verktøy (n pl)	['værkˌtøj]
adjustable wrench	skiftenøkkel (m)	['ʂiftəˌnøkəl]
to unscrew (lid, filter, etc.)	å skru ut	[ɔ 'skrʉ ʉt]
to screw (tighten)	å skru fast	[ɔ 'skrʉ 'fast]

to unclog (vt)	å rense	[ɔ 'rɛnsə]
plumber	rørlegger (m)	['rørˌlegər]
basement	kjeller (m)	['çɛlər]
sewerage (system)	avløp (n)	['avˌløp]

96. Fire. Conflagration

fire (accident)	ild (m)	['il]
flame	flamme (m)	['flamə]
spark	gnist (m)	['gnist]
smoke (from fire)	røyk (m)	['røjk]
torch (flaming stick)	fakkel (m)	['fakəl]
campfire	bål (n)	['bol]

gas, gasoline	bensin (m)	[bɛn'sin]
kerosene (type of fuel)	parafin (m)	[para'fin]
flammable (adj)	brennbar	['brɛnˌbar]
explosive (adj)	eksplosiv	['ɛkspluˌsiv]
NO SMOKING	RØYKING FORBUDT	['røjkiŋ for'bʉt]
safety	sikkerhet (m/f)	['sikərˌhet]
danger	fare (m)	['farə]

dangerous (adj)	**farlig**	['fɑːlị]
to catch fire	**å ta fyr**	[ɔ 'tɑ ˌfyr]
explosion	**eksplosjon** (m)	[ɛksplʉ'sʉn]
to set fire	**å sette fyr**	[ɔ 'sɛtə ˌfyr]
arsonist	**brannstifter** (m)	['brɑnˌstiftər]
arson	**brannstiftelse** (m)	['brɑnˌstiftəlsə]
to blaze (vi)	**å flamme**	[ɔ 'flɑmə]
to burn (be on fire)	**å brenne**	[ɔ 'brɛnə]
to burn down	**å brenne ned**	[ɔ 'brɛnə ne]
to call the fire department	**å ringe bransvesenet**	[ɔ 'riŋə 'brɑnsˌvesənə]
firefighter, fireman	**brannmann** (m)	['brɑnˌmɑn]
fire truck	**brannbil** (m)	['brɑnˌbil]
fire department	**brannkorps** (n)	['brɑnˌkɔrps]
fire truck ladder	**teleskopstige** (m)	['tele'skʉɽˌstiːə]
fire hose	**slange** (m)	['ʂlɑŋə]
fire extinguisher	**brannslukker** (n)	['brɑnˌʂlʉkər]
helmet	**hjelm** (m)	['jɛlm]
siren	**sirene** (m/f)	[si'renə]
to cry (for help)	**å skrike**	[ɔ 'skrikə]
to call for help	**å rope på hjelp**	[ɔ 'rʉpə pɔ 'jɛlp]
rescuer	**redningsmann** (m)	['rɛdniŋsˌmɑn]
to rescue (vt)	**å redde**	[ɔ 'rɛdə]
to arrive (vi)	**å ankomme**	[ɔ 'ɑnˌkɔmə]
to extinguish (vt)	**å slokke**	[ɔ 'ʂløkə]
water	**vann** (n)	['vɑn]
sand	**sand** (m)	['sɑn]
ruins (destruction)	**ruiner** (m pl)	[rʉ'inər]
to collapse (building, etc.)	**å falle sammen**	[ɔ 'fɑlə 'sɑmən]
to fall down (vi)	**å styrte ned**	[ɔ 'styːʈə ne]
to cave in (ceiling, floor)	**å styrte inn**	[ɔ 'styːʈə in]
piece of debris	**del** (m)	['del]
ash	**aske** (m/f)	['ɑskə]
to suffocate (die)	**å kveles**	[ɔ 'kveləs]
to be killed (perish)	**å omkomme**	[ɔ 'ɔmˌkɔmə]

HUMAN ACTIVITIES

Job. Business. Part 1

97. Banking

bank	**bank** (m)	['bɑnk]
branch (of bank, etc.)	**avdeling** (m)	['ɑvˌdeliŋ]
bank clerk, consultant	**konsulent** (m)	[kʊnsʉ'lent]
manager (director)	**forstander** (m)	[fɔ'ʂtɑndər]
bank account	**bankkonto** (m)	['bɑnkˌkɔntʉ]
account number	**kontonummer** (n)	['kɔntʉˌnʉmər]
checking account	**sjekkonto** (m)	['ʂɛkˌkɔntʉ]
savings account	**sparekonto** (m)	['spɑrəˌkɔntʉ]
to open an account	**å åpne en konto**	[ɔ 'ɔpnə en 'kɔntʉ]
to close the account	**å lukke kontoen**	[ɔ 'lʉkə 'kɔntʉən]
to deposit into the account	**å sette inn på kontoen**	[ɔ 'sɛtə in pɔ 'kɔntʉən]
to withdraw (vt)	**å ta ut fra kontoen**	[ɔ 'tɑ ʉt frɑ 'kɔntʉən]
deposit	**innskudd** (n)	['inˌskʉd]
to make a deposit	**å sette inn**	[ɔ 'sɛtə in]
wire transfer	**overføring** (m/f)	['ɔvərˌføriŋ]
to wire, to transfer	**å overføre**	[ɔ 'ɔvərˌførə]
sum	**sum** (m)	['sʉm]
How much?	**Hvor mye?**	[vʊr 'mye]
signature	**underskrift** (m/f)	['ʉnəˌskrift]
to sign (vt)	**å underskrive**	[ɔ 'ʉnəˌskrivə]
credit card	**kredittkort** (n)	[krɛ'ditˌkɔːʈ]
code (PIN code)	**kode** (m)	['kʊdə]
credit card number	**kreditkortnummer** (n)	[krɛ'ditˌkɔːʈ 'nʉmər]
ATM	**minibank** (m)	['miniˌbɑnk]
check	**sjekk** (m)	['ʂɛk]
to write a check	**å skrive en sjekk**	[ɔ 'skrivə en 'ʂɛk]
checkbook	**sjekkbok** (m/f)	['ʂɛkˌbʊk]
loan (bank ~)	**lån** (n)	['lɔn]
to apply for a loan	**å søke om lån**	[ɔ ˌsøkə ɔm 'lɔn]
to get a loan	**å få lån**	[ɔ 'fɔ 'lɔn]

| to give a loan | å gi lån | [ɔ 'ji 'lɔn] |
| guarantee | garanti (m) | [garan'ti] |

98. Telephone. Phone conversation

telephone	telefon (m)	[tele'fʊn]
cell phone	mobiltelefon (m)	[mʊ'bil tele fʊn]
answering machine	telefonsvarer (m)	[tele'fʊn‚svɔrər]

| to call (by phone) | å ringe | [ɔ 'riŋə] |
| phone call | telefonsamtale (m) | [tele'fʊn 'sam‚talə] |

to dial a number	å slå et nummer	[ɔ 'ṣlɔ et 'nʉmər]
Hello!	Hallo!	[ha'lʊ]
to ask (vt)	å spørre	[ɔ 'spørə]
to answer (vi, vt)	å svare	[ɔ 'svarə]

to hear (vt)	å høre	[ɔ 'hørə]
well (adv)	godt	['gɔt]
not well (adv)	dårlig	['dɔːli]
noises (interference)	støy (n)	['støj]

receiver	telefonrør (n)	[tele'fʊn‚rør]
to pick up (~ the phone)	å ta telefonen	[ɔ 'ta tele'fʊnən]
to hang up (~ the phone)	å legge på røret	[ɔ 'legə pɔ 'rørə]

busy (engaged)	opptatt	['ɔp‚tat]
to ring (ab. phone)	å ringe	[ɔ 'riŋə]
telephone book	telefonkatalog (m)	[tele'fʊn kata'lɔg]

local (adj)	lokal-	[lo'kal-]
local call	lokalsamtale (m)	[lo'kal 'sam‚talə]
long distance (~ call)	riks-	['riks-]
long-distance call	rikssamtale (m)	['riks 'sam‚talə]
international (adj)	internasjonal	['intɛ:ŋaṣʊ‚ŋal]
international call	internasjonal samtale (m)	['intɛ:ŋaṣʊ‚ŋal 'sam‚talə]

99. Cell phone

cell phone	mobiltelefon (m)	[mʊ'bil tele'fʊn]
display	skjerm (m)	['ṣærm]
button	knapp (m)	['knap]
SIM card	SIM-kort (n)	['sim‚kɔːt]

battery	batteri (n)	[batɛ'ri]
to be dead (battery)	å bli utladet	[ɔ 'bli ʉt‚ladət]
charger	lader (m)	['ladər]
menu	meny (m)	[me'ny]

settings	innstillinger (m/f pl)	['in,stiliŋər]
tune (melody)	melodi (m)	[melɔ'di]
to select (vt)	å velge	[ɔ 'vɛlgə]

calculator	regnemaskin (m)	['rɛjnə ma,ʂin]
voice mail	telefonsvarer (m)	[tele'fʊn,svarər]
alarm clock	vekkerklokka (m/f)	['vɛkər,klɔka]
contacts	kontakter (m pl)	[kʊn'taktər]

| SMS (text message) | SMS-beskjed (m) | [ɛsɛm'ɛs bɛ,ʂɛ] |
| subscriber | abonnent (m) | [abɔ'nɛnt] |

100. Stationery

| ballpoint pen | kulepenn (m) | ['kʉ:lə,pɛn] |
| fountain pen | fyllepenn (m) | ['fʏlə,pɛn] |

pencil	blyant (m)	['bly,ant]
highlighter	merkepenn (m)	['mærkə,pɛn]
felt-tip pen	tusjpenn (m)	['tʉʂ,pɛn]

| notepad | notatbok (m/f) | [nʊ'tat,bʊk] |
| agenda (diary) | dagbok (m/f) | ['dag,bʊk] |

ruler	linjal (m)	[li'njal]
calculator	regnemaskin (m)	['rɛjnə ma,ʂin]
eraser	viskelær (n)	['viskə,lær]
thumbtack	tegnestift (m)	['tæjnə,stift]
paper clip	binders (m)	['bindɛʂ]

glue	lim (n)	['lim]
stapler	stiftemaskin (m)	['stiftə ma,ʂin]
hole punch	hullemaskin (m)	['hʉlə ma,ʂin]
pencil sharpener	blyantspisser (m)	['blyant,spisər]

Job. Business. Part 2

101. Mass Media

newspaper	avis (m/f)	[ɑ'vis]
magazine	magasin, tidsskrift (n)	[mɑgɑ'sin], ['tid‚skrift]
press (printed media)	presse (m/f)	['prɛsə]
radio	radio (m)	['rɑdiʊ]
radio station	radiostasjon (m)	['rɑdiʊ‚stɑ'ʂʊn]
television	televisjon (m)	['televi‚ʂʊn]
presenter, host	programleder (m)	[prʊ'grɑm‚ledər]
newscaster	nyhetsoppleser (m)	['nyhets'ɔɔ‚lesər]
commentator	kommentator (m)	[kʊmən'tɑtʊr]
journalist	journalist (m)	[ʂuːɳɑ'list]
correspondent (reporter)	korrespondent (m)	[kʊrespor'dɛnt]
press photographer	pressefotograf (m)	['prɛsə fotʊ'grɑf]
reporter	reporter (m)	[re'pɔːtər]
editor	redaktør (m)	[rɛdɑk'tørˌ]
editor-in-chief	sjefredaktør (m)	['ʂɛf rɛdɑk'tør]
to subscribe (to ...)	å abonnere	[ɔ ɑbɔ'nerə]
subscription	abonnement (n)	[ɑbɔnə'mɑŋ]
subscriber	abonnent (m)	[ɑbɔ'nɛnt]
to read (vi, vt)	å lese	[ɔ 'lesə]
reader	leser (m)	['lesər]
circulation (of newspaper)	opplag (n)	['ɔp‚lɑg]
monthly (adj)	månedlig	['moːnədliˌ]
weekly (adj)	ukentlig	['ʉkəntli]
issue (edition)	nummer (n)	['nʉmər]
new (~ issue)	ny, fersk	['ny], ['fæʂk]
headline	overskrift (m)	['ɔvə‚skrift]
short article	notis (m)	[nʊ'tis]
column (regular article)	rubrikk (m)	[rʉ'brik]
article	artikkel (m)	[ɑː'tikəl]
page	side (m/f)	['sidə]
reportage, report	reportasje (m)	[repɔː'tɑʂə]
event (happening)	hendelse (m)	['hɛndəlsə]
sensation (news)	sensasjon (m)	[sɛnsɑ'ʂʊn]
scandal	skandale (m)	[skɑn'dɑlə]
scandalous (adj)	skandaløs	[skɑndɑ'løs]

great (~ scandal)	stor	['stʊr]
show (e.g., cooking ~)	program (n)	[prʊ'gram]
interview	intervju (n)	[intə'vjʉ:]
live broadcast	direktesending (m/f)	[di'rɛktə͵sɛniŋ]
channel	kanal (m)	[ka'nal]

102. Agriculture

agriculture	landbruk (n)	['lan͵brʉk]
peasant (masc.)	bonde (m)	['bɔnə]
peasant (fem.)	bondekone (m/f)	['bɔnə͵kʉnə]
farmer	gårdbruker, bonde (m)	['gɔ:r͵brʉkər], ['bɔnə]

| tractor (farm ~) | traktor (m) | ['traktʊr] |
| combine, harvester | skurtresker (m) | ['skʉ:͵trɛskər] |

plow	plog (m)	['plug]
to plow (vi, vt)	å pløye	[ɔ 'pløjə]
plowland	pløyemark (m/f)	['pløjə͵mark]
furrow (in field)	fure (m)	['fʉrə]

to sow (vi, vt)	å så	[ɔ 'sɔ]
seeder	såmaskin (m)	['so:ma͵ʂin]
sowing (process)	såing (m/f)	['so:iŋ]

| scythe | ljå (m) | ['ljo:] |
| to mow, to scythe | å meie, å slå | [ɔ 'mæjə], [ɔ 'slɔ] |

| spade (tool) | spade (m) | ['spadə] |
| to till (vt) | å grave | [ɔ 'gravə] |

hoe	hakke (m/f)	['hakə]
to hoe, to weed	å hakke	[ɔ 'hakə]
weed (plant)	ugras (n)	[ʉ'gras]

watering can	vannkanne (f)	['van͵kanə]
to water (plants)	å vanne	[ɔ 'vanə]
watering (act)	vanning (m/f)	['vaniŋ]

| pitchfork | greip (m) | ['græjp] |
| rake | rive (m/f) | ['rivə] |

fertilizer	gjødsel (m/f)	['jøtsəl]
to fertilize (vt)	å gjødsle	['ɔ 'jøtslə]
manure (fertilizer)	møkk (m/f)	['møk]

field	åker (m)	['o:ker]
meadow	eng (m/f)	['ɛŋ]
vegetable garden	kjøkkenhage (m)	['çœkən͵hagə]
orchard (e.g., apple ~)	frukthage (m)	['frʉkt͵hagə]

to graze (vt)	**å beite**	[ɔ 'bæjtə]
herder (herdsman)	**gjetər, hyrde** (m)	['jetər], ['hʏrdə]
pasture	**beitə** (n), **beitemark** (m/f)	['bæjtə], ['bæjtə‚mɑrk]
cattle breeding	**husdyrhold** (n)	['hʉsdyr‚hɔl]
sheep farming	**sauehold** (n)	['saʊə‚hɔl]
plantation	**plantasje** (m)	[plɑn'taʂə]
row (garden bed ~s)	**rad** (m/f)	['rɑd]
hothouse	**drivhus** (n)	['driv‚hʉs]
drought (lack of rain)	**tørkə** (m/f)	['tœrkə]
dry (~ summer)	**tørr**	['tœr]
grain	**korn** (n)	['kʉːn]
cereal crops	**cerealer** (n pl)	[sere'ɑlər]
to harvest, to gather	**å høste**	[ɔ 'høstə]
miller (person)	**møller** (m)	['mølər]
mill (e.g., gristmill)	**mølle** (m/f)	['mølə]
to grind (grain)	**å male**	[ɔ 'mɑlə]
flour	**mel** (n)	['mel]
straw	**halm** (m)	['hɑlm]

103. Building. Building process

construction site	**byggeplass** (m)	['bʏgə‚plɑs]
to build (vt)	**å bygge**	[ɔ 'bʏgə]
construction worker	**bygningsarbeider** (m)	['bʏgniŋs ‚ɑr‚bæjer]
project	**prosjekt** (n)	[prʉ'sɛkt]
architect	**arkitekt** (m)	[ɑrki'tɛkt]
worker	**arbeider** (m)	['ɑr‚bæjdər]
foundation (of a building)	**fundament** (n)	[fʉndɑ'mɛnt]
roof	**tak** (n)	['tɑk]
foundation pile	**pæl** (m)	['pæl]
wall	**mur, vegg** (m)	['mʉr], ['vɛɡ]
reinforcing bars	**armeringsjern** (n)	[ɑr'meriŋs‚jæːn]
scaffolding	**stillas** (n)	[sti'lɑs]
concrete	**betong** (m)	[be'tɔŋ]
granite	**granitt** (m)	[grɑ'nit]
stone	**stein** (m)	['stæjn]
brick	**tegl** (n), **murstein** (m)	['tæjl], ['mʉ‚stæjn]
sand	**sand** (m)	['sɑn]
cement	**sement** (m)	[se'mɛnt]
plaster (for walls)	**puss** (m)	['pʉs]

to plaster (vt)	å pusse	[ɔ 'pʉsə]
paint	maling (m/f)	['malɪŋ]
to paint (~ a wall)	å male	[ɔ 'malə]
barrel	tønne (m)	['tœnə]
crane	heisekran (m/f)	['hæjsə͵krɑn]
to lift, to hoist (vt)	å løfte	[ɔ 'lœftə]
to lower (vt)	å heise ned	[ɔ 'hæjsə ne]
bulldozer	bulldoser (m)	['bʉl͵dʉsər]
excavator	gravemaskin (m)	['grɑvə mɑ'ʂin]
scoop, bucket	skuffe (m/f)	['skʉfə]
to dig (excavate)	å grave	[ɔ 'grɑvə]
hard hat	hjelm (m)	['jɛlm]

Professions and occupations

104. Job search. Dismissal

job	**arbeid** (n), **jobb** (m)	['arbæj], ['job]
staff (work force)	**ansatte** (pl)	['an,satə]
personnel	**personale** (n)	[pæşu'nalə]
career	**karriere** (m)	[kari'ɛrə]
prospects (chances)	**utsikter** (m pl)	['ʉt,siktər]
skills (mastery)	**mesterskap** (n)	['mɛstæ,şkap]
selection (screening)	**utvelgelse** (m)	['ʉt,vɛlgəlsə]
employment agency	**rekrutteringsbyrå** (n)	['rekrʉ,teriŋgs by,ro]
résumé	**CV** (m/n)	['sɛvɛ]
job interview	**jobbintervju** (n)	['job ,intər'vjʉ]
vacancy, opening	**vakanse** (m)	['vakansə]
salary, pay	**lønn** (m/f)	['lœn]
fixed salary	**fastlønn** (m/f)	['fast,lœn]
pay, compensation	**betaling** (m/f)	[be'taliŋ]
position (job)	**stilling** (m/f)	['stiliŋ]
duty (of employee)	**plikt** (m/f)	['plikt]
range of duties	**arbeidsplikter** (m/f pl)	['arbæjds,pliktər]
busy (I'm ~)	**opptatt**	['ɔp,tat]
to fire (dismiss)	**å avskjedige**	[ɔ 'af,şedigə]
dismissal	**avskjedigelse** (m)	['afşe,digəlsə]
unemployment	**arbeidsløshet** (m)	['arbæjdsløs,het]
unemployed (n)	**arbeidsløs** (m)	['arbæjds,løs]
retirement	**pensjon** (m)	[pan'şun]
to retire (from job)	**å gå av med pensjon**	[ɔ 'gɔ a: me pan'şun]

105. Business people

director	**direktør** (m)	[dirɛk'tør]
manager (director)	**forstander** (m)	[fo'ştandər]
boss	**boss** (m)	['bɔs]
superior	**overordnet** (m)	['ɔvər,ɔrdnet]
superiors	**overordnede** (pl)	['ɔvər,ɔrdnedə]
president	**president** (m)	[prɛsi'dɛnt]

chairman	styreformann (m)	['styrə,formɑn]
deputy (substitute)	stedfortreder (m)	['stedfɔ:,tredər]
assistant	assistent (m)	[ɑsi'stɛnt]
secretary	sekretær (m)	[sɛkrə'tær]
personal assistant	privatsekretær (m)	[pri'vɑt sɛkrə'tær]

businessman	forretningsmann (m)	[fɔ'rɛtniŋs,mɑn]
entrepreneur	entreprenør (m)	[ɛntreprə'nør]
founder	grunnlegger (m)	['grʉn,legər]
to found (vt)	å grunnlegge, å stifte	[ɔ 'grʉn,legə], [ɔ 'stiftə]

incorporator	stifter (m)	['stiftər]
partner	partner (m)	['pɑ:ʈnər]
stockholder	aksjonær (m)	[ɑkʂʉ'nær]

millionaire	millionær (m)	[milju'nær]
billionaire	milliardær (m)	[miljɑ:'ɖær]
owner, proprietor	eier (m)	['æjər]
landowner	jordeier (m)	['juːr,æjər]

client	kunde (m)	['kʉndə]
regular client	fast kunde (m)	[,fɑst 'kʉndə]
buyer (customer)	kjøper (m)	['çœ:pər]
visitor	besøkende (m)	[be'søkenə]

professional (n)	yrkesmann (m)	['yrkəs,mɑn]
expert	ekspert (m)	[ɛks'pæ:ʈ]
specialist	spesialist (m)	[spesiɑ'list]

| banker | bankier (m) | [bɑnki'e] |
| broker | mekler, megler (m) | ['mɛklər] |

cashier, teller	kasserer (m)	[kɑ'serər]
accountant	regnskapsfører (m)	['rɛjnskɑps,førər]
security guard	sikkerhetsvakt (m/f)	['sikərhɛts,vɑkt]

investor	investor (m)	[in'vɛstʉr]
debtor	skyldner (m)	['ʂylnər]
creditor	kreditor (m)	['krɛditʉr]
borrower	låntaker (m)	['lɔn,tɑkər]

| importer | importør (m) | [impɔ:'tør] |
| exporter | eksportør (m) | [ɛkspɔ:'tør] |

manufacturer	produsent (m)	[prʉdʉ'sɛnt]
distributor	distributør (m)	[distribʉ'tør]
middleman	mellommann (m)	['mɛlɔ,mɑn]

consultant	konsulent (m)	[kʉnsʉ'lent]
sales representative	representant (m)	[represɛn'tɑnt]
agent	agent (m)	[ɑ'gɛnt]
insurance agent	forsikringsagent (m)	[fɔ'ʂikriŋs ɑ'gɛnt]

106. Service professions

cook	kokk (m)	['kʊk]
chef (kitchen chef)	sjefkokk (m)	['ʂɛfˌkʊk]
baker	baker (m)	['bɑkər]
bartender	bartender (m)	['bɑːˌtɛndər]
waiter	servitør (m)	['særvi'tør]
waitress	servitrise (m/f)	[særvi'trisə]
lawyer, attorney	advokat (m)	[ɑdvʊ'kɑt]
lawyer (legal expert)	jurist (m)	[jɵ'rist]
notary	notar (m)	[nʊ'tɑr]
electrician	elektriker (m)	[ɛ'lektrikər]
plumber	rørlegger (m)	['rørˌlegər]
carpenter	tømmermann (m)	['tœmərˌmɑn]
masseur	massør (m)	[mɑ'sør]
masseuse	massøse (m)	[mɑ'søsə]
doctor	lege (m)	['legə]
taxi driver	taxisjåfør (m)	['tɑksi ʂɔ'før]
driver	sjåfør (m)	[ʂɔ'før]
delivery man	bud (n)	['bʉd]
chambermaid	stuepike (m/f)	['stʉəˌpikə]
security guard	sikkerhetsvakt (m/f)	['sikərhɛtsˌvɑkt]
flight attendant (fem.)	flyvertinne (m/f)	[flyvɛː'tinə]
schoolteacher	lærer (m)	['lærər]
librarian	bibliotekar (m)	[bibliʊ'tekɑr]
translator	oversetter (m)	['ɔvəˌsɛtər]
interpreter	tolk (m)	['tɔlk]
guide	guide (m)	['gɑjd]
hairdresser	frisør (m)	[fri'sør]
mailman	postbud (n)	['pɔstˌbʉd]
salesman (store staff)	forselger (m)	[fɔ'ʂɛlər]
gardener	gartner (m)	['gɑːˌtnər]
domestic servant	tjener (m)	['tjenər]
maid (female servant)	tjenestepike (m/f)	['tjenɛstəˌpikə]
cleaner (cleaning lady)	vaskedame (m/f)	['vɑskəˌdɑmə]

107. Military professions and ranks

private	menig (m)	['meni]
sergeant	sersjant (m)	[sær'ʂɑnt]

lieutenant	**løytnant** (m)	['løjt,nant]
captain	**kaptein** (m)	[kap'tæjn]
major	**major** (m)	[ma'jɔr]
colonel	**oberst** (m)	['ʊbɛʂt]
general	**general** (m)	[gene'ral]
marshal	**marskalk** (m)	['marʂal]
admiral	**admiral** (m)	[admi'ral]
military (n)	**militær** (m)	[mili'tær]
soldier	**soldat** (m)	[sʊl'dat]
officer	**offiser** (m)	[ɔfi'sɛr]
commander	**befalshaver** (m)	[be'fals,havər]
border guard	**grensevakt** (m/f)	['grɛnsə,vakt]
radio operator	**radiooperatør** (m)	['radiʊ ʊpəra'tør]
scout (searcher)	**oppklaringssoldat** (m)	['ɔp,klariŋ sʊl'dat]
pioneer (sapper)	**pioner** (m)	[piʊ'ner]
marksman	**skytter** (m)	['ʂytər]
navigator	**styrmann** (m)	['styr,man]

108. Officials. Priests

king	**konge** (m)	['kʊŋə]
queen	**dronning** (m/f)	['drɔniŋ]
prince	**prins** (m)	['prins]
princess	**prinsesse** (m/f)	[prin'sɛsə]
czar	**tsar** (m)	['tsar]
czarina	**tsarina** (m)	[tsa'rina]
president	**president** (m)	[prɛsi'dɛnt]
Secretary (minister)	**minister** (m)	[mi'nistər]
prime minister	**statsminister** (m)	['stats mi'nistər]
senator	**senator** (m)	[se'natʊr]
diplomat	**diplomat** (m)	[diplʊ'mat]
consul	**konsul** (m)	['kʊn,sʉl]
ambassador	**ambassadør** (m)	[ambasa'dør]
counsilor (diplomatic officer)	**rådgiver** (m)	['rɔd,jivər]
official, functionary (civil servant)	**embetsmann** (m)	['ɛmbets,man]
prefect	**prefekt** (m)	[prɛ'fɛkt]
mayor	**borgermester** (m)	[bɔrgər'mɛstər]
judge	**dommer** (m)	['dɔmər]
prosecutor (e.g., district attorney)	**anklager** (m)	['an,klagər]

missionary	misjonær (m)	[miʂuˈnær]
monk	munk (m)	[ˈmʉnk]
abbot	abbed (m)	[ˈɑbed]
rabbi	rabbiner (m)	[rɑˈbinər]

vizier	vesir (m)	[vɛˈsir]
shah	sjah (m)	[ˈʂɑ]
sheikh	sjeik (m)	[ˈʂæjk]

109. Agricultural professions

beekeeper	birøkter (m)	[ˈbiˌrøktər]
herder, shepherd	gjeter, hyrde (m)	[ˈjetər], [ˈhʏrdə]
agronomist	agronom (m)	[ɑgrʉˈnʉm]
cattle breeder	husdyrholder (m)	[ˈhʉsdyrˌhɔldər]
veterinarian	dyrlege, veterinær (m)	[ˈdyrˌlegə] [vetəriˈnær]

farmer	gårdbruker, bonde (m)	[ˈgɔːrˌbrʉkər], [ˈbɔnə]
winemaker	vinmaker (m)	[ˈvinˌmɑkər]
zoologist	zoolog (m)	[sʉːˈlɔg]
cowboy	cowboy (m)	[ˈkɑwˌbɔj]

110. Art professions

actor	skuespiller (m)	[ˈskʉəˌspilər]
actress	skuespillerinne (m/f)	[ˈskʉəˌspiləˈrinə]

singer (masc.)	sanger (m)	[ˈsɑŋər]
singer (fem.)	sangerinne (m/f)	[sɑŋəˈrinə]

dancer (masc.)	danser (m)	[ˈdɑnsər]
dancer (fem.)	danserinne (m/f)	[dɑnseˈrinə]

performer (masc.)	skuespiller (m)	[ˈskʉəˌspilər]
performer (fem.)	skuespillerinne (m/f)	[ˈskʉəˌspiləˈrinə]

musician	musiker (m)	[ˈmʉsikər]
pianist	pianist (m)	[piɑˈnist]
guitar player	gitarspiller (m)	[giˈtɑrˌspilɛr]

conductor (orchestra ~)	dirigent (m)	[diriˈgɛnt]
composer	komponist (m)	[kʉmpʉˈnist]
impresario	impresario (m)	[impreˈsɑriʉ]

film director	regissør (m)	[rɛʂiˈsør]
producer	produsent (m)	[prʉdʉˈsɛnt]
scriptwriter	manusforfatter (m)	[ˈmɑnʉs fɔrˈfatər]
critic	kritiker (m)	[ˈkritikər]

writer	forfatter (m)	[fɔrˈfɑtər]
poet	poet, dikter (m)	[ˈpɔɛt], [ˈdiktər]
sculptor	skulptør (m)	[skʉlpˈtør]
artist (painter)	kunstner (m)	[ˈkʉnstnər]

juggler	sjonglør (m)	[ʂɔŋˈlør]
clown	klovn (m)	[ˈklɔvn]
acrobat	akrobat (m)	[ɑkrʊˈbɑt]
magician	tryllekunstner (m)	[ˈtrʏləˌkʉnstnər]

111. Various professions

doctor	lege (m)	[ˈlegə]
nurse	sykepleierske (m/f)	[ˈsykəˌplæjeʂkə]
psychiatrist	psykiater (m)	[syki'ɑtər]
dentist	tannlege (m)	[ˈtɑnˌlegə]
surgeon	kirurg (m)	[çiˈrʉrg]

| astronaut | astronaut (m) | [ɑstrʊˈnɑʊt] |
| astronomer | astronom (m) | [ɑstrʊˈnʊm] |

driver (of taxi, etc.)	fører (m)	[ˈførər]
engineer (train driver)	lokfører (m)	[ˈlʊkˌførər]
mechanic	mekaniker (m)	[meˈkɑnikər]

miner	gruvearbeider (m)	[ˈgrʉvəˈɑrˌbæjdər]
worker	arbeider (m)	[ˈɑrˌbæjdər]
locksmith	låsesmed (m)	[ˈloːsəˌsme]
joiner (carpenter)	snekker (m)	[ˈsnɛkər]
turner (lathe machine operator)	dreier (m)	[ˈdræjər]
construction worker	bygningsarbeider (m)	[ˈbʏgniŋs ˈɑrˌbæjər]
welder	sveiser (m)	[ˈsvæjsər]

professor (title)	professor (m)	[prʊˈfɛsʉr]
architect	arkitekt (m)	[ɑrkiˈtɛkt]
historian	historiker (m)	[hiˈstʉrikər]
scientist	vitenskapsmann (m)	[ˈvitənˌskɑps mɑn]
physicist	fysiker (m)	[ˈfysikər]
chemist (scientist)	kjemiker (m)	[ˈçemikər]

archeologist	arkeolog (m)	[ˌɑrkeʊˈlɔg]
geologist	geolog (m)	[geʊˈlɔg]
researcher (scientist)	forsker (m)	[ˈfɔʂkər]

| babysitter | babysitter (m) | [ˈbɛbyˌsitər] |
| teacher, educator | lærer, pedagog (m) | [ˈlærər], [pedɑˈgɔg] |

| editor | redaktør (m) | [rɛdakˈtør] |
| editor-in-chief | sjefredaktør (m) | [ˈʂɛf rɛdakˈtør] |

| correspondent | korrespondent (m) | [kʊrespɔn'dɛnt] |
| typist (fem.) | maskinskriverske (m) | [ma'ʂin ˌskrivɛʂkə] |

designer	designer (m)	[de'sɑjnər]
computer expert	dataekspert (m)	['dɑtɑ ɛks'pɛːt̩]
programmer	programmerer (m)	[prʊgrɑ'meˀər]
engineer (designer)	ingeniør (m)	[inʂə'njør]

sailor	sjømann (m)	['ʂø ˌmɑn]
seaman	matros (m)	[mɑ'trʊs]
rescuer	redningsmann (m)	['rɛdniŋs ˌmɑn]

fireman	brannmann (m)	['brɑn ˌmɑn]
police officer	politi (m)	[pʊli'ti]
watchman	nattvakt (m)	['nɑt ˌvɑkt]
detective	detektiv (m)	[detɛk'tiv]

customs officer	tollbetjent (m)	['tɔlbe ˌtjɛnt]
bodyguard	livvakt (m/f)	['liv ˌvɑkt]
prison guard	fangevokter (m)	['fɑŋə ˌvɔktər]
inspector	inspektør (m)	[inspɛk'tør]

sportsman	idrettsmann (m)	['idrɛts ˌmɑn]
trainer, coach	trener (m)	['trenər]
butcher	slakter (m)	['ʂlɑktər]
cobbler (shoe repairer)	skomaker (m)	['skʊ ˌmɑkər]
merchant	handelsmann (m)	['hɑndəls ˌmɑn]
loader (person)	lastearbeider (m)	['lɑstə'ɑr ˌbæjdər]

| fashion designer | moteskaper (m) | ['mʊtə ˌskɑɾər] |
| model (fem.) | modell (m) | [mʊ'dɛl] |

112. Occupations. Social status

| schoolboy | skolegutt (m) | ['skʊlə ˌgʊt] |
| student (college ~) | student (m) | [stʉ'dɛnt] |

philosopher	filosof (m)	[filu'sʊf]
economist	økonom (m)	[økʊ'nʊm]
inventor	oppfinner (m)	['ɔp ˌfinər]

unemployed (n)	arbeidsløs (m)	['ɑrbæjds ˌløs]
retiree	pensjonist (m)	[pɑnʂʉ'nist̩]
spy, secret agent	spion (m)	[spi'un]

prisoner	fange (m)	['fɑŋə]
striker	streiker (m)	['stræjkər]
bureaucrat	byråkrat (m)	[byro'krɑt]
traveler (globetrotter)	reisende (m)	['ræjsenə]
gay, homosexual (n)	homofil (m)	['hʊmʊ ˌfil]

hacker	**hacker** (m)	['hakər]
hippie	**hippie** (m)	['hipi]
bandit	**banditt** (m)	[ban'dit]
hit man, killer	**leiemorder** (m)	['læjə͵mʊrdər]
drug addict	**narkoman** (m)	[narkʊ'man]
drug dealer	**narkolanger** (m)	['narkɔ͵laŋər]
prostitute (fem.)	**prostituert** (m)	[prʊstitʉ'e:t]
pimp	**hallik** (m)	['halik]
sorcerer	**trollmann** (m)	['trɔl͵man]
sorceress (evil ~)	**trollkjerring** (m/f)	['trɔl͵çæriŋ]
pirate	**pirat, sjørøver** (m)	['pi'rat], ['ʂø͵røvər]
slave	**slave** (m)	['slavə]
samurai	**samurai** (m)	[samʉ'raj]
savage (primitive)	**villmann** (m)	['vil͵man]

Sports

113. Kinds of sports. Sportspersons

sportsman	idrettsmann (m)	['idrɛts͵mɑn]
kind of sports	idrettsgren (m/f)	['idrɛts͵grεn]
basketball	basketball (m)	['bɑsketbɑl]
basketball player	basketballspiller (m)	['bɑsketbɑl͵spilər]
baseball	baseball (m)	['bɛjsbɔl]
baseball player	baseballspiller (m)	['bɛjsbɔl͵sɔilər]
soccer	fotball (m)	['fʊtbɑl]
soccer player	fotballspiller (m)	['fʊtbɑl͵sp lər]
goalkeeper	målmann (m)	['mo:l͵mɑn]
hockey	ishockey (m)	['is͵hɔki]
hockey player	ishockeyspiller (m)	['is͵hɔki 'sɔilər]
volleyball	volleyball (m)	['vɔlibɑl]
volleyball player	volleyballspiller (m)	['vɔlibɑl͵spilər]
boxing	boksing (m)	['bɔksiŋ]
boxer	bokser (m)	['bɔksər]
wrestling	bryting (m/f)	['brytiŋ]
wrestler	bryter (m)	['brytər]
karate	karate (m)	[kɑ'rɑte]
karate fighter	karateutøver (m)	[kɑ'rɑtə 'ʉ͵tøvər]
judo	judo (m)	['jʉdɔ]
judo athlete	judobryter (m)	['jʉdɔ͵brytər]
tennis	tennis (m)	['tεnis]
tennis player	tennisspiller (m)	['tεnis͵spilər]
swimming	svømming (m/f)	['svœmiŋ]
swimmer	svømmer (m)	['svœmər]
fencing	fekting (m)	['fεktiŋ]
fencer	fekter (m)	['fεktər]
chess	sjakk (m)	['ʂɑk]
chess player	sjakkspiller (m)	['ʂɑk͵spilər]

| alpinism | alpinisme (m) | [alpi'nismə] |
| alpinist | alpinist (m) | [alpi'nist] |

| running | løp (n) | ['løp] |
| runner | løper (m) | ['løpər] |

| athletics | friidrett (m) | ['fri: 'iˌdrɛt] |
| athlete | atlet (m) | [at'let] |

| horseback riding | ridesport (m) | ['ridəˌspɔːt] |
| horse rider | rytter (m) | ['rʏtər] |

figure skating	kunstløp (n)	['kʉnstˌløp]
figure skater (masc.)	kunstløper (m)	['kʉnstˌløpər]
figure skater (fem.)	kunstløperske (m/f)	['kʉnstˌløpəşkə]

| powerlifting | vektløfting (m/f) | ['vɛktˌlœftiŋ] |
| powerlifter | vektløfter (m) | ['vɛktˌlœftər] |

| car racing | billøp (m), bilrace (n) | ['bilˌløp], ['bilˌras] |
| racing driver | racerfører (m) | ['resəˌførər] |

| cycling | sykkelsport (m) | ['sʏkəlˌspɔːt] |
| cyclist | syklist (m) | [sʏk'list] |

broad jump	lengdehopp (n pl)	['leŋdəˌhɔp]
pole vault	stavhopp (n)	['stavˌhɔp]
jumper	hopper (m)	['hɔpər]

114. Kinds of sports. Miscellaneous

football	amerikansk fotball (m)	[ameri'kansk 'fʉtbal]
badminton	badminton (m)	['bɛdmintɔn]
biathlon	skiskyting (m/f)	['şiˌşytiŋ]
billiards	biljard (m)	[bil'jaːd]

bobsled	bobsleigh (m)	['bobslej]
bodybuilding	kroppsbygging (m/f)	['krɔpsˌbʏgiŋ]
water polo	vannpolo (m)	['vanˌpʉlʉ]
handball	håndball (m)	['hɔnˌbal]
golf	golf (m)	['gɔlf]

rowing, crew	roing (m/f)	['rʉiŋ]
scuba diving	dykking (m/f)	['dʏkiŋ]
cross-country skiing	langrenn (n), skirenn (n)	['laŋˌrɛn], ['şiˌrɛn]
table tennis (ping-pong)	bordtennis (m)	['bʉrˌtɛnis]

sailing	seiling (m/f)	['sæjliŋ]
rally racing	rally (n)	['rɛli]
rugby	rugby (m)	['rygbi]

| snowboarding | snøbrett (n) | ['snøˌbrɛt] |
| archery | bueskyting (m/f) | ['bʉːəˌsytiŋ] |

115. Gym

| barbell | vektstang (m/f) | ['vɛktˌstɑŋ] |
| dumbbells | manualer (m pl) | ['mɑnʉˌɑlər] |

training machine	treningsapparat (n)	['treniŋs ɑpɑ'rɑt]
exercise bicycle	trimsykkel (m)	['trimˌsʏkɛl]
treadmill	løpebånd (n)	['løpəˌbɔːn]

horizontal bar	svingstang (m/f)	['sviŋstɑŋ]
parallel bars	barre (m)	['bɑrə]
vault (vaulting horse)	hest (m)	['hɛst]
mat (exercise ~)	matte (m/f)	['mɑtə]

jump rope	hoppetau (n)	['hɔpəˌtaʊ]
aerobics	aerobic (m)	[ɑɛ'rɔbik]
yoga	yoga (m)	['joga]

116. Sports. Miscellaneous

Olympic Games	de olympiske leker	[de u'lʏmpiskə 'lekər]
winner	seierherre (m)	['sæjərˌhɛˑə]
to be winning	å vinne, å seire	[ɔ 'vinə], [ɔ 'sæjrə]
to win (vi)	å vinne	[ɔ 'vinə]

| leader | leder (m) | ['ledər] |
| to lead (vi) | å lede | [ɔ 'ledə] |

first place	førsteplass (m)	['fœʂtəˌplɑs]
second place	annenplass (m)	['ɑnənˌplɑs]
third place	tredjeplass (m)	['trɛdjəˌplɑs]

medal	medalje (m)	[me'dɑljə]
trophy	trofé (m/n)	[trɔ'fe]
prize cup (trophy)	pokal (m)	[pɔ'kɑl]
prize (in game)	pris (m)	['pris]
main prize	hovedpris (m)	['hʊvədˌpris]

| record | rekord (m) | [re'kɔrd] |
| to set a record | å sette rekord | [ɔ 'sɛtə re'kɔrd] |

final	finale (m)	[fi'nɑlə]
final (adj)	finale-	[fi'nɑlə-]
champion	mester (m)	['mɛstər]
championship	mesterskap (n)	['mɛstæˌsˑɑp]

stadium	**stadion** (m/n)	['stɑdiɔn]
stand (bleachers)	**tribune** (m)	[tri'bʉnə]
fan, supporter	**fan** (m)	['fæn]
opponent, rival	**motstander** (m)	['mʊt‚stɑnər]
start (start line)	**start** (m)	['stɑːt]
finish line	**mål** (n), **målstrek** (m)	['moːl], ['moːl‚strek]
defeat	**nederlag** (n)	['nedə‚lɑg]
to lose (not win)	**å tape**	[ɔ 'tɑpə]
referee	**dommer** (m)	['dɔmər]
jury (judges)	**jury** (m)	['jʉry]
score	**resultat** (n)	[resʉl'tɑt]
tie	**uavgjort** (m)	[ʉːav'jɔːt]
to tie (vi)	**å spille uavgjort**	[ɔ 'spilə ʉːav'jɔːt]
point	**poeng** (n)	[pɔ'ɛŋ]
result (final score)	**resultat** (n)	[resʉl'tɑt]
period	**periode** (m)	[pæri'ʊdə]
half-time	**halvtid** (m)	['hɑl‚tid]
doping	**doping** (m)	['dʊpiŋ]
to penalize (vt)	**å straffe**	[ɔ 'strɑfə]
to disqualify (vt)	**å diskvalifisere**	[ɔ 'diskvɑlifi‚serə]
apparatus	**redskap** (m/n)	['rɛd‚skɑp]
javelin	**spyd** (n)	['spyd]
shot (metal ball)	**kule** (m/f)	['kʉːlə]
ball (snooker, etc.)	**kule** (m/f), **ball** (m)	['kʉːlə], ['bɑl]
aim (target)	**mål** (n)	['mol]
target	**målskive** (m/f)	['moːl‚ʂivə]
to shoot (vi)	**å skyte**	[ɔ 'ʂytə]
accurate (~ shot)	**fulltreffer**	['fʉl‚trɛfər]
trainer, coach	**trener** (m)	['trenər]
to train (sb)	**å trene**	[ɔ 'trenə]
to train (vi)	**å trene**	[ɔ 'trenə]
training	**trening** (m/f)	['treniŋ]
gym	**idrettssal** (m)	['idrɛts‚sɑl]
exercise (physical)	**øvelse** (m)	['øvəlsə]
warm-up (athlete ~)	**oppvarming** (m/f)	['ɔp‚vɑrmiŋ]

Education

117. School

school	skole (m/f)	['skʊlə]
principal (headmaster)	rektor (m)	['rektʊr]
pupil (boy)	elev (m)	[e'lev]
pupil (girl)	elev (m)	[e'lev]
schoolboy	skolegutt (m)	['skʊlə‚gʊt]
schoolgirl	skolepike (m)	['skʊlə‚pikə]
to teach (sb)	å undervise	[ɔ 'ʉnər‚visə]
to learn (language, etc.)	å lære	[ɔ 'lærə]
to learn by heart	å lære utenat	[ɔ 'lærə 'ʉtənat]
to learn (~ to count, etc.)	å lære	[ɔ 'lærə]
to be in school	å gå på skolen	[ɔ 'gɔ pɔ 'skʊlən]
to go to school	å gå på skolen	[ɔ 'gɔ pɔ 'skʊlən]
alphabet	alfabet (n)	[alfa'bet]
subject (at school)	fag (n)	['fag]
classroom	klasserom (m/f)	['klasə‚rʊm]
lesson	time (n)	['timə]
recess	frikvarter (n)	['frikvɑ:‚tər]
school bell	skoleklokke (m/f)	['skʊlə‚klɔkə]
school desk	skolepult (m)	['skʊlə‚pʉlt]
chalkboard	tavle (n/f)	['tavlə]
grade	karakter (m)	[karak'ter]
good grade	god karakter (m)	['gʊ karak'ter]
bad grade	dårlig karakter (m)	['dɔ:‚li karak'ter]
to give a grade	å gi en karakter	[ɔ 'ji en karak'ter]
mistake, error	feil (m)	['fæjl]
to make mistakes	å gjøre feil	[ɔ 'jørə ‚fæjl]
to correct (an error)	å rette	[ɔ 'rɛtə]
cheat sheet	fuskelapp (m)	['fʉskə‚lap]
homework	lekser (m/f pl)	['leksər]
exercise (in education)	øvelse (m)	['øvəlsə]
to be present	å være til stede	[ɔ 'værə til 'stedə]
to be absent	å være fraværende	[ɔ 'værə 'frɑ‚værənə]
to miss school	å skulke skolen	[ɔ 'skʉlkə 'skʊlən]

to punish (vt)	å straffe	[ɔ 'strɑfə]
punishment	straff, avstraffelse (m)	['strɑf], ['ɑf,strɑfəlsə]
conduct (behavior)	oppførsel (m)	['ɔp,fœʂəl]

report card	karakterbok (m/f)	[kɑrɑk'ter,bʊk]
pencil	blyant (m)	['bly,ɑnt]
eraser	viskelær (n)	['viskə,lær]
chalk	kritt (n)	['krit]
pencil case	pennal (n)	[pɛ'nɑl]

schoolbag	skoleveske (m/f)	['skʊlə,vɛskə]
pen	penn (m)	['pɛn]
school notebook	skrivebok (m/f)	['skrivə,bʊk]
textbook	lærebok (m/f)	['lærə,bʊk]
compasses	passer (m)	['pɑsər]

| to make technical drawings | å tegne | [ɔ 'tæjnə] |
| technical drawing | teknisk tegning (m/f) | ['tɛknisk ,tæjniŋ] |

poem	dikt (n)	['dikt]
by heart (adv)	utenat	['ʉtən,ɑt]
to learn by heart	å lære utenat	[ɔ 'lærə 'ʉtənɑt]

school vacation	skoleferie (m)	['skʊlə,feriə]
to be on vacation	å være på ferie	[ɔ 'værə pɔ 'feriə]
to spend one's vacation	å tilbringe ferien	[ɔ 'til,briŋə 'feriən]

test (written math ~)	prøve (m/f)	['prøvə]
essay (composition)	essay (n)	[ɛ'sɛj]
dictation	diktat (m)	[dik'tɑt]
exam (examination)	eksamen (m)	[ɛk'sɑmən]
to take an exam	å ta eksamen	[ɔ 'tɑ ɛk'sɑmən]
experiment (e.g., chemistry ~)	forsøk (n)	['fɔ'ʂøk]

118. College. University

academy	akademi (n)	[ɑkɑde'mi]
university	universitet (n)	[ʉnivæʂi'tet]
faculty (e.g., ~ of Medicine)	fakultet (n)	[fɑkʉl'tet]

student (masc.)	student (m)	[stʉ'dɛnt]
student (fem.)	kvinnelig student (m)	['kvinəli stʉ'dɛnt]
lecturer (teacher)	lærer, foreleser (m)	['lærər], ['fʊrə,lesər]

lecture hall, room	auditorium (n)	[,aʊdi'tʊrium]
graduate	alumn (m)	[ɑ'lʉmn]
diploma	diplom (n)	[di'plʊm]

dissertation	avhandling (m/f)	['av‚handliŋ]
study (report)	studie (m)	['studiə]
laboratory	laboratorium (n)	[labura'torium]

lecture	forelesning (m)	['forə‚lesniŋ]
coursemate	studiekamerat (m)	['studiə kame‚rat]
scholarship	stipendium (n)	[sti'pɛndium]
academic degree	akademisk grad (m)	[aka'demisk ‚grad]

119. Sciences. Disciplines

mathematics	matematikk (m)	[matəma'tik]
algebra	algebra (m)	['algə‚bra]
geometry	geometri (m)	[geume'tr]

astronomy	astronomi (m)	[astrunu'mi]
biology	biologi (m)	[biulu'gi]
geography	geografi (m)	[geugra'fi˙]
geology	geologi (m)	[geulu'gi]
history	historie (m/f)	[hi'sturiə]

medicine	medsin (m)	[medi'sin]
pedagogy	pedagogikk (m)	[pedagu'çik]
law	rett (m)	['rɛt]

physics	fysikk (m)	[fy'sik]
chemistry	kjemi (m)	[çe'mi]
philosophy	filosofi (m)	[filusu'fi]
psychology	psykologi (m)	[sikulu'gi]

120. Writing system. Orthography

grammar	grammatikk (m)	[grama'tik]
vocabulary	ordforråd (n)	['u:rfu‚rod]
phonetics	fonetikk (m)	[fune'tik]

noun	substantiv (n)	['substan tiv]
adjective	adjektiv (n)	['adjɛk‚tiv˙]
verb	verb (n)	['værb]
adverb	adverb (n)	[ad'væ:b]

pronoun	pronomen (n)	[pru'numən]
interjection	interjeksjon (m)	[interjɛk'ʂun]
preposition	preposisjon (m)	[prɛpusi'ʂun]

root	rot (n/f)	['rut]
ending	endelse (m)	['ɛnəlsə]
prefix	prefiks (n)	[prɛ'fiks]

| syllable | stavelse (m) | ['stɑvəlsə] |
| suffix | suffiks (n) | [sʉ'fiks] |

| stress mark | betoning (m), trykk (n) | ['be'toniŋ], ['trʏk] |
| apostrophe | apostrof (m) | [ɑpʉ'strɔf] |

period, dot	punktum (n)	['pʉnktum]
comma	komma (n)	['kɔmɑ]
semicolon	semikolon (n)	[ˌsemikʉ'lɔn]
colon	kolon (n)	['kʉlɔn]
ellipsis	tre prikker (m pl)	['tre 'prikər]

| question mark | spørsmålstegn (n) | ['spœʂmolsˌtæjn] |
| exclamation point | utropstegn (n) | ['ʉtrʊpsˌtæjn] |

quotation marks	anførselstegn (n pl)	[ɑn'fœʂɛlsˌtejn]
in quotation marks	i anførselstegn	[i ɑn'fœʂɛlsˌtejn]
parenthesis	parentes (m)	[pɑrɛn'tes]
in parenthesis	i parentes	[i pɑrɛn'tes]

hyphen	bindestrek (m)	['binəˌstrek]
dash	tankestrek (m)	['tɑnkəˌstrek]
space (between words)	mellomrom (n)	['mɛlɔmˌrʊm]

| letter | bokstav (m) | ['bʊkstɑv] |
| capital letter | stor bokstav (m) | ['stʊr 'bʊkstɑv] |

| vowel (n) | vokal (m) | [vʉ'kɑl] |
| consonant (n) | konsonant (m) | [kʊnsʉ'nɑnt] |

sentence	setning (m)	['sɛtniŋ]
subject	subjekt (n)	[sʉb'jɛkt]
predicate	predikat (n)	[prɛdi'kɑt]

line	linje (m)	['linjə]
on a new line	på ny linje	[pɔ ny 'linjə]
paragraph	avsnitt (n)	['ɑfˌsnit]

word	ord (n)	['uːr]
group of words	ordgruppe (m/f)	['uːrˌgrʉpə]
expression	uttrykk (n)	['ʉtˌtrʏk]
synonym	synonym (n)	[synʉ'nym]
antonym	antonym (n)	[ɑntʉ'nym]

rule	regel (m)	['rɛgəl]
exception	unntak (n)	['ʉnˌtɑk]
correct (adj)	riktig	['rikti]

conjugation	bøyning (m/f)	['bøjniŋ]
declension	bøyning (m/f)	['bøjniŋ]
nominal case	kasus (m)	['kɑsʉs]
question	spørsmål (n)	['spœʂˌmol]

| to underline (vt) | å understreke | [ɔ 'ʉnəˌstrəkə] |
| dotted line | prikket linje (m) | ['prikət 'linjə] |

121. Foreign languages

language	språk (n)	['sprɔk]
foreign (adj)	fremmed-	['fremə-]
foreign language	fremmedspråk (n)	['fremedˌsprɔk]
to study (vt)	å studere	[ɔ stʉ'derə]
to learn (language, etc.)	å lære	[ɔ 'lærə]

to read (vi, vt)	å lese	[ɔ 'lesə]
to speak (vi, vt)	å tale	[ɔ 'talə]
to understand (vt)	å forstå	[ɔ fɔ'ʂtɔ]
to write (vt)	å skrive	[ɔ 'skrivə]

fast (adv)	fort	['fʉːt]
slowly (adv)	langsomt	['laŋsɔmt]
fluently (adv)	flytende	['flytnə]

rules	regler (m pl)	['rɛglər]
grammar	grammatikk (m)	[grɑmɑ'tik]
vocabulary	ordforråd (n)	['uːrfʉˌrɔd]
phonetics	fonetikk (m)	[fʉne'tik]

textbook	lærebok (m/f)	['lærəˌbʉk]
dictionary	ordbok (m/f)	['uːrˌbʉk]
teach-yourself book	lærebok (m/f)	['lærəˌbʉk
	for selvstudium	fɔ 'selˌstʉdium]
phrasebook	parler (m)	[pɑː'lør]

cassette, tape	kassett (m)	[kɑ'sɛt]
videotape	videokassett (m)	['videʉ kɑ sɛt]
CD, compact disc	CD-rom (m)	['sɛdɛˌrʉm]
DVD	DVD (m)	[deve'de]

alphabet	alfabet (n)	[ɑlfɑ'bet]
to spell (vt)	å stave	[ɔ 'stavə]
pronunciation	uttale (m)	['ʉtˌtɑlə]

accent	aksent (m)	[ɑk'sɑŋ]
with an accent	med aksent	[me ɑk'sɑŋ]
without an accent	uten aksent	['ʉtən ɑk'sɑŋ]

| word | ord (n) | ['uːr] |
| meaning | betydning (m) | [be'tʏdniŋ] |

course (e.g., a French ~)	kurs (n)	['kʉʂ]
to sign up	å anmelde seg	[ɔ 'ɑnˌmɛlə sæj]
teacher	lærer (m)	['lærər]

translation (process)	oversettelse (m)	['ɔvəˌsɛtəlsə]
translation (text, etc.)	oversettelse (m)	['ɔvəˌsɛtəlsə]
translator	oversetter (m)	['ɔvəˌsɛtər]
interpreter	tolk (m)	['tɔlk]
polyglot	polyglott (m)	[pʊlʏ'glɔt]
memory	minne (n),	['minə],
	hukommelse (m)	[hʉ'kɔmǝlsə]

122. Fairy tale characters

Santa Claus	Julenissen	['jʉləˌnisǝn]
Cinderella	Askepott	['askəˌpɔt]
mermaid	havfrue (m/f)	['havˌfrʉə]
Neptune	Neptun	[nɛp'tʉn]
magician, wizard	trollmann (m)	['trɔlˌmɑn]
fairy	fe (m)	['fe]
magic (adj)	trylle-	['trʏlə-]
magic wand	tryllestav (m)	['trʏləˌstɑv]
fairy tale	eventyr (n)	['ɛvənˌtyr]
miracle	mirakel (n)	[mi'rɑkəl]
dwarf	gnom, dverg (m)	['gnʊm], ['dvɛrg]
to turn into ...	å forvandle seg til ...	[ɔ fɔr'vɑndlə sæj til ...]
ghost	spøkelse (n)	['spøkəlsə]
phantom	fantom (m)	[fɑn'tɔm]
monster	monster (n)	['mɔnstər]
dragon	drage (m)	['drɑgə]
giant	gigant (m)	[gi'gɑnt]

123. Zodiac Signs

Aries	Væren (m)	['væərən]
Taurus	Tyren (m)	['tyrən]
Gemini	Tvillingene (m pl)	['tviliŋənə]
Cancer	Krepsen (m)	['krɛpsən]
Leo	Løven (m)	['løvən]
Virgo	Jomfruen (m)	['ʉmfrʉən]
Libra	Vekten (m)	['vɛktən]
Scorpio	Skorpionen	[skɔrpi'ʊnən]
Sagittarius	Skytten (m)	['ʂytən]
Capricorn	Steinbukken (m)	['stæjnˌbʉkən]
Aquarius	Vannmannen (m)	['vɑnˌmɑnən]
Pisces	Fiskene (pl)	['fiskenə]
character	karakter (m)	[kɑrɑk'ter]

character traits	**karaktertrekk** (n pl)	[karɑk'ter,trɛk]
behavior	**oppførsel** (m)	['ɔp,fœşəl]
to tell fortunes	**å spå**	[ɔ 'spɔ]
fortune-teller	**spåkone** (m/f)	['spoː,kɔnə]
horoscope	**horoskop** (n)	[hʊrʊ'skɔp]

Arts

124. Theater

theater	teater (n)	[te'atər]
opera	opera (m)	['ʊpera]
operetta	operette (m)	[ʊpe'rɛtə]
ballet	ballett (m)	[ba'let]
theater poster	plakat (m)	[pla'kat]
troupe	teatertrupp (m)	[te'atər‚trʉp]
(theatrical company)		
tour	turné (m)	[tʉr'ne:]
to be on tour	å være på turné	[ɔ 'værə pɔ tʉr'ne:]
to rehearse (vi, vt)	å repetere	[ɔ repe'terə]
rehearsal	repetisjon (m)	[repeti'ʂʊn]
repertoire	repertoar (n)	[repæ:tʊ'ar]
performance	forestilling (m/f)	['fɔrə‚stiliŋ]
theatrical show	teaterstykke (n)	[te'atər‚stʏkə]
play	skuespill (n)	['skʉə‚spil]
ticket	billett (m)	[bi'let]
box office (ticket booth)	billettluke (m/f)	[bi'let‚lʉkə]
lobby, foyer	lobby, foajé (m)	['lɔbi], [fʊa'je]
coat check (cloakroom)	garderobe (m)	[ga:də'rʊbə]
coat check tag	garderobemerke (n)	[ga:də'rʊbə 'mærkə]
binoculars	kikkert (m)	['çikɛ:t]
usher	plassanviser (m)	['plas an‚visər]
orchestra seats	parkett (m)	[par'kɛt]
balcony	balkong (m)	[bal'kɔŋ]
dress circle	første losjerad (m)	['fœʂtə ‚luʂɛrad]
box	losje (m)	['lʊʂə]
row	rad (m/f)	['rad]
seat	plass (m)	['plas]
audience	publikum (n)	['pʉblikum]
spectator	tilskuer (m)	['til‚skʉər]
to clap (vi, vt)	å klappe	[ɔ 'klapə]
applause	applaus (m)	[a'plaʊs]
ovation	bifall (n)	['bi‚fal]
stage	scene (m)	['se:nə]
curtain	teppe (n)	['tɛpə]
scenery	dekorasjon (m)	[dekʊra'ʂʊn]

backstage	**kulisser** (m pl)	[kʉ'lisər]
scene (e.g., the last ~)	**scene** (m)	['se:nə]
act	**akt** (m)	['akt]
intermission	**mellomakt** (m)	['mɛlɔmˌakt]

125. Cinema

actor	**skuespiller** (m)	['skʉəˌspilər]
actress	**skuespillerinne** (m/f)	['skʉəˌspilə'rinə]
movies (industry)	**filmindustri** (m)	['film indʉ'stri]
movie	**film** (m)	['film]
episode	**del** (m)	['del]
detective movie	**kriminalfilm** (m)	[krimi'nalˌfilm]
action movie	**actionfilm** (m)	['ɛkʂənˌfilm]
adventure movie	**eventyrfilm** (m)	['ɛvəntyrˌflm]
science fiction movie	**Sci-Fi film** (m)	['sajˌfaj film]
horror movie	**skrekkfilm** (m)	['skrɛkˌfilm]
comedy movie	**komedie** (m)	['kʉ'mediə]
melodrama	**melodrama** (n)	[melɔ'drama]
drama	**drama** (n)	['drama]
fictional movie	**spillefilm** (m)	['spiləˌfilm]
documentary	**dokumentarfilm** (m)	[dɔkʉmɛn'tar ˌfilm]
cartoon	**tegnefilm** (m)	['tæjnəˌfilm]
silent movies	**stumfilm** (m)	['stʉmˌfilm]
role (part)	**rolle** (m/f)	['rɔlə]
leading role	**hovedrolle** (m)	['hʉvədˌrɔle]
to play (vi, vt)	**å spille**	[ɔ 'spilə]
movie star	**filmstjerne** (m)	['filmˌstjæːnə]
well-known (adj)	**kjent**	['çɛnt]
famous (adj)	**berømt**	[be'rømt]
popular (adj)	**populær**	[pʉpʉ'lær]
script (screenplay)	**manus** (n)	['manʉs]
scriptwriter	**manusforfatter** (m)	['manʉs fɔr'fatər]
movie director	**regissør** (m)	[rɛʂi'sør]
producer	**produsent** (m)	[prʉdʉ'sɛnt]
assistant	**assistent** (m)	[asi'stɛnt]
cameraman	**kameramann** (m)	['kamerɑˌman]
stuntman	**stuntmann** (m)	['stantˌmɛn]
double (stuntman)	**stand-in** (m)	[ˌstand'in]
to shoot a movie	**å spille inn en film**	[ɔ 'spilə in en 'film]
audition, screen test	**prøve** (m/f)	['prøvə]
shooting	**opptak** (n)	['ɔpˌtak]

movie crew	filmteam (n)	['film,tim]
movie set	opptaksplass (m)	['ɔptaks,plas]
camera	filmkamera (n)	['film,kamera]

movie theater	kino (m)	['çinʊ]
screen (e.g., big ~)	filmduk (m)	['film,dʉk]
to show a movie	å vise en film	[ɔ 'visə en 'film]

soundtrack	lydspor (n)	['lyd,spʊr]
special effects	spesialeffekter (m pl)	['spesi'al e'fɛktər]
subtitles	undertekster (m/f)	['ʉnə,tɛkstər]
credits	rulletekst (m)	['rʉlə,tɛkst]
translation	oversettelse (m)	['ɔvə,sɛtəlsə]

126. Painting

art	kunst (m)	['kʉnst]
fine arts	de skjønne kunster	[de 'ʂønə 'kʉnstər]
art gallery	kunstgalleri (n)	['kʉnst gale'ri]
art exhibition	maleriutstilling (m/f)	[,male'ri ʉt,stiliŋ]

painting (art)	malerkunst (m)	['malər,kʉnst]
graphic art	grafikk (m)	[gra'fik]
abstract art	abstrakt kunst (m)	[ab'strakt 'kʉnst]
impressionism	impresjonisme (m)	[imprɛʂʊ'nisme]

picture (painting)	maleri (m/f)	[,male'ri]
drawing	tegning (m/f)	['tæjniŋ]
poster	plakat, poster (m)	['pla,kat], ['pɔstər]

illustration (picture)	illustrasjon (m)	[ilʉstra'ʂʊn]
miniature	miniatyr (m)	[minia'tyr]
copy (of painting, etc.)	kopi (m)	[kʊ'pi]
reproduction	reproduksjon (m)	[reprʊdʉk'ʂʊn]

mosaic	mosaikk (m)	[mʊsa'ik]
stained glass window	glassmaleri (n)	['glas,male'ri]
fresco	freske (m)	['frɛskə]
engraving	gravyr (m)	[gra'vyr]

bust (sculpture)	byste (m)	['bystə]
sculpture	skulptur (m)	[skʉlp'tʉr]
statue	statue (m)	['statʉə]
plaster of Paris	gips (m)	['jips]
plaster (as adj)	gips-	['jips-]

portrait	portrett (n)	[pɔ:'ʈrɛt]
self-portrait	selvportrett (n)	['sɛl,pɔ:'ʈrɛt]
landscape painting	landskapsmaleri (n)	['lanskaps,male'ri]
still life	stilleben (n)	['stil,lebən]

| caricature | kari<atur (m) | [kɑrikɑˈtʉr] |
| sketch | skisse (m/f) | [ˈʂisə] |

paint	maling (m/f)	[ˈmɑliŋ]
watercolor paint	akvarell (m)	[ɑkvɑˈrɛl]
oil (paint)	olje (m)	[ˈɔljə]
pencil	blyant (m)	[ˈblyˌɑnt]
India ink	tusj (m/n)	[ˈtʉʂ]
charcoal	kull (n)	[ˈkʉl]

| to draw (vi, vt) | å tegne | [ɔ ˈtæjnə] |
| to paint (vi, vt) | å male | [ɔ ˈmɑlə] |

to pose (vi)	å posere	[ɔ poˈserə]
artist's model (masc.)	mocell (m)	[mʉˈdɛl]
artist's model (fem.)	mocell (m)	[mʉˈdɛl]

artist (painter)	kunstner (m)	[ˈkʉnstnər]
work of art	kunstverk (n)	[ˈkʉnstˌværk]
masterpiece	mesterverk (n)	[ˈmɛstɛrˌværk]
studio (artist's workroom)	atelier (n)	[ɑteˈlje]

canvas (cloth)	kanvas (m/n), lerret (n)	[ˈkɑnvɑs], [ˈleret]
easel	staffeli (n)	[stɑfeˈli]
palette	palett (m)	[pɑˈlet]

frame (picture ~, etc.)	ramme (m/f)	[ˈrɑmə]
restoration	restaurering (m)	[rɛstɑʉˈreriŋ]
to restore (vt)	å restaurere	[ɔ rɛstɑʉˈrərə]

127. Literature & Poetry

literature	litteratur (m)	[litərɑˈtʉr]
author (writer)	forfatter (m)	[forˈfɑtər]
pseudonym	pseudonym (n)	[sewdʉˈnym]

book	bok (m/f)	[ˈbʉk]
volume	bind (n)	[ˈbin]
table of contents	innholdsfortegnelse (m)	[ˈinhɔls fɔːˈʈæjnəlsə]
page	side (m/f)	[ˈsidə]
main character	hovedperson (m)	[ˈhʉvəd pæˈʂʉn]
autograph	autograf (m)	[ɑʉtʉˈgrɑf]

short story	novelle (m/f)	[nʉˈvɛlə]
story (novella)	kortroman (m)	[ˈkʉːʈ rʉˌmɑn]
novel	roman (m)	[rʉˈmɑn]
work (writing)	verk (n)	[ˈværk]
fable	fabel (m)	[ˈfɑbəl]
detective novel	kriminalroman (m)	[krimiˈnɑl rʉˌmɑn]
poem (verse)	dikt (n)	[ˈdikt]

poetry	**poesi** (m)	[pɔɛ'si]
poem (epic, ballad)	**epos** (n)	['ɛpɔs]
poet	**poet, dikter** (m)	['pɔɛt], ['diktər]
fiction	**skjønnlitteratur** (m)	['ʂøn literɑ'tʉr]
science fiction	**science fiction** (m)	['sɑjəns ˌfikʂn]
adventures	**eventyr** (n pl)	['ɛvənˌtyr]
educational literature	**undervisnings-litteratur** (m)	['ʉnərˌvisniŋs literɑ'tʉr]
children's literature	**barnelitteratur** (m)	['bɑːŋə literɑ'tʉr]

128. Circus

circus	**sirkus** (m/n)	['sirkʉs]
traveling circus	**ambulerende sirkus** (n)	['ɑmbʉˌlerɛnə 'sirkʉs]
program	**program** (n)	[prʉ'grɑm]
performance	**forestilling** (m/f)	['fɔrəˌstiliŋ]
act (circus ~)	**nummer** (n)	['nʉmər]
circus ring	**manesje, arena** (m)	[mɑ'neʂə], [ɑ'renɑ]
pantomime (act)	**pantomime** (m)	[pɑntʉ'mimə]
clown	**klovn** (m)	['klɔvn]
acrobat	**akrobat** (m)	[ɑkrʉ'bɑt]
acrobatics	**akrobatikk** (m)	[ɑkrʉbɑ'tik]
gymnast	**gymnast** (m)	[gʏm'nɑst]
gymnastics	**gymnastikk** (m)	[gʏmnɑ'stik]
somersault	**salto** (m)	['sɑltʉ]
athlete (strongman)	**atlet** (m)	[ɑt'let]
tamer (e.g., lion ~)	**dyretemmer** (m)	['dyrəˌtɛmər]
rider (circus horse ~)	**rytter** (m)	['rʏtər]
assistant	**assistent** (m)	[ɑsi'stɛnt]
stunt	**trikk, triks** (n)	['trik], ['triks]
magic trick	**trylletriks** (n)	['trʏləˌtriks]
conjurer, magician	**tryllekunstner** (m)	['trʏləˌkʉnstnər]
juggler	**sjonglør** (m)	[ʂɔŋ'lør]
to juggle (vi, vt)	**å sjonglere**	[ɔ 'ʂɔŋˌlerə]
animal trainer	**dressør** (m)	[drɛ'sør]
animal training	**dressur** (m)	[drɛ'sʉr]
to train (animals)	**å dressere**	[ɔ drɛ'serə]

129. Music. Pop music

music	**musikk** (m)	[mʉ'sik]
musician	**musiker** (m)	['mʉsikər]

| musical instrument | musikkinstrument (n) | [mʉ'sik instrʉ'mɛnt] |
| to play ... | å spille ... | [ɔ 'spilə ...] |

guitar	gitar (m)	['giˌtar]
violin	fiolin (m)	[fiʊ'lin]
cello	cello (m)	['sɛlʊ]
double bass	kontrabass (m)	['kʊntraˌbas]
harp	harpe (m)	['harpə]

piano	piano (n)	[pi'anʊ]
grand piano	flygel (n)	['flygəl]
organ	orgel (n)	['ɔrgəl]

wind instruments	blåseinstrumenter (n pl)	['blo:sə instrʉ'mɛntər]
oboe	obo (m)	[ʊ'bʊ]
saxophone	saksofon (m)	[saksʊ'fʊn]
clarinet	klarinett (m)	[klari'nɛt]
flute	fløyte (m)	['fløjtə]
trumpet	trompet (m)	[trʊm'pet]

accordion	trekkspill (n)	['trɛkˌspil]
drum	tromme (m)	['trʊmə]
duo	duett (m)	[dʉ'ɛt]
trio	trio (m)	['triʊ]
quartet	kvartett (m)	[kva:'tɛt]
choir	kor (r)	['kʊr]
orchestra	orkester (n)	[ɔr'kɛstər]

pop music	popmusikk (m)	['pɔp mʉ'sik]
rock music	rockmusikk (m)	['rɔk mʉ'sik]
rock group	rockeband (n)	['rɔkəˌbɛnd|
jazz	jazz (m)	['jas]

| idol | idol (n) | [i'dʊl] |
| admirer, fan | beundrer (m) | [be'ʉndrər] |

concert	konsert (m)	[kʊn'sæ:t]
symphony	symfoni (m)	[symfʊ'ni]
composition	komposisjon (m)	[kʊmpʊzi'sʉn]
to compose (write)	å komponere	[ɔ kʊmpʊ'rerə]

singing (n)	synging (m/f)	['syŋiŋ]
song	sang (m)	['saŋ]
tune (melody)	melodi (m)	[melʊ'di]
rhythm	rytme (m)	['rʏtmə]
blues	blues (m)	['blʉs]

sheet music	noter (m pl)	['nʊtər]
baton	taktstokk (m)	['taktˌstɔk]
bow	bue, boge (m)	['bʉ:ə], ['bɔgə]
string	streng (m)	['strɛŋ]
case (e.g., guitar ~)	futteral (n), kasse (m/f)	['fʉte'ral], [kasə]

Rest. Entertainment. Travel

130. Trip. Travel

tourism, travel	turisme (m)	[tʉ'rismə]
tourist	turist (m)	[tʉ'rist]
trip, voyage	reise (m/f)	['ræjsə]
adventure	eventyr (n)	['ɛvən‚tyr]
trip, journey	tripp (m)	['trip]
vacation	ferie (m)	['fɛriə]
to be on vacation	å være på ferie	[ɔ 'værə pɔ 'fɛriə]
rest	hvile (m/f)	['vilə]
train	tog (n)	['tɔg]
by train	med tog	[me 'tɔg]
airplane	fly (n)	['fly]
by airplane	med fly	[me 'fly]
by car	med bil	[me 'bil]
by ship	med skip	[me 'ṣip]
luggage	bagasje (m)	[bɑ'gɑṣə]
suitcase	koffert (m)	['kʊfɛːt]
luggage cart	bagasjetralle (m/f)	[bɑ'gɑṣə‚trɑlə]
passport	pass (n)	['pɑs]
visa	visum (n)	['visʉm]
ticket	billett (m)	[bi'let]
air ticket	flybillett (m)	['fly bi'let]
guidebook	reisehåndbok (m/f)	['ræjsə‚hɔnbʊk]
map (tourist ~)	kart (n)	['kɑːt]
area (rural ~)	område (n)	['ɔm‚roːdə]
place, site	sted (n)	['sted]
exotic (adj)	eksotisk	[ɛk'sʉtisk]
amazing (adj)	forunderlig	[fɔ'rʉnde:lị]
group	gruppe (m)	['grʉpə]
excursion, sightseeing tour	utflukt (m/f)	['ʉt‚flʉkt]
guide (person)	guide (m)	['gɑjd]

131. Hotel

hotel	hotell (n)	[hʊ'tɛl]
motel	motell (n)	[mʊ'tɛl]

three-star (~ hotel)	trestjernet	['treˌstjæːŋə]
five-star	femstjernet	['fɛmˌstjæ ŋə]
to stay (in a hotel, etc.)	å bo	[ɔ 'buː]
room	rom (n)	['rʊm]
single room	enkeltrom (n)	['ɛnkeltˌrʊːn]
double room	dobbeltrom (n)	['dobeltˌrʊm]
to book a room	å reservere rom	[ɔ resɛr'verə 'rʊm]
half board	halvpensjon (m)	['hɑl panˌsʊn]
full board	fullpensjon (m)	['fʉl panˌsʊn]
with bath	med badekar	[me 'bɑdəˌkar]
with shower	med dusj	[me 'dʉʂ]
satellite television	satellitt-TV (m)	[sɑtɛ'lit 'tɛvɛ]
air-conditioner	klimaanlegg (n)	['klimɑ'ɑn leg]
towel	håndkle (n)	['hɔnˌkle]
key	nøkkel (m)	['nøkəl]
administrator	administrator (m)	[admini'strɑːtʊr]
chambermaid	stuepike (m/f)	['stʉeˌpikə]
porter, bellboy	pikkolo (m)	['pikɔlɔ]
doorman	portier (m)	[pɔː'tje]
restaurant	restaurant (m)	[rɛstʉ'ranˑ]
pub, bar	bar (m)	['bar]
breakfast	frokost (m)	['frʊkɔst]
dinner	middag (m)	['miˌdɑ]
buffet	buffet (m)	[bʉ'fɛ]
lobby	hall, lobby (m)	['hɑl], ['lɔbi]
elevator	heis (m)	['hæjs]
DO NOT DISTURB	VENNLIGST IKKE FORSTYRR!	['vɛnligt ikə fɔ'ʂtyr]
NO SMOKING	RØYKING FORBUDT	['røjkiŋ fɔr'bʉt]

132. Books. Reading

book	bok (m/f)	['bʊk]
author	forfatter (m)	[fɔr'fatər]
writer	forfatter (m)	[fɔr'fatər]
to write (~ a book)	å skrive	[ɔ 'skrivə]
reader	leser (m)	['lesər]
to read (vi, vt)	å lese	[ɔ 'lesə]
reading (activity)	lesning (m/f)	['lesniŋ]
silently (to oneself)	for seg selv	[fɔr sæj 'sɛl]
aloud (adv)	høyt	['højt]

to publish (vt)	å publisere	[ɔ pʉbli'serə]
publishing (process)	publisering (m/f)	[pʉbli'serin]
publisher	forlegger (m)	['fɔːˌlegər]
publishing house	forlag (n)	['fɔːˌlɑg]

to come out (be released)	å komme ut	[ɔ 'kɔmə ʉt]
release (of a book)	utgivelse (m)	['ʉtjivəlsə]
print run	opplag (n)	['ɔpˌlɑg]

| bookstore | bokhandel (m) | ['bʊkˌhɑndəl] |
| library | bibliotek (n) | [bibliʊ'tek] |

story (novella)	kortroman (m)	['kʊːt rʊˌmɑn]
short story	novelle (m/f)	[nʊ'vɛlə]
novel	roman (m)	[rʊ'mɑn]
detective novel	kriminalroman (m)	[krimi'nɑl rʊˌmɑn]

memoirs	memoarer (pl)	[memʊ'ɑrər]
legend	legende (m)	['le'gɛndə]
myth	myte (m)	['myːtə]

poetry, poems	dikt (n pl)	['dikt]
autobiography	selvbiografi (m)	['sɛlˌbiʊgrɑ'fi]
selected works	utvalgte verker (n pl)	['ʉtˌvɑlgtə 'værkər]
science fiction	science fiction (m)	['sɑjəns ˌfikʂn]

title	tittel (m)	['titəl]
introduction	innledning (m)	['inˌlednin]
title page	tittelblad (n)	['titəlˌblɑ]

chapter	kapitel (n)	[kɑ'pitəl]
extract	utdrag (n)	['ʉtˌdrɑg]
episode	episode (m)	[ɛpi'sʊdə]

plot (storyline)	handling (m/f)	['hɑndlin]
contents	innhold (n)	['inˌhɔl]
table of contents	innholdsfortegnelse (m)	['inhɔls fɔː'tæjnəlsə]
main character	hovedperson (m)	['hʊvəd pæ'ʂʊn]

volume	bind (n)	['bin]
cover	omslag (n)	['ɔmˌslɑg]
binding	bokbind (n)	['bʊkˌbin]
bookmark	bokmerke (n)	['bʊkˌmærkə]

page	side (m/f)	['sidə]
to page through	å bla	[ɔ 'blɑ]
margins	marger (m pl)	['mɑrgər]
annotation (marginal note, etc.)	annotering (n)	[anʊ'tɛrin]
footnote	anmerkning (m)	['anˌmærknin]
text	tekst (m/f)	['tɛkst]
type, font	skrift, font (m)	['skrift], ['fɔnt]

misprint, typo	trykkfeil (m)	['trʏkˌfæjl]
translation	oversettelse (m)	['ɔvəˌsɛtəlsə]
to translate (vt)	å oversette	[ɔ 'ɔvəˌsɛtə]
original (n)	original (m)	[ɔrigiˈnal]
famous (adj)	berømt	[beˈrømt]
unknown (not famous)	ukjemt	['ʉˌçɛnt]
interesting (adj)	interessant	[intereˈsan]
bestseller	bestselger (m)	['bɛstˌsɛləˈ]
dictionary	ordbok (m/f)	['uːrˌbʉk]
textbook	lærebok (m/f)	['læɾəˌbʉk]
encyclopedia	encyklopedi (m)	[ɛnsʏklopeˈdi]

133. Hunting. Fishing

hunting	jakt (n/f)	['jakt]
to hunt (vi, vt)	å jage	[ɔ 'jagə]
hunter	jeger (m)	['jɛːgər]
to shoot (vi)	å skyte	[ɔ 'sytə]
rifle	gevær (n)	[geˈvær]
bullet (shell)	patron (m)	[paˈtrʉn]
shot (lead balls)	hagl (n)	['hagl]
steel trap	saks (m/f)	['saks]
snare (for birds, etc.)	felle (m/f)	['fɛlə]
to fall into the steel trap	å fanges i felle	[ɔ 'faŋəs i 'fɛlə]
to lay a steel trap	å sette opp felle	[ɔ 'sɛtə ɔp 'fɛlə]
poacher	tyvskytter (m)	['tyfˌsytər]
game (in hunting)	vilt (r)	['vilt]
hound dog	jakthund (m)	['jaktˌhʉn]
safari	safari (m)	[saˈfari]
mounted animal	utstoppet dyr (n)	['ʉtˌstopet ˌdyr]
fisherman, angler	fisker (m)	['fiskər]
fishing (angling)	fiske (n)	['fiskə]
to fish (vi)	å fiske	[ɔ 'fiskə]
fishing rod	fiskestang (m/f)	['fiskəˌstaŋ]
fishing line	fiskesnøre (n)	['fiskəˌsnørə]
hook	krok (m)	['krʉk]
float, bobber	dupp (m)	['dʉp]
bait	agn (m)	['aŋn]
to cast a line	å kaste ut	[ɔ 'kastə ʉt]
to bite (ab. fish)	å bite	[ɔ 'bitə]
catch (of fish)	fangst (m)	['faŋst]
ice-hole	hull (n) i isen	['hʉl i ˌisəˈ]
fishing net	nett (n)	['nɛt]

boat	**båt** (m)	['bot]
to net (to fish with a net)	**å fiske med nett**	[ɔ 'fiskə me 'nɛt]
to cast[throw] the net	**å kaste nettet**	[ɔ 'kastə 'nɛtə]
to haul the net in	**å hale opp nettet**	[ɔ 'halə ɔp 'nɛtə]
to fall into the net	**å bli fanget i nett**	[ɔ 'bli 'faŋət i 'nɛt]

whaler (person)	**hvalfanger** (m)	['val̩faŋər]
whaleboat	**hvalbåt** (m)	['val̩bot]
harpoon	**harpun** (m)	[har'pʉn]

134. Games. Billiards

billiards	**biljard** (m)	[bil'ja:ɖ]
billiard room, hall	**biljardsalong** (m)	[bil'ja:ɖsɑˌlɔŋ]
ball (snooker, etc.)	**biljardkule** (m/f)	[bil'ja:ɖˌkʉ:lə]
to pocket a ball	**å støte en kule**	[ɔ 'støtə en 'kʉ:lə]
cue	**kø** (m)	['kø]
pocket	**hull** (n)	['hʉl]

135. Games. Playing cards

diamonds	**ruter** (m pl)	['rʉtər]
spades	**spar** (m pl)	['spɑr]
hearts	**hjerter** (m)	['jæːᴛ̩ər]
clubs	**kløver** (m)	['kløvər]

ace	**ess** (n)	['ɛs]
king	**konge** (m)	['kuŋə]
queen	**dame** (m/f)	['damə]
jack, knave	**knekt** (m)	['knɛkt]

playing card	**kort** (n)	['kɔ:ᴛ]
cards	**kort** (n pl)	['kɔ:ᴛ]
trump	**trumf** (m)	['trʉmf]
deck of cards	**kortstokk** (m)	['kɔ:ᴛ̩stɔk]

point	**poeng** (n)	[pɔ'ɛŋ]
to deal (vi, vt)	**å gi, å dele ut**	[ɔ 'ji], [ɔ 'delə ʉt]
to shuffle (cards)	**å blande**	[ɔ 'blanə]
lead, turn (n)	**trekk** (n)	['trɛk]
cardsharp	**falskspiller** (m)	['falskˌspilər]

136. Rest. Games. Miscellaneous

| to stroll (vi, vt) | **å spasere** | [ɔ spɑ'serə] |
| stroll (leisurely walk) | **spasertur** (m) | [spɑ'sɛːˌtʉr] |

car ride	kjøretur (m)	['çœ:rə,tʉr]
adventure	eventyr (n)	['evən,tyr]
picnic	piknik (m)	['piknik]

game (chess, etc.)	spill (r)	['spil]
player	spiller (m)	['spilər]
game (one ~ of chess)	parti (1)	[pɑ:'ti]

collector (e.g., philatelist)	samler (m)	['sɑmlər]
to collect (stamps, etc.)	å samle	[ɔ 'sɑmlə]
collection	samling (m/f)	['sɑmliŋ]

crossword puzzle	kryssord (n)	['krʏs,u:r]
racetrack (horse racing venue)	travbane (m)	['trɑv,bɑnə]
disco (discotheque)	diskotek (n)	[diskʊ'tek]

| sauna | sauna (m) | ['sɑʊnɑ] |
| lottery | lotteri (n) | [lote'ri] |

camping trip	campingtur (m)	['kɑmpiŋ,tʉr]
camp	leir (n)	['læjr]
tent (for camping)	telt (r)	['tɛlt]
compass	kompass (m/n)	[kʊm'pɑs]
camper	camper (m)	['kɑmpər]

to watch (movie, etc.)	å se på	[ɔ 'se pɔ]
viewer	TV-seer (m)	['tɛvɛ ,se:ər]
TV show (TV program)	TV-show (n)	['tɛvɛ ,ɕo:w]

137. Photography

| camera (photo) | kamera (n) | ['kɑmerɑ] |
| photo, picture | foto, fotografi (n) | ['fɔtɔ], ['fɔtɔgrɑ'fi] |

photographer	fotograf (m)	[fɔtɔ'grɑf]
photo studio	fotostudio (n)	['fɔtɔ,stʉdiɔ]
photo album	fotoalbum (n)	['fɔtɔ,ɑlbʉm]

camera lens	objektiv (n)	[ɔbjɛk'tiv]
telephoto lens	teleobjektiv (n)	['teleɔbjek'tiv]
filter	filter (n)	['filtər]
lens	linse (m/f)	['linsə]

optics (high-quality ~)	optikk (m)	[ɔp'tik]
diaphragm (aperture)	blender (m)	['blenər]
exposure time (shutter speed)	eksponeringstid (m/f)	[ɛkspʊ'neriŋs,tid]
viewfinder	søker (m)	['søkər]
digital camera	digitalkamera (n)	[digi'tal ,kɑmerɑ]

139

tripod	**stativ** (m)	[sta'tiv]
flash	**blits** (m)	['blits]
to photograph (vt)	**å fotografere**	[ɔ fɔtɔgra'ferə]
to take pictures	**å ta bilder**	[ɔ 'ta 'bildər]
to have one's picture taken	**å bli fotografert**	[ɔ 'bli fɔtɔgra'fɛːt]
focus	**fokus** (n)	['fɔkʉs]
to focus	**å stille skarphet**	[ɔ 'stilə 'skarp,het]
sharp, in focus (adj)	**skarp**	['skarp]
sharpness	**skarphet** (m)	['skarp,het]
contrast	**kontrast** (m)	[kʉn'trast]
contrast (as adj)	**kontrast-**	[kʉn'trast-]
picture (photo)	**bilde** (n)	['bildə]
negative (n)	**negativ** (m/n)	['nega,tiv]
film (a roll of ~)	**film** (m)	['film]
frame (still)	**bilde** (n)	['bildə]
to print (photos)	**å skrive ut**	[ɔ skrivə ʉt]

138. Beach. Swimming

beach	**badestrand** (m/f)	['badə,stran]
sand	**sand** (m)	['san]
deserted (beach)	**øde**	['ødə]
suntan	**solbrenthet** (m)	['sʉlbrɛnt,het]
to get a tan	**å sole seg**	[ɔ 'sʉlə sæj]
tan (adj)	**solbrent**	['sʉl,brɛnt]
sunscreen	**solkrem** (m)	['sʉl,krɛm]
bikini	**bikini** (m)	[bi'kini]
bathing suit	**badedrakt** (m/f)	['badə,drakt]
swim trunks	**badebukser** (m/f)	['badə,bʉksər]
swimming pool	**svømmebasseng** (n)	['svœmə,ba'sɛŋ]
to swim (vi)	**å svømme**	[ɔ 'svœmə]
shower	**dusj** (m)	['dʉʃ]
to change (one's clothes)	**å kle seg om**	[ɔ 'kle sæj ,ɔm]
towel	**håndkle** (n)	['hɔn,kle]
boat	**båt** (m)	['bɔt]
motorboat	**motorbåt** (m)	['mɔtʉr,bɔt]
water ski	**vannski** (m pl)	['van,ʃi]
paddle boat	**pedalbåt** (m)	['pe'dal,bɔt]
surfing	**surfing** (m/f)	['sørfiŋ]
surfer	**surfer** (m)	['sørfər]
scuba set	**scuba** (n)	['skʉba]

flippers (swim fins)	**svømmeføtter** (m pl)	['svœmə‚fœtər]
mask (diving ~)	**maske** (m/f)	['maskə]
diver	**dykker** (m)	['dʏkər]
to dive (vi)	**å dykke**	[ɔ 'dʏkə]
underwater (adv)	**under vannet**	['ʉnər 'vɑnə]
beach umbrella	**parasoll** (m)	[parɑ'sɔl]
sunbed (lounger)	**liggestol** (m)	['ligə‚stʉl]
sunglasses	**solbriller** (m pl)	['sʉl‚brilər]
air mattress	**luftmadrass** (m)	['lʉftmɑ‚drɑs]
to play (amuse oneself)	**å leke**	[ɔ 'lekə]
to go for a swim	**å bade**	[ɔ 'bɑdə]
beach ball	**ball** m)	['bɑl]
to inflate (vt)	**å blåse opp**	[ɔ 'blɔːsə ɔp]
inflatable, air (adj)	**luft-‚ oppblåsbar**	['lʉft-], [ɔp'blɔːsbɑr]
wave	**bølge** (m)	['bølgə]
buoy (line of ~s)	**bøye** (m)	['bøjə]
to drown (ab. person)	**å drukne**	[ɔ 'drʉknə‚
to save, to rescue	**å redde**	[ɔ 'rɛdə]
life vest	**redningsvest** (m)	['rɛdniŋs‚vɛst]
to observe, to watch	**å observere**	[ɔ ɔbsɛr'verə]
lifeguard	**badevakt** (m/f)	['bɑdə‚vɑk-]

TECHNICAL EQUIPMENT. TRANSPORTATION

Technical equipment

139. Computer

computer	datamaskin (m)	['dɑtɑ mɑˌṣin]
notebook, laptop	bærbar, laptop (m)	['bærˌbɑr], ['lɑptɔp]
to turn on	å slå på	[ɔ 'ṣlɔ pɔ]
to turn off	å slå av	[ɔ 'ṣlɔ ɑ:]
keyboard	tastatur (n)	[tɑstɑ'tʉr]
key	tast (m)	['tɑst]
mouse	mus (m/f)	['mʉs]
mouse pad	musematte (m/f)	['mʉsəˌmɑtə]
button	knapp (m)	['knɑp]
cursor	markør (m)	[mɑr'kør]
monitor	monitor (m)	['mɔnitɔr]
screen	skjerm (m)	['ṣærm]
hard disk	harddisk (m)	['hɑrˌdisk]
hard disk capacity	harddiskkapasitet (m)	['hɑrˌdisk kɑpɑsi'tet]
memory	minne (n)	['minə]
random access memory	hovedminne (n)	['hɔvədˌminə]
file	fil (m)	['fil]
folder	mappe (m/f)	['mɑpə]
to open (vt)	å åpne	[ɔ 'ɔpnə]
to close (vt)	å lukke	[ɔ 'lʉkə]
to save (vt)	å lagre	[ɔ 'lɑgrə]
to delete (vt)	å slette, å fjerne	[ɔ 'ṣletə], [ɔ 'fjæ:ŋə]
to copy (vt)	å kopiere	[ɔ kʉ'pjerə]
to sort (vt)	å sortere	[ɔ sɔ:'ʈerə]
to transfer (copy)	å overføre	[ɔ 'ɔvərˌførə]
program	program (n)	[prʉ'grɑm]
software	programvare (m/f)	[prʉ'grɑmˌvɑrə]
programmer	programmerer (m)	[prʉgrɑ'merər]
to program (vt)	å programmere	[ɔ prʉgrɑ'merə]
hacker	hacker (m)	['hɑkər]
password	passord (n)	['pɑsˌu:r]

| virus | virus (m) | ['virus] |
| to find, to detect | å oppdage | [ɔ 'ɔpˌdɑgɛ] |

| byte | byte (n) | ['bɑjt] |
| megabyte | megabyte (m) | ['megaˌbɑjt] |

| data | data (n pl) | ['dɑtɑ] |
| database | database (m) | ['dɑtɑˌbɑsə] |

cable (USB, etc.)	kabel (m)	['kɑbəl]
to disconnect (vt)	å koble fra	[ɔ 'koblə frɔ]
to connect (sth to sth)	å koble	[ɔ 'koblə]

140. Internet. E-mail

Internet	Internett	['intəˌnɛt]
browser	nettleser (m)	['nɛtˌlesər]
search engine	søkemotor (m)	['søkəˌmotʊr]
provider	leverandør (m)	[levəran'dør]

webmaster	webmaster (m)	['vɛbˌmɑstər]
website	webside, hjemmeside (m/f)	['vɛbˌsidə], ['jɛməˌsidə]
webpage	nettside (m)	['nɛtˌsidə]

| address (e-mail ~) | adresse (m) | [ɑ'drɛsə] |
| address book | adressebok (f) | [ɑ'drɛsəˌbʊk] |

mailbox	postkasse (m/f)	['pɔstˌkɑsə]
mail	post (m)	['pɔst]
full (adj)	full	['fʉl]

message	melding (m/f)	['mɛliŋ]
incoming messages	innkommende meldinger	['inˌkɔmenə 'mɛliŋər]
outgoing messages	utgående meldinger	['ʉtˌgɔənə 'mɛliŋər]
sender	avsender (m)	['ɑfˌsɛnər]
to send (vt)	å sende	[ɔ 'sɛnə]
sending (of mail)	avsending (m)	['ɑfˌsɛniŋ]

| receiver | mottaker (m) | ['mɔtˌtɑkər] |
| to receive (vt) | å motta | [ɔ 'mɔtɑ] |

| correspondence | korrespondanse (m) | [kʊrespɔn'dɑnsə] |
| to correspond (vi) | å brevveksle | [ɔ 'brɛvˌvɛkslə] |

file	fil (m)	['fil]
to download (vt)	å laste ned	[ɔ 'lɑstə 'ne]
to create (vt)	å opprette	[ɔ 'ɔpˌrɛtə]
to delete (vt)	å slette, å fjerne	[ɔ 'ʂletə], ɔ 'fjæ:ɳə]
deleted (adj)	slettet	['ʂletət]
connection (ADSL, etc.)	forbindelse (m)	[fɔr'binəlsə]

speed	**hastighet** (m/f)	['hɑstiˌhet]
modem	**modem** (n)	['mʊ'dɛm]
access	**tilgang** (m)	['tilˌgɑŋ]
port (e.g., input ~)	**port** (m)	['pɔːt]

| connection (make a ~) | **tilkobling** (m/f) | ['tilˌkɔbliŋ] |
| to connect to … (vi) | **å koble** | [ɔ 'kɔblə] |

| to select (vt) | **å velge** | [ɔ 'vɛlgə] |
| to search (for …) | **å søke etter …** | [ɔ 'søkə ˌɛtər …] |

Transportation

141. Airplane

airplane	**fly** (n)	['fly]
air ticket	**flybilett** (m)	['fly bi'let]
airline	**flyselskap** (n)	['flysəl,skap]
airport	**flyplass** (m)	['fly,plas]
supersonic (adj)	**overlyds-**	['ɔvə,lyds-]
captain	**kaptein** (m)	[kap'tæjn]
crew	**besetning** (m/f)	[be'sɛtniŋ]
pilot	**pilot** (m)	[pi'lot]
flight attendant (fem.)	**flyvertinne** (m/f)	[flyvɛːˈtinə]
navigator	**styrmann** (m)	['styr,man]
wings	**vinger** (m pl)	['viŋər]
tail	**hale** (m)	['halə]
cockpit	**cockpit, førerkabin** (m)	['kɔkpit], ['førərka,bin]
engine	**motor** (m)	['motʉr]
undercarriage (landing gear)	**landingshjul** (n)	['laniŋs,jʉl]
turbine	**turbin** (m)	[tʉr'bin]
propeller	**propell** (m)	[prʊ'pɛl]
black box	**svart boks** (m)	['svɑːt̪ bɔks]
yoke (control column)	**ratt** (r)	['rat]
fuel	**brensel** (n)	['brɛnsəl]
safety card	**sikkerhetsbrosjyre** (m)	['sikərhɛts,brɔ'syrə]
oxygen mask	**oksygenmaske** (m/f)	['ɔksygən,maskə]
uniform	**uniform** (m)	[ʉni'fɔrm]
life vest	**redningsvest** (m)	['rɛdniŋs,vɛst]
parachute	**fallskjerm** (m)	['fal,særm]
takeoff	**start** (m)	['stɑːt̪]
to take off (vi)	**å løfte**	[ɔ 'lœftə]
runway	**startbane** (m)	['stɑːt̪,banə]
visibility	**siktbarhet** (m)	['siktbar,het]
flight (act of flying)	**flyging** (m/f)	['flygiŋ]
altitude	**høyde** (m)	['højdə]
air pocket	**lufthull** (n)	['lʉft,hʉl]
seat	**plass** (m)	['plas]
headphones	**hodetelefoner** (n pl)	['hɔdətelə,fʊnər]

folding tray (tray table)	klappbord (n)	['klɑpˌbʊr]
airplane window	vindu (n)	['vindʉ]
aisle	midtgang (m)	['mitˌɡɑŋ]

142. Train

train	tog (n)	['tɔɡ]
commuter train	lokaltog (n)	[lɔ'kɑlˌtɔɡ]
express train	ekspresstog (n)	[ɛks'prɛsˌtɔɡ]
diesel locomotive	diesellokomotiv (n)	['disəl lʊkɔmɔ'tiv]
steam locomotive	damplokomotiv (n)	['dɑmp lʊkɔmɔ'tiv]

| passenger car | vogn (m) | ['vɔŋn] |
| dining car | restaurantvogn (m/f) | [rɛstʉ'rɑŋˌvɔŋn] |

rails	skinner (m/f pl)	['ʂinər]
railroad	jernbane (m)	['jæːɳˌbɑnə]
railway tie	sville (m/f)	['svilə]

platform (railway ~)	perrong, plattform (m/f)	[pɛ'rɔŋ], ['plɑtfɔrm]
track (~ 1, 2, etc.)	spor (n)	['spʊr]
semaphore	semafor (m)	[semɑ'fʊr]
station	stasjon (m)	[stɑ'ʂʊn]

engineer (train driver)	lokfører (m)	['lʊkˌførər]
porter (of luggage)	bærer (m)	['bærər]
car attendant	betjent (m)	['be'tjɛnt]
passenger	passasjer (m)	[pɑsɑ'ʂɛr]
conductor (ticket inspector)	billett inspektør (m)	[bi'let inspɛk'tør]

| corridor (in train) | korridor (m) | [kʊri'dɔr] |
| emergency brake | nødbrems (m) | ['nødˌbrɛms] |

compartment	kupé (m)	[kʉ'pe]
berth	køye (m/f)	['køjə]
upper berth	overkøye (m/f)	['ɔvərˌkøjə]
lower berth	underkøye (m/f)	['ʉnərˌkøjə]
bed linen, bedding	sengetøy (n)	['sɛŋəˌtøj]

ticket	billett (m)	[bi'let]
schedule	rutetabell (m)	['rʉtəˌtɑ'bɛl]
information display	informasjonstavle (m/f)	[infɔrmɑ'ʂʊns ˌtɑvlə]

to leave, to depart	å avgå	[ɔ 'ɑvɡɔ]
departure (of train)	avgang (m)	['ɑvˌɡɑŋ]
to arrive (ab. train)	å ankomme	[ɔ 'ɑnˌkɔmə]
arrival	ankomst (m)	['ɑnˌkɔmst]
to arrive by train	å ankomme med toget	[ɔ 'ɑnˌkɔmə me 'tɔɡe]
to get on the train	å gå på toget	[ɔ 'ɡɔ pɔ 'tɔɡe]

to get off the train	å gå av toget	[ɔ 'gɔ ɑ: 'tɔge]
train wreck	togulykke (m/n)	['tɔg ʉ'lʏkə]
to derail (vi)	å spore av	[ɔ 'spʉrə ɑ:]
steam locomotive	damplokomotiv (n)	['dɑmp lʊkɔmɔ'tiv]
stoker, fireman	fyrbøter (m)	['fyr̩bøtər]
firebox	fyrrom (n)	['fyr̩rʊm]
coal	kull (n)	['kʉl]

143. Ship

ship	skip (n)	['ʂip]
vessel	fartøy (n)	['fɑ:ˌtøj]
steamship	dampskip (n)	['dɑmpˌʂip]
riverboat	elvebåt (m)	['ɛlvəˌbɔt]
cruise ship	cruiseskip (n)	['krʉsˌʂip]
cruiser	krysser (m)	['krʏsər]
yacht	jakt (n/f)	['jɑkt]
tugboat	bukserbåt (m)	[bʉk'serˌbɔt]
barge	lastepram (m)	['lɑstəˌprɑm]
ferry	ferje ferge (m/f)	['færjə], ['fˤærgə]
sailing ship	seilbåt (n)	['sæjlˌbɔt]
brigantine	brigantin (m)	[brigɑn'tir]
ice breaker	isbryter (m)	['isˌbrytər]
submarine	ubåt (m)	['ʉ:ˌbɔt]
boat (flat-bottomed ~)	båt (m)	['bɔt]
dinghy	jolle (m/f)	['jɔlə]
lifeboat	livbåt (m)	['livˌbɔt]
motorboat	motorbåt (m)	['mɔtʊrˌbɔt]
captain	kaptein (m)	[kɑp'tæjn]
seaman	matros (m)	[mɑ'trʊs]
sailor	sjømann (m)	['ʂøˌmɑn]
crew	besetning (m/f)	[be'sɛtniŋ]
boatswain	båtsmann (m)	['bɔsˌmɑn]
ship's boy	skipsgutt, jungmann (m)	['ʂipsˌgʉt], ['jʉŋˌmɑn]
cook	kokk (m)	['kʊk]
ship's doctor	skipslege (m)	['ʂipsˌlegə]
deck	dekk (n)	['dɛk]
mast	mast (m/f)	['mɑst]
sail	seil (n)	['sæjl]
hold	lasterom (n)	['lɑstəˌrʊm]
bow (prow)	baug (m)	['bæu]

stern	**akterende** (m)	['aktə‚rɛnə]
oar	**åre** (m)	['oːrə]
screw propeller	**propell** (m)	[prʊ'pɛl]
cabin	**hytte** (m)	['hʏtə]
wardroom	**offisersmesse** (m/f)	[ɔfi'sɛrs‚mɛsə]
engine room	**maskinrom** (n)	[ma'ʂin‚rʊm]
bridge	**kommandobro** (m/f)	[kɔ'mandʊ‚brʊ]
radio room	**radiorom** (m)	['radiʊ‚rʊm]
wave (radio)	**bølge** (m)	['bølgə]
logbook	**loggbok** (m/f)	['lɔg‚bʊk]
spyglass	**langkikkert** (m)	['laŋ‚kike:t]
bell	**klokke** (m/f)	['klɔkə]
flag	**flagg** (n)	['flag]
hawser (mooring ~)	**trosse** (m/f)	['trʊsə]
knot (bowline, etc.)	**knute** (m)	['knʉtə]
deckrails	**rekkverk** (n)	['rɛk‚værk]
gangway	**landgang** (m)	['lan‚gaŋ]
anchor	**anker** (n)	['ankər]
to weigh anchor	**å lette anker**	[ɔ 'letə 'ankər]
to drop anchor	**å kaste anker**	[ɔ 'kastə 'ankər]
anchor chain	**ankerkjetting** (m)	['ankər‚çɛtiŋ]
port (harbor)	**havn** (m/f)	['havn]
quay, wharf	**kai** (m/f)	['kaj]
to berth (moor)	**å fortøye**	[ɔ fɔː'tøjə]
to cast off	**å kaste loss**	[ɔ 'kastə lɔs]
trip, voyage	**reise** (m/f)	['ræjsə]
cruise (sea trip)	**cruise** (n)	['krʉs]
course (route)	**kurs** (m)	['kʉʂ]
route (itinerary)	**rute** (m/f)	['rʉtə]
fairway	**seilrende** (m)	['sæjl‚rɛnə]
(safe water channel)		
shallows	**grunne** (m/f)	['grʉnə]
to run aground	**å gå på grunn**	[ɔ 'gɔ pɔ 'grʉn]
storm	**storm** (m)	['stɔrm]
signal	**signal** (n)	[siŋ'nal]
to sink (vi)	**å synke**	[ɔ 'sʏnkə]
Man overboard!	**Mann over bord!**	['man ‚ovər 'bʊr]
SOS (distress signal)	**SOS** (n)	[ɛsʊ'ɛs]
ring buoy	**livbøye** (m/f)	['liv‚bøjə]

144. Airport

airport	**flyplass** (m)	['fly,plɑs]
airplane	**fly** (n)	['fly]
airline	**flyselskap** (n)	['flysəl,skɑp]
air traffic controller	**flygeleder** (m)	['flygə,ledər]
departure	**avgang** (m)	['ɑv,gɑŋ]
arrival	**ankomst** (m)	['ɑn,kɔmst]
to arrive (by plane)	**å ankomme**	[ɔ 'ɑn,kɔmə]
departure time	**avgangstid** (m/f)	['ɑvgɑŋs,t d]
arrival time	**ankomsttid** (m/f)	[ɑn'kɔms,tid]
to be delayed	**å bli forsinket**	[ɔ 'bli fɔ'ʂiŋkət]
flight delay	**avgangsforsinkelse** (m)	['ɑvgɑŋs fɔ'ʂiŋkəlsə]
information board	**informasjonstavle** (m/f)	[infɔrmɑ'ʂʊns ,tɑvlə]
information	**informasjon** (m)	[infɔrmɑ'ʂʊn]
to announce (vt)	**å meddele**	[ɔ 'mɛd,delə]
flight (e.g., next ~)	**fly** (r)	['fly]
customs	**toll** (m)	['tɔl]
customs officer	**tollbetjent** (m)	['tɔlbe,tjɛnt]
customs declaration	**tolldeklarasjon** (m)	['tɔldɛklɑrɑ'ʂʊn]
to fill out (vt)	**å utfylle**	[ɔ 'ʉt,fylə]
to fill out the declaration	**å utfylle en tolldeklarasjon**	[ɔ 'ʉt,fylə en 'tɔldɛklɑrɑ,ʂʊn]
passport control	**passkontroll** (m)	['pɑskʊn,trɔl]
luggage	**bagasje** (m)	[bɑ'gɑʂə]
hand luggage	**håndbagasje** (m)	['hɔn,bɑ'gɑʂə]
luggage cart	**bagasjetralle** (m/f)	[bɑ'gɑʂə,tʰɑlə]
landing	**lancing** (m)	['lɑniŋ]
landing strip	**lancingsbane** (m)	['lɑniŋs,bɑnə]
to land (vi)	**å lande**	[ɔ 'lɑnə]
airstairs	**trapp** (m/f)	['trɑp]
check-in	**innsjekking** (m/f)	['in,ʂɛkiŋ]
check-in counter	**innsjekkingsskranke** (m)	['in,ʂɛkiŋs ,skrɑnkə]
to check-in (vi)	**å sjekke inn**	[ɔ 'ʂɛkə in]
boarding pass	**boardingkort** (n)	['bɔːdiŋ,kɔːt]
departure gate	**gate** (m/f)	['gejt]
transit	**transitt** (m)	[trɑn'sit]
to wait (vt)	**å vente**	[ɔ 'vɛntə]
departure lounge	**ventehall** (m)	['vɛntə,hɑl]
to see off	**å ta avskjed**	[ɔ 'tɑ 'ɑf,ʂɛd]
to say goodbye	**å si farvel**	[ɔ 'si fɑr'vɛl]

145. Bicycle. Motorcycle

bicycle	sykkel (m)	['sʏkəl]
scooter	skooter (m)	['skutər]
motorcycle, bike	motorsykkel (m)	['motʊrˌsʏkəl]
to go by bicycle	å sykle	[ɔ 'sʏklə]
handlebars	styre (n)	['styrə]
pedal	pedal (m)	[pe'dɑl]
brakes	bremser (m pl)	['brɛmsər]
bicycle seat (saddle)	sete (n)	['setə]
pump	pumpe (m/f)	['pʉmpə]
luggage rack	bagasjebrett (n)	[bɑ'gɑʂəˌbrɛt]
front lamp	lykt (m/f)	['lʏkt]
helmet	hjelm (m)	['jɛlm]
wheel	hjul (n)	['jʉl]
fender	skjerm (m)	['ʂærm]
rim	felg (m)	['fɛlg]
spoke	eik (m/f)	['æjk]

Cars

146. Types of cars

automobile, car	bil (m	['bil]
sports car	sportsbil (m)	['spɔ:ʦˌbil]
limousine	limousin (m)	[limʉ'sin]
off-road vehicle	terrengbil (m)	[tɛ'rɛŋˌbil]
convertible (n)	kabriolet (m)	[kabriʉ'le]
minibus	minibuss (m)	['miniˌbʉs]
ambulance	ambulanse (m)	[ambʉ'lanѕə]
snowplow	snøplog (m)	['snøˌplɔg]
truck	lastebil (m)	['lastəˌbil]
tanker truck	tankbil (m)	['tɑnkˌbil]
van (small truck)	skapbil (m)	['skɑpˌbil]
road tractor (trailer truck)	trekkvogn (m/f)	['trɛkˌvɔŋn]
trailer	tilhenger (m)	['tilˌhɛŋər]
comfortable (adj)	komfortabel	[kʊmfɔ:'ʈabəl]
used (adj)	brukt	['brʉkt]

147. Cars. Bodywork

hood	panser (n)	['panѕər]
fender	skjerm (m)	['ʂærm]
roof	tak (n	['tɑk]
windshield	frontrute (m/f)	['frontˌrʉtə]
rear-view mirror	bakspeil (n)	['bɑkˌspæjl]
windshield washer	vindusspyler (m)	['vindʉsˌspylər]
windshield wipers	viskerblader (n pl)	['viskəblɑər]
side window	siderute (m/f)	['sidəˌrʉtə]
window lift (power window)	vindusheis (m)	['vindʉsˌhæjs]
antenna	antenne (m)	[ɑn'tɛnə]
sunroof	takluke (m/f), soltak (n)	['tɑkˌlʉkə], ['sʊlˌtɑk]
bumper	støtfanger (m)	['støtˌfɑŋər]
trunk	bagasjerom (n)	[ba'gaѕəˌrʊm]
roof luggage rack	takgrind (m/f)	['tɑkˌgrin]
door	dør (m/f)	['dœr]

door handle	dørhåndtak (n)	['dœr,hɔntak]
door lock	dørlås (m/n)	['dœr,lɔs]
license plate	nummerskilt (n)	['nʉmər,ʂilt]
muffler	lyddemper (m)	['lyd,dɛmpər]
gas tank	bensintank (m)	[bɛn'sin,tank]
tailpipe	eksosrør (n)	['ɛksʉs,rør]
gas, accelerator	gass (m)	['gɑs]
pedal	pedal (m)	[pe'dal]
gas pedal	gasspedal (m)	['gɑs pe'dal]
brake	brems (m)	['brɛms]
brake pedal	bremsepedal (m)	['brɛmsə pe'dal]
to brake (use the brake)	å bremse	[ɔ 'brɛmsə]
parking brake	håndbrekk (n)	['hɔn,brɛk]
clutch	koppling (m)	['kɔpliŋ]
clutch pedal	kopplingspedal (m)	['kɔpliŋs pe'dal]
clutch disc	koplingsskive (m/f)	['kɔpliŋs,ʂivə]
shock absorber	støtdemper (m)	['støt,dɛmpər]
wheel	hjul (n)	['jʉl]
spare tire	reservehjul (n)	[re'sɛrvə,jʉl]
tire	dekk (n)	['dɛk]
hubcap	hjulkapsel (m)	['jʉl,kapsəl]
driving wheels	drivhjul (n pl)	['driv,jʉl]
front-wheel drive (as adj)	forhjulsdrevet	['fɔrjʉls,drevət]
rear-wheel drive (as adj)	bakhjulsdrevet	['bakjʉls,drevət]
all-wheel drive (as adj)	firehjulsdrevet	['firəjʉls,drevət]
gearbox	girkasse (m/f)	['gir,kasə]
automatic (adj)	automatisk	[aʉtʉ'matisk]
mechanical (adj)	mekanisk	[me'kanisk]
gear shift	girspak (m)	['gi,spak]
headlight	lyskaster (m)	['lys,kastər]
headlights	lyskastere (m pl)	['lys,kastərə]
low beam	nærlys (n)	['nær,lys]
high beam	fjernlys (n)	['fjæːn̩,lys]
brake light	stopplys, bremselys (n)	['stɔp,lys], ['brɛmsə,lys]
parking lights	parkeringslys (n)	[par'keriŋs,lys]
hazard lights	varselblinklys (n)	['vaʂəl,blink lys]
fog lights	tåkelys (n)	['toːkə,lys]
turn signal	blinklys (n)	['blink,lys]
back-up light	baklys (n)	['bak,lys]

148. Cars. Passenger compartment

car inside (interior)	interiør (n), innredning (m/f)	[inter'jør], ['in,rɛdniŋ]
leather (as adj)	lær-	['lær-]
velour (as adj)	velur	[ve'lʉr]
upholstery	trekk (n)	['trɛk]
instrument (gage)	instrument (n)	[instrʉ'mɛnt]
dashboard	dashbord (n)	['daʂbɔːd]
speedometer	speedometer (n)	[spidʉ'metər]
needle (pointer)	viser (m)	['visər]
odometer	kilometerteller (m)	[çilu'metər,tɛlər]
indicator (sensor)	indikator (m)	[indi'katʊr]
level	nivå (n)	[ni'vo]
warning light	varsellampe (m/f)	['vaʂəl,lampə]
steering wheel	ratt (n)	['rat]
horn	horn (n)	['hʊːn]
button	knapp (m)	['knap]
switch	bryter (m)	['brytər]
seat	sete (n)	['setə]
backrest	seterygg (m)	['setə,rʏg]
headrest	nakkestøtte (m/f)	['nakə,stœtə]
seat belt	sikkerhetsbelte (m)	['sikərhɛts,bɛltə]
to fasten the belt	å spenne fast sikkerhetsbeltet	[ɔ 'spɛnə fast 'sikərhets,bɛltə]
adjustment (of seats)	justering (m/f)	[jʉ'steriŋ]
airbag	kollisjonspute (m/f)	['kʊliʂʊns pʉtə]
air-conditioner	klimaanlegg (n)	['klima'an leg]
radio	radio (m)	['radiʊ]
CD player	CD-spiller (m)	['sɛdɛ ,spilər]
to turn on	å slå på	[ɔ 'ʂlɔ pɔ]
antenna	antenne (m)	[an'tɛnə]
glove box	hanskerom (n)	['hanskə,rʊm]
ashtray	askebeger (n)	['askə,begər]

149. Cars. Engine

engine, motor	motor (m)	['motʊr]
diesel (as adj)	diesel-	['disəl-]
gasoline (as adj)	bensin-	[bɛn'sin-]
engine volume	motorvolum (n)	['motʊr vɔ'lʉm]
power	styrke (m)	['styrkə]

horsepower	hestekraft (m/f)	['hɛstə‚kraft]
piston	stempel (n)	['stɛmpəl]
cylinder	sylinder (m)	[sy'lindər]
valve	ventil (m)	[vɛn'til]

injector	injektor (m)	[i'njɛktʊr]
generator (alternator)	generator (m)	[gene'ratʊr]
carburetor	forgasser (m)	[fɔr'gasər]
motor oil	motorolje (m)	['mɔtʊr‚ɔljə]

radiator	radiator (m)	[radi'atʊr]
coolant	kjølevæske (m/f)	['çœlə‚væskə]
cooling fan	vifte (m/f)	['viftə]

battery (accumulator)	batteri (n)	[batɛ'ri]
starter	starter (m)	['staːʈər]
ignition	tenning (m/f)	['tɛniŋ]
spark plug	tennplugg (m)	['tɛn‚plʉg]

terminal (of battery)	klemme (m/f)	['klemə]
positive terminal	plussklemme (m/f)	['plʉs‚klemə]
negative terminal	minusklemme (m/f)	['minʉs‚klemə]
fuse	sikring (m)	['sikriŋ]

air filter	luftfilter (n)	['lʉft‚filtər]
oil filter	oljefilter (n)	['ɔljə‚filtər]
fuel filter	brenselsfilter (n)	['brɛnsəls‚filtər]

150. Cars. Crash. Repair

car crash	bilulykke (m/f)	['bil ʉ'lʏkə]
traffic accident	trafikkulykke (m/f)	[tra'fik ʉ'lʏkə]
to crash (into the wall, etc.)	å kjøre inn i ...	[ɔ 'çœːrə in i ...]

to get smashed up	å havarere	[ɔ hava'rerə]
damage	skade (m)	['skadə]
intact (unscathed)	uskadd	['ʉ‚skad]

breakdown	havari (n)	[hava'ri]
to break down (vi)	å bryte sammen	[ɔ 'brytə 'samən]
towrope	slepetau (n)	['ʂlepə‚taʉ]

puncture	punktering (m)	[pʉn'teriŋ]
to be flat	å være punktert	[ɔ 'værə pʉnk'tɛːʈ]
to pump up	å pumpe opp	[ɔ 'pʉmpə ɔp]
pressure	trykk (n)	['trʏk]
to check (to examine)	å sjekke	[ɔ 'ʂɛkə]

| repair | reparasjon (m) | [repara'ʂʊn] |
| auto repair shop | bilverksted (n) | ['bil 'værk‚sted] |

spare part	reservedel (m)	[re'sɛrvəˌdel]
part	del (m)	['del]
bolt (with nut)	bolt (m)	['bɔlt]
screw (fastener)	skrue (m)	['skrʉə]
nut	mutter (m)	['mʉtər]
washer	skive (m/f)	['ʂivə]
bearing	lager (n)	['lagər]
tube	rør (n)	['rør]
gasket (head ~)	pakning (m/f)	['paknin]
cable, wire	ledring (m)	['lednin]
jack	jekk (m), donkraft (m/f)	['jɛk], ['dɔnˌkrɑft]
wrench	skrunøkkel (m)	['skrʉˌnøkəl]
hammer	hammer (m)	['hamər]
pump	pumpe (m/f)	['pʉmpə]
screwdriver	skrutrekker (m)	['skrʉˌtrɛkər]
fire extinguisher	brannslukker (n)	['branˌslʉkər]
warning triangle	varseltrekant (m)	['vaʂəl 'trɛ kant]
to stall (vi)	å skjære	[ɔ 'ʂæːrə]
stall (n)	stans (m), stopp (m/n)	['stans], ['stɔp]
to be broken	å være ødelagt	[ɔ 'værə 'ødəˌlakt]
to overheat (vi)	å bli overopphetet	[ɔ 'bli 'ovə-ɔpˌhetət]
to be clogged up	å bli tilstoppet	[ɔ 'bli til'stɔpət]
to freeze up (pipes, etc.)	å fryse	[ɔ 'frysə]
to burst (vi, ab. tube)	å sprekke, å briste	[ɔ 'sprɛkə], [ɔ 'bristə]
pressure	trykk (n)	['trʏk]
level	nivå (n)	[ni'vo]
slack (~ belt)	slakk	['ʂlak]
dent	bulk (m)	['bʉlk]
knocking noise (engine)	bankelyd (m), dunk (m/n)	['bankəˌlyd], ['dʉnk]
crack	sprekk (m)	['sprɛk]
scratch	ripe (m/f)	['ripə]

151. Cars. Road

road	vei (m)	['væj]
highway	hovedvei (m)	['hʉvədˌvæj]
freeway	motorvei (m)	['mɔtʉrˌvæj]
direction (way)	retning (m/f)	['rɛtnin]
distance	avstand (m)	['afˌstan]
bridge	bro (m/f)	['brʉ]
parking lot	parkeringsplass (m)	[par'kerinsˌplas]

square	**torg** (n)	['tɔr]
interchange	**trafikkmaskin** (m)	[tra'fik ma͵ʂin]
tunnel	**tunnel** (m)	['tʉnəl]

gas station	**bensinstasjon** (m)	[bɛn'sin͵sta'ʂʉn]
parking lot	**parkeringsplass** (m)	[par'keriŋs͵plas]
gas pump (fuel dispenser)	**bensinpumpe** (m/f)	[bɛn'sin͵pʉmpə]
auto repair shop	**bilverksted** (n)	['bil 'værk͵sted]
to get gas (to fill up)	**å tanke opp**	[ɔ 'tankə ɔp]
fuel	**brensel** (n)	['brɛnsəl]
jerrycan	**bensinkanne** (m/f)	[bɛn'sin͵kanə]

asphalt	**asfalt** (m)	['asfalt]
road markings	**vegoppmerking** (m/f)	['veg 'ɔp͵mærkiŋ]
curb	**fortauskant** (m)	['fɔːtaʊs͵kant]
guardrail	**autovern, veirekkverk** (n)	['aʊto͵væːŋ], ['væj͵rekværk]
ditch	**veigrøft** (m/f)	['væj͵grœft]
roadside (shoulder)	**veikant** (m)	['væj͵kant]
lamppost	**lyktestolpe** (m)	['lʏktə͵stɔlpə]

to drive (a car)	**å kjøre**	[ɔ 'çœːrə]
to turn (e.g., ~ left)	**å svinge**	[ɔ 'sviŋə]
to make a U-turn	**å ta en U-sving**	[ɔ 'ta en 'ʉː͵sviŋ]
reverse (~ gear)	**revers** (m)	[re'væʂ]

to honk (vi)	**å tute**	[ɔ 'tʉtə]
honk (sound)	**tut** (n)	['tʉt]
to get stuck (in the mud, etc.)	**å kjøre seg fast**	[ɔ 'çœːrə sæj 'fast]
to spin the wheels	**å spinne**	[ɔ 'spinə]
to cut, to turn off (vt)	**å stanse**	[ɔ 'stansə]

speed	**hastighet** (m/f)	['hasti͵het]
to exceed the speed limit	**å overskride fartsgrensen**	[ɔ 'ɔvə͵skridə 'faːts͵grɛnsən]
to give a ticket	**å gi bot**	[ɔ 'ji 'bʉt]
traffic lights	**trafikklys** (n)	[tra'fik͵lys]
driver's license	**førerkort** (n)	['førər͵kɔːt]

grade crossing	**planovergang** (m)	['plan 'ɔvər͵gaŋ]
intersection	**veikryss** (n)	['væjkrʏs]
crosswalk	**fotgjengerovergang** (m)	['fʉt͵jɛŋər 'ɔvər͵gaŋ]
bend, curve	**kurve** (m)	['kʉrvə]
pedestrian zone	**gågate** (m/f)	['goː͵gatə]

PEOPLE. LIFE EVENTS

Life events

152. Holidays. Event

celebration, holiday	**fest** (m)	['fɛst]
national day	**nasjonaldag** (m)	[naʂu'nal,dɔ]
public holiday	**festdag** (m)	['fɛst,da]
to commemorate (vt)	**å feire**	[ɔ 'fæjrə]
event (happening)	**begivenhet** (m/f)	[be'jiven,het]
event (organized activity)	**evenement** (n)	[ɛvenə'maŋ]
banquet (party)	**bankett** (m)	[ban'kɛt]
reception (formal party)	**resepsjon** (m)	[resɛp'ʂun]
feast	**fest** (ŋ)	['fɛst]
anniversary	**årsdag** (m)	['o:ʂ,da]
jubilee	**jubileum** (n)	[jʉbi'leʉm]
to celebrate (vt)	**å feire**	[ɔ 'fæjrə]
New Year	**nytt år** (n)	['nʏt ,o:r]
Happy New Year!	**Godt nytt år!**	['gɔt nʏt ,o:r]
Santa Claus	**Julenissen**	['jʉlə,nisən]
Christmas	**Jul** (m/f)	['jʉl]
Merry Christmas!	**Gledelig jul!**	['gledəli 'jʉ]
Christmas tree	**juletre** (n)	['jʉlə,trɛ]
fireworks (fireworks show)	**fyrverkeri** (n)	[,fyrværkə'ri]
wedding	**bryllup** (n)	['brʏlʉp]
groom	**brudgom** (m)	['brʉd,gɔm]
bride	**brud** (m/f)	['brʉd]
to invite (vt)	**å innby, å invitere**	[ɔ 'inby], [ɔ invi'terə]
invitation card	**innbydelse** (m)	[in'bydəlse]
guest	**gjest** (m)	['jɛst]
to visit	**å besøke**	[ɔ be'søkə]
(~ your parents, etc.)		
to meet the guests	**å hilse på gjestene**	[ɔ 'hilsə pɔ 'jɛstenə]
gift, present	**gave** (m/f)	['gavə]
to give (sth as present)	**å gi**	[ɔ 'ji]
to receive gifts	**å få gaver**	[ɔ 'fɔ 'gavər]

bouquet (of flowers)	bukett (m)	[bʉ'kɛt]
congratulations	lykkønskning (m/f)	['lʏk,ønskniŋ]
to congratulate (vt)	å gratulere	[ɔ gratʉ'lerə]

greeting card	gratulasjonskort (n)	[gratʉla'sʉns,kɔːt]
to send a postcard	å sende postkort	[ɔ 'sɛnə 'pɔst,kɔːt]
to get a postcard	å få postkort	[ɔ 'fɔ 'pɔst,kɔːt]

toast	skål (m/f)	['skɔl]
to offer (a drink, etc.)	å tilby	[ɔ 'tilby]
champagne	champagne (m)	[ʂam'panjə]

to enjoy oneself	å more seg	[ɔ 'mʉrə sæj]
merriment (gaiety)	munterhet (m)	['mʉntər,het]
joy (emotion)	glede (m/f)	['gledə]

| dance | dans (m) | ['dans] |
| to dance (vi, vt) | å danse | [ɔ 'dansə] |

| waltz | vals (m) | ['vals] |
| tango | tango (m) | ['taŋgʉ] |

153. Funerals. Burial

cemetery	gravplass, kirkegård (m)	['grav,plas], ['çirkə,gɔːr]
grave, tomb	grav (m)	['grav]
cross	kors (n)	['kɔːʂ]
gravestone	gravstein (m)	['graf,stæjn]
fence	gjerde (n)	['jærə]
chapel	kapell (n)	[ka'pɛl]

death	død (m)	['dø]
to die (vi)	å dø	[ɔ 'dø]
the deceased	den avdøde	[den 'av,dødə]
mourning	sorg (m/f)	['sɔr]
to bury (vt)	å begrave	[ɔ be'gravə]
funeral home	begravelsesbyrå (n)	[be'gravəlsəs by,ro]
funeral	begravelse (m)	[be'gravəlsə]

wreath	krans (m)	['krans]
casket, coffin	likkiste (m/f)	['lik,çistə]
hearse	likbil (m)	['lik,bil]
shroud	likklede (n)	['lik,kledə]

funeral procession	gravfølge (n)	['grav,følgə]
funerary urn	askeurne (m/f)	['askə,ʉːnə]
crematory	krematorium (n)	[krɛma'tʉrium]
obituary	nekrolog (m)	[nekrʉ'lɔg]
to cry (weep)	å gråte	[ɔ 'groːtə]
to sob (vi)	å hulke	[ɔ 'hʉlkə]

154. War. Soldiers

platoon	tropp (m)	['trɔp]
company	kompani (n)	[kʊmpɑ'ni]
regiment	regiment (n)	[rɛgi'mɛnt]
army	hær (m)	['hær]
division	divisjon (m)	[divi'ʂʊn]
section, squad	tropp (m)	['trɔp]
host (army)	hær (m)	['hær]
soldier	soldat (m)	[sʊl'dɑt]
officer	offiser (m)	[ɔfi'sɛr]
private	menig (m)	['meni]
sergeant	sersjant (m)	[sær'ʂɑnt]
lieutenant	løytnant (m)	['løjt,nɑnt]
captain	kaptein (m)	[kɑp'tæjn]
major	major (m)	[mɑ'jɔr]
colonel	oberst (m)	['ʊbɛʂt]
general	general (m)	[gene'rɑl]
sailor	sjømann (m)	['ʂø,mɑn]
captain	kaptein (m)	[kɑp'tæjn]
boatswain	båtsmann (m)	['bɔs,mɑn]
artilleryman	artillerist (m)	[,ɑːʈile'rist]
paratrooper	fallskjermjeger (m)	['fal,ʂærm 'jɛ:gər]
pilot	flyger, flyver (m)	['flygər], ['flyvər]
navigator	styrmann (m)	['styr,mɑn]
mechanic	mekaniker (m)	[me'kɑnikər]
pioneer (sapper)	pioner (m)	[piʊ'ner]
parachutist	fallskjermhopper (m)	['fal,ʂærm 'hɔpər]
reconnaissance scout	oppklaringssoldat (m)	['ɔp,klɑriŋ sʊl'dɑt]
sniper	skarpskytte (m)	['skɑrp,ʂʏtə]
patrol (group)	patrulje (m)	[pɑ'trʊlje]
to patrol (vt)	å patruljere	[ɔ patrʊ'ljerə]
sentry, guard	vakt (m)	['vɑkt]
warrior	kriger (m)	['krigər]
hero	helt (m)	['hɛlt]
heroine	heltinne (m)	['hɛlt,inə]
patriot	patriot (m)	[pɑtri'ɔt]
traitor	forræder (m)	[fɔ'rædər]
to betray (vt)	å forråde	[ɔ fɔ'rɔ:de]
deserter	desertør (m)	[desæ:'tør]
to desert (vi)	å desertere	[ɔ desæ:'ʈerə]
mercenary	leiesoldat (m)	['læjəsʊl,dɑt]

recruit	**rekrutt** (m)	[re'krʉt]
volunteer	**frivillig** (m)	['fri,vili]
dead (n)	**drept** (m)	['drɛpt]
wounded (n)	**såret** (m)	['soːrə]
prisoner of war	**fange** (m)	['faŋə]

155. War. Military actions. Part 1

war	**krig** (m)	['krig]
to be at war	**å være i krig**	[ɔ 'værə i ˌkrig]
civil war	**borgerkrig** (m)	['bɔrgər,krig]
treacherously (adv)	**lumsk, forræderisk**	['lʉmsk], [fɔ'rædərisk]
declaration of war	**krigserklæring** (m)	['krigs ær,klæriŋ]
to declare (~ war)	**å erklære**	[ɔ ær'klærə]
aggression	**aggresjon** (m)	[agre'ʂʉn]
to attack (invade)	**å angripe**	[ɔ 'an,gripə]
to invade (vt)	**å invadere**	[ɔ inva'derə]
invader	**angriper** (m)	['an,gripər]
conqueror	**erobrer** (m)	[ɛ'rʉbrər]
defense	**forsvar** (n)	['fʉ,svar]
to defend (a country, etc.)	**å forsvare**	[ɔ fo'ʂvarə]
to defend (against ...)	**å forsvare seg**	[ɔ fo'ʂvarə sæj]
enemy	**fiende** (m)	['fiɛndə]
foe, adversary	**motstander** (m)	['mʉt,stanər]
enemy (as adj)	**fiendtlig**	['fjɛntli]
strategy	**strategi** (m)	[strate'gi]
tactics	**taktikk** (m)	[tak'tik]
order	**ordre** (m)	['ɔrdrə]
command (order)	**ordre, kommando** (m/f)	['ɔrdrə], ['kʉ'mandʉ]
to order (vt)	**å beordre**	[ɔ be'ɔrdrə]
mission	**oppdrag** (m)	['ɔpdrag]
secret (adj)	**hemmelig**	['hɛməli]
battle	**batalje** (m)	[ba'taljə]
battle	**slag** (n)	['ʂlag]
combat	**kamp** (m)	['kamp]
attack	**angrep** (n)	['an,grɛp]
charge (assault)	**storm** (m)	['stɔrm]
to storm (vt)	**å storme**	[ɔ 'stɔrmə]
siege (to be under ~)	**beleiring** (m/f)	[be'læjriŋ]
offensive (n)	**offensiv** (m), **angrep** (n)	['ɔfen,sif], ['an,grɛp]
to go on the offensive	**å angripe**	[ɔ 'an,gripə]

retreat	retrett (m)	[rɛ'trɛt]
to retreat (vi)	å retirere	[ɔ reti'rerə]

encirclement	omringing (m/f)	['ɔm,riŋiŋ]
to encircle (vt)	å omringe	[ɔ 'ɔm,riŋə]

bombing (by aircraft)	bombing (m/f)	['bʊmbiŋ]
to drop a bomb	å slippe bombe	[ɔ 'ʂlipə 'bʊmbə]
to bomb (vt)	å bombardere	[ɔ bʊmbɑː'dɛrə]
explosion	eksplosjon (m)	[ɛksplʊ'ʂʊn]

shot	skudd (n)	['skʊd]
to fire (~ a shot)	å skyte av	[ɔ 'ʂytə ɑː]
firing (burst of ~)	skyting (m/f)	['ʂytiŋ]

to aim (to point a weapon)	å sikte på ...	[ɔ 'siktə pɔ ...]
to point (a gun)	å rette	[ɔ 'rɛtə]
to hit (the target)	å treffe	[ɔ 'trɛfə]

to sink (~ a ship)	å senke	[ɔ 'sɛnkə]
hole (in a ship)	hull (n)	['hʊl]
to founder, to sink (vi)	å synke	[ɔ 'sʏnkə]

front (war ~)	front (m)	['frɔnt]
evacuation	evakuering (m/f)	[ɛvɑkʉ'eriŋ]
to evacuate (vt)	å evakuere	[ɔ ɛvɑkʉ'erə]

trench	skyttergrav (m)	['ʂytə,grɑv]
barbwire	piggtråd (m)	['pig,trɔd]
barrier (anti tank ~)	hinder (n), sperring (m/f)	['hindər], ['spɛriŋ]
watchtower	vakttårn (n)	['vɑkt,tɔːn]

military hospital	militærsykehus (n)	[mili'tær,sykə'hʊs]
to wound (vt)	å såre	[ɔ 'soːrə]
wound	sår (r)	['sɔr]
wounded (n)	såret (n)	['soːrə]
to be wounded	å bli såret	[ɔ 'bli 'soːrət]
serious (wound)	alvorlig	[ɑl'vɔːli]

156. Weapons

weapons	våpen (n)	['vɔpən]
firearms	skytevåpen (n)	['ʂytə,vɔpən]
cold weapons (knives, etc.)	blankvåpen (n)	['blɑnk,vɔɔən]

chemical weapons	kjemisk våpen (n)	['çemisk ,vɔpən]
nuclear (adj)	kjerne-	['çæːnə-]
nuclear weapons	kjernevåpen (n)	['çæːnə,vɔpən]
bomb	bombe (m)	['bʊmbə]

atomic bomb	atombombe (m)	[a'tʊm,bʊmbə]
pistol (gun)	pistol (m)	[pi'stʊl]
rifle	gevær (n)	[ge'vær]
submachine gun	maskinpistol (m)	[ma'ʂin pi,stʊl]
machine gun	maskingevær (n)	[ma'ʂin ge,vær]
muzzle	munning (m)	['mʉniŋ]
barrel	løp (n)	['løp]
caliber	kaliber (m/n)	[ka'libər]
trigger	avtrekker (m)	['av,trɛkər]
sight (aiming device)	sikte (n)	['siktə]
magazine	magasin (n)	[maga'sin]
butt (shoulder stock)	kolbe (m)	['kɔlbə]
hand grenade	håndgranat (m)	['hɔn,gra'nat]
explosive	sprengstoff (n)	['sprɛŋ,stɔf]
bullet	kule (m/f)	['kʉ:lə]
cartridge	patron (m)	[pa'trʊn]
charge	ladning (m)	['ladniŋ]
ammunition	ammunisjon (m)	[amʉni'ʂʊn]
bomber (aircraft)	bombefly (n)	['bʊmbə,fly]
fighter	jagerfly (n)	['jagər,fly]
helicopter	helikopter (n)	[heli'kɔptər]
anti-aircraft gun	luftvernkanon (m)	['lʉftvɛ:ɳ ka'nʊn]
tank	stridsvogn (m/f)	['strids,vɔŋn]
tank gun	kanon (m)	[ka'nʊn]
artillery	artilleri (n)	[,a:ʈile'ri]
gun (cannon, howitzer)	kanon (m)	[ka'nʊn]
to lay (a gun)	å rette	[ɔ 'rɛtə]
shell (projectile)	projektil (m)	[prʊek'til]
mortar bomb	granat (m/f)	[gra'nat]
mortar	granatkaster (m)	[gra'nat,kastər]
splinter (shell fragment)	splint (m)	['splint]
submarine	ubåt (m)	['ʉ:,bot]
torpedo	torpedo (m)	[tʊr'pedʊ]
missile	rakett (m)	[ra'kɛt]
to load (gun)	å lade	[ɔ 'ladə]
to shoot (vi)	å skyte	[ɔ 'ʂytə]
to point at (the cannon)	å sikte på ...	[ɔ 'siktə pɔ ...]
bayonet	bajonett (m)	[bajo'nɛt]
rapier	kårde (m)	['ko:rdə]
saber (e.g., cavalry ~)	sabel (m)	['sabəl]
spear (weapon)	spyd (n)	['spyd]

bow	**bue** (m)	['bʉːə]
arrow	**pil** (m/f)	['pil]
musket	**muskett** (m)	[mʉ'skɛt]
crossbow	**armbrøst** (m)	['arm͵brøst]

157. Ancient people

primitive (prehistoric)	**ur-**	['ʉr-]
prehistoric (adj)	**forhistorisk**	['forhi͵stʉrisk]
ancient (~ civilization)	**oldtidens, antikkens**	['ɔl͵tidəns], [an'tikəns]

Stone Age	**Steinalderen**	['stæjn͵alderən]
Bronze Age	**bronsealder** (m)	['brɔnsə͵aldər]
Ice Age	**istid** (m/f)	['is͵tid]

tribe	**stamme** (m)	['stamə]
cannibal	**kannibal** (m)	[kani'bal]
hunter	**jeger** (m)	['jɛːgər]
to hunt (vi, vt)	**å jage**	[ɔ 'jagə]
mammoth	**mammut** (m)	['mamʉt]

cave	**grotte** (m/f)	['grɔtə]
fire	**ild** (m	['il]
campfire	**bål** (n	['bɔl]
cave painting	**helleristning** (m/f)	['hɛlə͵ristniŋ]

tool (e.g., stone ax)	**redskap** (m/n)	['rɛd͵skap]
spear	**spyd** (n)	['spyd]
stone ax	**steinøks** (m/f)	['stæjn͵øks]
to be at war	**å være i krig**	[ɔ 'væra i ͵krig]
to domesticate (vt)	**å temme**	[ɔ 'tɛmə]

idol	**idol** (n)	[i'dʉl]
to worship (vt)	**å dyrke**	[ɔ 'dyrkə]
superstition	**overtro** (m)	['ɔvə͵trʉ]
rite	**ritual** (n)	[ritʉ'al]

evolution	**evolusjon** (m)	[ɛvɔlʉ'ʂʊn]
development	**utvikling** (m/f)	['ʉt͵vikliŋ]
disappearance (extinction)	**forsvinning** (m/f)	[fo'ʂviniŋ]
to adapt oneself	**å tilpasse seg**	[ɔ 'til͵pasə sæj]

archeology	**arkeologi** (m)	[͵arkeʉlʉ'gi]
archeologist	**arkeolog** (m)	[͵arkeʉ'lɔg]
archeological (adj)	**arkeologisk**	[͵arkeʉ'lɔgisk]

excavation site	**utgravingssted** (n)	['ʉt͵graviŋs ͵sted]
excavations	**utgravinger** (m/f pl)	['ʉt͵graviŋər]
find (object)	**funn** (n)	['fʉn]
fragment	**fragment** (n)	[frag'mɛnt]

158. Middle Ages

people (ethnic group)	folk (n)	['fɔlk]
peoples	folk (n pl)	['fɔlk]
tribe	stamme (m)	['stɑmə]
tribes	stammer (m pl)	['stɑmər]

barbarians	barbarer (m pl)	[bɑr'bɑrər]
Gauls	gallere (m pl)	['gɑlere]
Goths	gotere (m pl)	['gɔterə]
Slavs	slavere (m pl)	['slɑvɛrə]
Vikings	vikinger (m pl)	['vikiŋər]

Romans	romere (m pl)	['rʊmerə]
Roman (adj)	romersk	['rʊmæʂk]

Byzantines	bysantiner (m pl)	[bysɑn'tinər]
Byzantium	Bysants	[by'sɑnts]
Byzantine (adj)	bysantinsk	[bysɑn'tinsk]

emperor	keiser (m)	['kæjsər]
leader, chief (tribal ~)	høvding (m)	['høvdiŋ]
powerful (~ king)	mektig	['mɛkti]
king	konge (m)	['kʊŋə]
ruler (sovereign)	hersker (m)	['hæʂkər]

knight	ridder (m)	['ridər]
feudal lord	føydalherre (m)	['føjdɑl‚hɛrə]
feudal (adj)	føydal	['føjdɑl]
vassal	vasall (m)	[vɑ'sɑl]

duke	hertug (m)	['hæːʈʉg]
earl	greve (m)	['grevə]
baron	baron (m)	[bɑ'rʊn]
bishop	biskop (m)	['biskɔp]

armor	rustning (m/f)	['rʉstniŋ]
shield	skjold (n)	['ʂɔl]
sword	sverd (n)	['svæːrd]
visor	visir (n)	[vi'sir]
chainmail	ringbrynje (m/f)	['riŋ‚brynje]

Crusade	korstog (n)	['kɔːʂ‚tɔg]
crusader	korsfarer (m)	['kɔːʂ‚fɑrər]

territory	territorium (n)	[tɛri'tʊrium]
to attack (invade)	å angripe	[ɔ 'ɑn‚gripə]
to conquer (vt)	å erobre	[ɔ ɛ'rʊbrə]
to occupy (invade)	å okkupere	[ɔ ɔkʉ'perə]
siege (to be under ~)	beleiring (m/f)	[be'læjriŋ]
besieged (adj)	beleiret	[be'læjrət]

to besiege (vt)	å beleire	[ɔ be'læjre]
inquisition	inkvisisjon (m)	[inkvisi'ʂʊn]
inquisitor	inkvisitor (m)	[inkvi'sitʊr]
torture	tortur (m)	[tɔ:'tʉr]
cruel (adj)	brutal	[brʉ'tal]
heretic	kjetter (m)	['çɛtər]
heresy	kjetteri (n)	[çɛtə'ri]

seafaring	sjøfart (m)	['ʂøˌfɑ:t]
pirate	pirat, sjørøver (m)	['pi'rɑt], ['ʂøˌrøvər]
piracy	sjørøveri (n)	['ʂø røvɛ'ri]
boarding (attack)	entring (m/f)	['ɛntriŋ]
loot, booty	bytte (n)	['bytə]
treasures	skatter (m pl)	['skatər]

discovery	oppdagelse (m)	['ɔpˌdagəlsə]
to discover (new land, etc.)	å oppdage	[ɔ 'ɔpˌdagə]
expedition	ekspedisjon (m)	[ɛkspedi'ʂʊn]

musketeer	musketer (m)	[mʉskə'ter]
cardinal	kardinal (m)	[kɑːdi'nɑl]
heraldry	heraldikk (m)	[herɑl'dik]
heraldic (adj)	heraldisk	[he'rɑldisk]

159. Leader. Chief. Authorities

king	konge (m)	['kʊŋə]
queen	dronning (m/f)	['drɔniŋ]
royal (adj)	kongelig	['kʊŋəli]
kingdom	kongerike (n)	['kʊŋəˌrikə]

| prince | prins (m) | ['prins] |
| princess | prinsesse (m/f) | [prin'sɛsə] |

president	president (m)	[prɛsi'dɛnt]
vice-president	visepresident (m)	['visə prɛsi'dɛnt]
senator	senator (m)	[se'nɑtʊr]

monarch	monark (m)	[mʊ'nɑrk]
ruler (sovereign)	hersker (m)	['hæʂkər]
dictator	diktator (m)	[dik'tɑtʊr]
tyrant	tyrann (m)	[ty'rɑn]
magnate	magnat (m)	[maɲ'nɑt]

director	direktør (m)	[dirɛk'tør]
chief	sjef (m)	['ʂɛf]
manager (director)	forstander (m)	[fɔ'ʂtandər]
boss	boss (m)	['bɔs]
owner	eier (m)	['æjər]
leader	leder (m)	['ledər]

head (~ of delegation)	leder (m)	['ledər]
authorities	myndigheter (m pl)	['mʏndiˌhetər]
superiors	overordnede (pl)	['ɔvərˌɔrdnedə]
governor	guvernør (m)	[gʉver'nør]
consul	konsul (m)	['kʊnˌsʉl]
diplomat	diplomat (m)	[diplʉ'mɑt]
mayor	borgermester (m)	[bɔrgər'mɛstər]
sheriff	sheriff (m)	[ʂɛ'rif]
emperor	keiser (m)	['kæjsər]
tsar, czar	tsar (m)	['tsɑr]
pharaoh	farao (m)	['fɑrɑu]
khan	khan (m)	['kɑn]

160. Breaking the law. Criminals. Part 1

bandit	banditt (m)	[bɑn'dit]
crime	forbrytelse (m)	[fɔr'brytəlsə]
criminal (person)	forbryter (m)	[fɔr'brytər]
thief	tyv (m)	['tyv]
to steal (vi, vt)	å stjele	[ɔ 'stjelə]
to kidnap (vt)	å kidnappe	[ɔ 'kidˌnɛpə]
kidnapping	kidnapping (m)	['kidˌnɛpiŋ]
kidnapper	kidnapper (m)	['kidˌnɛpər]
ransom	løsepenger (m pl)	['løsəˌpɛŋər]
to demand ransom	å kreve løsepenger	[ɔ 'krevə 'løsəˌpɛŋər]
to rob (vt)	å rane	[ɔ 'rɑnə]
robbery	ran (n)	['rɑn]
robber	raner (m)	['rɑnər]
to extort (vt)	å presse ut	[ɔ 'prɛsə ʉt]
extortionist	utpresser (m)	['ʉtˌprɛsər]
extortion	utpressing (m/f)	['ʉtˌprɛsiŋ]
to murder, to kill	å myrde	[ɔ 'mʏːɖə]
murder	mord (n)	['mʊr]
murderer	morder (m)	['mʊrdər]
gunshot	skudd (n)	['skʉd]
to fire (~ a shot)	å skyte av	[ɔ 'ʂytə ɑ:]
to shoot to death	å skyte ned	[ɔ 'ʂytə ne]
to shoot (vi)	å skyte	[ɔ 'ʂytə]
shooting	skyting, skytning (m/f)	['ʂytiŋ], ['ʂytniŋ]
incident (fight, etc.)	hendelse (m)	['hɛndəlsə]
fight, brawl	slagsmål (n)	['ʂlɑksˌmol]

Help!	**Hjelp!**	['jɛlp]
victim	**offer** (n)	['ɔfər]
to damage (vt)	**å skade**	[ɔ 'skɑdə]
damage	**skade** (m)	['skɑdə]
dead body, corpse	**lik** (r)	['lik]
grave (~ crime)	**alvcrlig**	[ɑl'vɔː[i]
to attack (vt)	**å arfalle**	[ɔ 'ɑnˌfɑlə]
to beat (to hit)	**å slå**	[ɔ 'ʂlɔ]
to beat up	**å klå opp**	[ɔ 'klɔ ɔp]
to take (rob of sth)	**å berøve**	[ɔ be'røvə]
to stab to death	**å stikke i hjel**	[ɔ 'stikə i 'jel]
to maim (vt)	**å lemleste**	[ɔ 'lemˌlestə]
to wound (vt)	**å såre**	[ɔ 'sɔːrə]
blackmail	**utpressing** (m/f)	['ʉtˌprɛsiŋ]
to blackmail (vt)	**å utpresse**	[ɔ 'ʉtˌprɛsə]
blackmailer	**utpresser** (m)	['ʉtˌprɛsər]
protection racket	**utpressing** (m/f)	['ʉtˌprɛsiŋ]
racketeer	**utpresser** (m)	['ʉtˌprɛsər]
gangster	**gangster** (m)	['gɛŋstər]
mafia, Mob	**mafia** (m)	['mɑfiɑ]
pickpocket	**lommetyv** (m)	['lʊməˌtyv]
burglar	**innbruddstyv** (m)	['inbrʉdsˌtyv]
smuggling	**smugling** (m/f)	['smʉgliŋ]
smuggler	**smugler** (m)	['smʉglər]
forgery	**forfalskning** (m/f)	[fɔr'fɑlskniŋ]
to forge (counterfeit)	**å forfalske**	[ɔ for'fɑlskə]
fake (forged)	**falsk**	['fɑlsk]

161. Breaking the law. Criminals. Part 2

rape	**voldtekt** (m)	['vɔlˌtɛkt]
to rape (vt)	**å voldta**	[ɔ 'vɔlˌtɑ]
rapist	**voldtektsmann** (m)	['vɔlˌtɛkts mɑn]
maniac	**maniker** (m)	['mɑnikər]
prostitute (fem.)	**prostituert** (m)	[prʊstitʉ'eːt]
prostitution	**prostitusjon** (m)	[prʊstitʉ'ʂʊn]
pimp	**hallk** (m)	['hɑlik]
drug addict	**narkoman** (m)	[nɑrkʊ'mɑn]
drug dealer	**narkolanger** (m)	['nɑrkɔˌlɑŋər]
to blow up (bomb)	**å sprenge**	[ɔ 'sprɛŋə]
explosion	**eksplosjon** (m)	[ɛksplʊ'ʂʊn]

to set fire	å sette fyr	[ɔ 'sɛtə ˌfyr]
arsonist	brannstifter (m)	['branˌstiftər]
terrorism	terrorisme (m)	[tɛrʊ'rismə]
terrorist	terrorist (m)	[tɛrʊ'rist]
hostage	gissel (m)	['jisəl]
to swindle (deceive)	å bedra	[ɔ be'dra]
swindle, deception	bedrag (n)	[be'drag]
swindler	bedrager, svindler (m)	[be'dragər], ['svindlər]
to bribe (vt)	å bestikke	[ɔ be'stikə]
bribery	bestikkelse (m)	[be'stikəlsə]
bribe	bestikkelse (m)	[be'stikəlsə]
poison	gift (m/f)	['jift]
to poison (vt)	å forgifte	[ɔ for'jiftə]
to poison oneself	å forgifte seg selv	[ɔ for'jiftə sæj sɛl]
suicide (act)	selvmord (n)	['sɛlˌmʊr]
suicide (person)	selvmorder (m)	['sɛlˌmʊrdər]
to threaten (vt)	å true	[ɔ 'trʉə]
threat	trussel (m)	['trʉsəl]
to make an attempt	å begå mordforsøk	[ɔ be'gɔ 'mʊrdfɔˌsøk]
attempt (attack)	mordforsøk (n)	['mʊrdfɔˌsøk]
to steal (a car)	å stjele	[ɔ 'stjelə]
to hijack (a plane)	å kapre	[ɔ 'kaprə]
revenge	hevn (m)	['hɛvn]
to avenge (get revenge)	å hevne	[ɔ 'hɛvnə]
to torture (vt)	å torturere	[ɔ tɔːtʉ'rerə]
torture	tortur (m)	[tɔː'tʉr]
to torment (vt)	å plage	[ɔ 'plagə]
pirate	pirat, sjørøver (m)	['pi'rat], ['ʂøˌrøvər]
hooligan	bølle (m)	['bølə]
armed (adj)	bevæpnet	[be'væpnət]
violence	vold (m)	['vɔl]
illegal (unlawful)	illegal	['ileˌgal]
spying (espionage)	spionasje (m)	[spiʊ'naʂə]
to spy (vi)	å spionere	[ɔ spiʊ'nerə]

162. Police. Law. Part 1

justice	justis (m), rettspleie (m/f)	['jʉ'stis], ['rɛtsˌplæje]
court (see you in ~)	rettssal (m)	['rɛtsˌsal]

judge	**dommer** (m)	['dɔmər]
jurors	**lagrettemedlemmer** (n pl)	['lag‚rɛtə medle'mer]
jury trial	**lagrette, juryordning** (m)	['lag‚rɛtə], ['jʉri‚ɔrdniŋ]
to judge (vt)	**å dømme**	[ɔ 'dœmə]
lawyer, attorney	**advokat** (m)	[advʉ'kat]
defendant	**anklaget** (m)	['an‚klaget]
dock	**anklagebenk** (m)	[an'klagə‚bɛnk]
charge	**anklage** (m)	['an‚klagə]
accused	**anklagede** (m)	['an‚klagedə]
sentence	**dom** (m)	['dɔm]
to sentence (vt)	**å dømme**	[ɔ 'dœmə]
guilty (culprit)	**skyldige** (m)	['şyldiə]
to punish (vt)	**å straffe**	[ɔ 'strafə]
punishment	**straff, avstraffelse** (m)	['straf], ['af strafəlsə]
fine (penalty)	**bot** (m f)	['bʉt]
life imprisonment	**livsvarig fengsel** (n)	['lifs‚vari 'fɛŋsəl]
death penalty	**dødsstraff** (m/f)	['død‚straf]
electric chair	**elektrisk stol** (m)	[ɛ'lektrisk ‚stʉl]
gallows	**galge** (m)	['galgə]
to execute (vt)	**å henrette**	[ɔ 'hɛn‚rɛtə]
execution	**henrettelse** (m)	['hɛn‚rɛtəlsə]
prison, jail	**fengsel** (n)	['fɛŋsəl]
cell	**celle** (m)	['sɛlə]
escort	**eskorte** (m)	[ɛs'kɔːtə]
prison guard	**fangevokter** (m)	['faŋə‚vɔktər]
prisoner	**fange** (m)	['faŋə]
handcuffs	**håndjern** (n pl)	['hɔn‚jæːŋ]
to handcuff (vt)	**å sette håndjern**	[ɔ 'sɛtə 'hɔn‚jæːŋ]
prison break	**flykt** (m/f)	['flʏkt]
to break out (vi)	**å flykte, å rømme**	[ɔ 'flʏktə], [ɔ 'rœmə]
to disappear (vi)	**å forsvinne**	[ɔ fɔ'şvinə]
to release (from prison)	**å løslate**	[ɔ 'løs‚latə]
amnesty	**amnesti** (m)	[amnɛ'sti]
police	**politi** (n)	[pʉli'ti]
police officer	**politi** (m)	[pʉli'ti]
police station	**politistasjon** (m)	[pʉli'ti‚sta'şʉn]
billy club	**gummikølle** (m/f)	['gʉmi‚kølə]
bullhorn	**megafon** (m)	[mega'fʉn]
patrol car	**patruljebil** (m)	[pɑ'trʉljə‚bil]
siren	**sirene** (m/f)	[si'renə]

| to turn on the siren | å slå på sirenen | [ɔ 'slɔ pɔ si'renən] |
| siren call | sirene hyl (n) | [si'renə ˌhyl] |

crime scene	åsted (n)	['ɔsted]
witness	vitne (n)	['vitnə]
freedom	frihet (m)	['friˌhet]
accomplice	medskyldig (m)	['mɛˌsyldi]
to flee (vi)	å flykte	[ɔ 'flʏktə]
trace (to leave a ~)	spor (n)	['spʊr]

163. Police. Law. Part 2

search (investigation)	ettersøking (m/f)	['ɛtəˌsøkiŋ]
to look for ...	å søke etter ...	[ɔ 'søkə ˌɛtər ...]
suspicion	mistanke (m)	['misˌtɑnkə]
suspicious (e.g., ~ vehicle)	mistenkelig	[mis'tɛnkəli]
to stop (cause to halt)	å stoppe	[ɔ 'stɔpə]
to detain (keep in custody)	å anholde	[ɔ 'ɑnˌhɔlə]

case (lawsuit)	sak (m/f)	['sɑk]
investigation	etterforskning (m/f)	['ɛtərˌfɔs*kniŋ]
detective	detektiv (m)	[detɛk'tiv]
investigator	etterforsker (m)	['ɛtərˌfɔs*kər]
hypothesis	versjon (m)	[væ'sʊn]

motive	motiv (n)	[mʊ'tiv]
interrogation	forhør (n)	[fɔr'hør]
to interrogate (vt)	å forhøre	[ɔ fɔr'hørə]
to question (~ neighbors, etc.)	å avhøre	[ɔ 'ɑvˌhørə]
check (identity ~)	sjekking (m/f)	['ʂɛkiŋ]

round-up	rassia, razzia (m)	['rɑsiɑ]
search (~ warrant)	ransakelse (m)	['rɑnˌsɑkəlsə]
chase (pursuit)	jakt (m/f)	['jɑkt]
to pursue, to chase	å forfølge	[ɔ fɔr'følə]
to track (a criminal)	å spore	[ɔ 'spʊrə]

arrest	arrest (m)	[ɑ'rɛst]
to arrest (sb)	å arrestere	[ɔ ɑrɛ'sterə]
to catch (thief, etc.)	å fange	[ɔ 'faŋə]
capture	pågripelse (m)	['pɔˌgripəlsə]

document	dokument (n)	[dɔkʉ'mɛnt]
proof (evidence)	bevis (n)	[be'vis]
to prove (vt)	å bevise	[ɔ be'visə]
footprint	fotspor (n)	['fʊtˌspʊr]
fingerprints	fingeravtrykk (n pl)	['fiŋərˌɑvtrʏk]
piece of evidence	bevis (n)	[be'vis]
alibi	alibi (n)	['ɑlibi]

innocent (not guilty)	**uskyldig**	[ʉˈʂyldi]
injustice	**urettferdighet** (m)	[ˈʉrɛtfærdiˌhet]
unjust, unfair (adj)	**urettferdig**	[ˈʉrɛtˌfærdi]

criminal (adj)	**kriminell**	[krimiˈnɛl]
to confiscate (vt)	**å konfiskere**	[ɔ kʊnfiˈskerə]
drug (illegal substance)	**narkotika** (m)	[narˈkotika]
weapon, gun	**våpen** (n)	[ˈvopən]
to disarm (vt)	**å avvæpne**	[ɔ ˈavˌvæpnə]
to order (command)	**å befale**	[ɔ beˈfaləˑ]
to disappear (vi)	**å forsvinne**	[ɔ fɔˈʂvinə]

law	**lov** (n)	[ˈlɔv]
legal, lawful (adj)	**lovlig**	[ˈlɔvli]
illegal, illicit (adj)	**ulovlig**	[ʉˈlɔvli]

| responsibility (blame) | **ansvar** (n) | [ˈanˌsvar] |
| responsible (adj) | **ansvarlig** | [ansˈvaːli] |

NATURE

The Earth. Part 1

164. Outer space

space	rommet, kosmos (n)	['rʊmə], ['kɔsmɔs]
space (as adj)	rom-	['rʊm-]
outer space	ytre rom (n)	['ytrə ˌrʊm]
world	verden (m)	['værdən]
universe	univers (n)	[ʉni'væʂ]
galaxy	galakse (m)	[gɑ'lɑksə]

star	stjerne (m/f)	['stjæ:ŋə]
constellation	stjernebilde (n)	['stjæ:ŋəˌbildə]
planet	planet (m)	[plɑ'net]
satellite	satellitt (m)	[sɑtɛ'lit]

meteorite	meteoritt (m)	[meteʊ'rit]
comet	komet (m)	[kʊ'met]
asteroid	asteroide (n)	[ɑsterʊ'idə]

orbit	bane (m)	['bɑnə]
to revolve (~ around the Earth)	å rotere	[ɔ rɔ'terə]
atmosphere	atmosfære (m)	[ɑtmʊ'sfærə]

the Sun	Solen	['sʊlən]
solar system	solsystem (n)	['sʊl sʏ'stem]
solar eclipse	solformørkelse (m)	['sʊl fɔr'mœrkəlsə]

the Earth	Jorden	['ju:rən]
the Moon	Månen	['mo:nən]

Mars	Mars	['mɑʂ]
Venus	Venus	['venʉs]
Jupiter	Jupiter	['jʉpitər]
Saturn	Saturn	['sɑˌtʉ:ŋ]

Mercury	Merkur	[mær'kʉr]
Uranus	Uranus	[ʉ'rɑnʉs]
Neptune	Neptun	[nɛp'tʉn]
Pluto	Pluto	['plʉtʊ]
Milky Way	Melkeveien	['mɛlkəˌvæjən]
Great Bear (Ursa Major)	den Store Bjørn	['dən 'stʊrə ˌbjœ:ŋ]

North Star	Nordstjernen, Polaris	['nuːrˌstjæːŋən], [poˈlaris]
Martian	marsbeboer (m)	['maʂˌbebʊər]
extraterrestrial (n)	uteromjordisk vesen (n)	['ʉtənɔmˌjᴊːrdisk 'vesən]
alien	romvesen (n)	['rʊmˌvesən]
flying saucer	flygende tallerken (m)	['flygənə tɑ'lærkən]
spaceship	romskip (n)	['rʊmˌsip]
space station	romstasjon (m)	['rʊmˌsta'ʂʊn]
blast-off	start (m), oppskyting (m/f)	['stɑːt], ['ɔpˌʂytiŋ]
engine	motor (m)	['motʊr]
nozzle	dyse (m)	['dysə]
fuel	brensel (n), drivstoff (n)	['brɛnsəl], ['drifˌstɔf]
cockpit, flight deck	cockpit (m), flydekk (n)	['kɔkpit], ['flyˌdɛk]
antenna	antenne (m)	[ɑn'tɛnə]
porthole	koøye (n)	['kʊˌøjə]
solar panel	solbatteri (n)	['sʊl batɛ'ri]
spacesuit	romdrakt (m/f)	['rʊmˌdrakt]
weightlessness	vektløshet (m/f)	['vɛktløsˌhet]
oxygen	oksygen (n)	['ɔksy'gen]
docking (in space)	dokking (m/f)	['dɔkiŋ]
to dock (vi, vt)	å dokke	[ɔ 'dɔkə]
observatory	observatorium (n)	[ɔbsɛrva'tʊrium]
telescope	teleskop (n)	[tele'skʊp]
to observe (vt)	å observere	[ɔ ɔbsɛr'vərə]
to explore (vt)	å utforske	[ɔ 'ʉtˌføʂkə]

165. The Earth

the Earth	Jorden	['juːrən]
the globe (the Earth)	jordklode (m)	['juːrˌklɔdə]
planet	planet (m)	[plɑ'net]
atmosphere	atmosfære (m)	[atmʊ'sfærə]
geography	geografi (m)	[geʊgra'fi]
nature	natur (m)	[na'tʉr]
globe (table ~)	globus (m)	['glɔbʉs]
map	kart (n)	['kɑːt]
atlas	atlas (n)	['atlɑs]
Europe	Europa	[ɛʉ'rʊpa]
Asia	Asia	['asia]
Africa	Afrika	['afrika]
Australia	Australia	[aʊ'stralic]
America	Amerika	[a'merika]

North America	Nord-Amerika	['nʊːr ɑ'merikɑ]
South America	Sør-Amerika	['sør ɑ'merikɑ]
Antarctica	Antarktis	[ɑn'tɑrktis]
the Arctic	Arktis	['ɑrktis]

166. Cardinal directions

north	nord (n)	['nʊːr]
to the north	mot nord	[mʊt 'nʊːr]
in the north	i nord	[i 'nʊːr]
northern (adj)	nordlig	['nʊːrli]
south	syd, sør	['syd], ['sør]
to the south	mot sør	[mʊt 'sør]
in the south	i sør	[i 'sør]
southern (adj)	sydlig, sørlig	['sydli], ['søː[i]
west	vest (m)	['vɛst]
to the west	mot vest	[mʊt 'vɛst]
in the west	i vest	[i 'vɛst]
western (adj)	vestlig, vest-	['vɛstli]
east	øst (m)	['øst]
to the east	mot øst	[mʊt 'øst]
in the east	i øst	[i 'øst]
eastern (adj)	østlig	['østli]

167. Sea. Ocean

sea	hav (n)	['hɑv]
ocean	verdenshav (n)	[værdəns'hɑv]
gulf (bay)	bukt (m/f)	['bʉkt]
straits	sund (n)	['sʉn]
land (solid ground)	fastland (n)	['fɑst̩lɑn]
continent (mainland)	fastland, kontinent (n)	['fɑst̩lɑn], [kʊnti'nɛnt]
island	øy (m/f)	['øj]
peninsula	halvøy (m/f)	['hɑl̩øːj]
archipelago	skjærgård (m), arkipelag (n)	['ʂær̩gɔr], [ɑrkipe'lɑg]
bay, cove	bukt (m/f)	['bʉkt]
harbor	havn (m/f)	['hɑvn]
lagoon	lagune (m)	[lɑ'gʉnə]
cape	nes (n), kapp (n)	['nes], ['kɑp]
atoll	atoll (m)	[ɑ'tɔl]
reef	rev (n)	['rev]

coral	korall (m)	[ku'ral]
coral reef	korallrev (n)	[ku'ral,rɛv]
deep (adj)	dyp	['dyp]
depth (deep water)	dybde (m)	['dʏbdə]
abyss	avgrunn (m)	['av,grʉn]
trench (e.g., Mariana ~)	dyphavsgrop (m/f)	['dyphɑfs,gɔp]
current (Ocean ~)	strøm (m)	['strøm]
to surround (bathe)	å omgi	[ɔ 'ɔm,ji]
shore	kyst (m)	['çyst]
coast	kyst (m)	['çyst]
flow (flood tide)	flo (m f)	['flʊ]
ebb (ebb tide)	ebbe (m), fjære (m/f)	['ɛbə], ['fjæ-ə]
shoal	sandbanke (m)	['san,bankə]
bottom (~ of the sea)	bunn (m)	['bʉn]
wave	bølge (m)	['bølgə]
crest (~ of a wave)	bølgekam (m)	['bølgə,kam]
spume (sea foam)	skum (n)	['skʉm]
storm (sea storm)	storm (m)	['stɔrm]
hurricane	orkan (m)	[ɔr'kan]
tsunami	tsunami (m)	[tsʉ'nami]
calm (dead ~)	stille (m/f)	['stilə]
quiet, calm (adj)	stille	['stilə]
pole	pol (m)	['pʊl]
polar (adj)	pol-, polar	['pʊl-], [pʊ'lar]
latitude	bredde, latitude (m)	['brɛdə], ['lati,tʉdə]
longitude	lengde (m/f)	['leŋdə]
parallel	breddegrad (m)	['brɛdə,grad]
equator	ekvator (m)	[ɛ'kvatʊr]
sky	himmel (m)	['himəl]
horizon	horisont (m)	[hʊri'sɔnt]
air	luft (f)	['lʉft]
lighthouse	fyr (n)	['fyr]
to dive (vi)	å dykke	[ɔ 'dʏkə]
to sink (ab. boat)	å synke	[ɔ 'sʏnkə]
treasures	skatter (m pl)	['skatər]

168. Mountains

mountain	fjell (n)	['fjɛl]
mountain range	fjellkjede (m)	['fjɛl,çɛ:də]

mountain ridge	fjellrygg (m)	['fjɛl.rʏg]
summit, top	topp (m)	['tɔp]
peak	tind (m)	['tin]
foot (~ of the mountain)	fot (m)	['fʊt]
slope (mountainside)	skråning (m)	['skrɔniŋ]

volcano	vulkan (m)	[vʉl'kan]
active volcano	virksom vulkan (m)	['virksɔm vʉl'kan]
dormant volcano	utslukt vulkan (m)	['ʉt.ʂlʉkt vʉl'kan]

eruption	utbrudd (n)	['ʉt.brʉd]
crater	krater (n)	['kratər]
magma	magma (m/n)	['magma]
lava	lava (m)	['lava]
molten (~ lava)	glødende	['glødenə]

canyon	canyon (m)	['kanjən]
gorge	gjel (n), kløft (m)	['jel], ['klœft]
crevice	renne (m/f)	['rɛnə]
abyss (chasm)	avgrunn (m)	['av.grʉn]

pass, col	pass (n)	['pas]
plateau	platå (n)	[pla'to]
cliff	klippe (m)	['klipə]
hill	ås (m)	['ɔs]

glacier	bre, jøkel (m)	['bre], ['jøkəl]
waterfall	foss (m)	['fɔs]
geyser	geysir (m)	['gɛjsir]
lake	innsjø (m)	['in'ʂø]

plain	slette (m/f)	['ʂletə]
landscape	landskap (n)	['lan.skap]
echo	ekko (n)	['ɛkʊ]

alpinist	alpinist (m)	[alpi'nist]
rock climber	fjellklatrer (m)	['fjɛl.klatrər]
to conquer (in climbing)	å erobre	[ɔ ɛ'rʊbrə]
climb (an easy ~)	bestigning (m/f)	[be'stigniŋ]

169. Rivers

river	elv (m/f)	['ɛlv]
spring (natural source)	kilde (m)	['çildə]
riverbed (river channel)	elveleie (n)	['ɛlvə.læje]
basin (river valley)	flodbasseng (n)	['flʊd ba.seŋ]
to flow into ...	å munne ut ...	[ɔ 'mʉnə ʉt ...]

| tributary | bielv (m/f) | ['bi.elv] |
| bank (of river) | bredd (m) | ['brɛd] |

current (stream)	**strøm** (m)	['strøm]
downstream (adv)	**medstrøms**	['me‚strøms]
upstream (adv)	**motstrøms**	['mʊt‚strøms]
inundation	**oversvømmelse** (m)	['ɔvə‚svœməlsə]
flooding	**flom** (m)	['flɔm]
to overflow (vi)	**å overflø**	[ɔ 'ɔvər‚flø]
to flood (vt)	**å oversvømme**	[ɔ 'ɔvə‚svœmə]
shallow (shoal)	**grunne** (m/f)	['grʉnə]
rapids	**stryk** (m/n)	['stryk]
dam	**demning** (m)	['dɛmniŋ]
canal	**kanal** (m)	[ka'nɑl]
reservoir (artificial lake)	**reservoar** (n)	[resɛrvʊ'ɑˑ]
sluice, lock	**sluse** (m)	['slʉsə]
water body (pond, etc.)	**vannmasse** (m)	['vɑn‚mɑsə]
swamp (marshland)	**myr, sump** (m)	['myr], ['sʉmp]
bog, marsh	**hengemyr** (m)	['hɛŋe‚myr]
whirlpool	**virvel** (m)	['virvəl]
stream (brook)	**bekk** (m)	['bɛk]
drinking (ab. water)	**drikke-**	['drikə-]
fresh (~ water)	**fersk-**	['fæʂk-]
ice	**is** (m)	['is]
to freeze over	**å fryse til**	[ɔ 'frysə til]
(ab. river, etc.)		

170. Forest

forest, wood	**skog** (m)	['skʊg]
forest (as adj)	**skog-**	['skʊg-]
thick forest	**tett skog** (n)	['tɛt ‚skʊg]
grove	**lund** (m)	['lʉn]
forest clearing	**glenne** (m/f)	['glenə]
thicket	**krattskog** (m)	['krɑt‚skʊg]
scrubland	**kratt** (n)	['krɑt]
footpath (troddenpath)	**sti** (m)	['sti]
gully	**ravine** (m)	[ra'vinə]
tree	**tre** (n)	['trɛ]
leaf	**blad** (n)	['blɑ]
leaves (foliage)	**løv** (n)	['løv]
fall of leaves	**løvfall** (n)	['løv‚fɑl]
to fall (ab. leaves)	**å falle**	[ɔ 'fɑlə]

top (of the tree)	tretopp (m)	['trɛˌtɔp]
branch	kvist, gren (m)	['kvist], ['grɛn]
bough	gren, grein (m/f)	['grɛn], ['græjn]
bud (on shrub, tree)	knopp (m)	['knɔp]
needle (of pine tree)	nål (m/f)	['nɔl]
pine cone	kongle (m/f)	['kʊŋlə]

hollow (in a tree)	trehull (n)	['trɛˌhʉl]
nest	reir (n)	['ræjr]
burrow (animal hole)	hule (m/f)	['hʉlə]

trunk	stamme (m)	['stɑmə]
root	rot (m/f)	['rʊt]
bark	bark (m)	['bɑrk]
moss	mose (m)	['mʊsə]

to uproot (remove trees or tree stumps)	å rykke opp med roten	[ɔ 'rʏkə ɔp me 'rutən]
to chop down	å felle	[ɔ 'fɛlə]
to deforest (vt)	å hogge ned	[ɔ 'hɔgə 'ne]
tree stump	stubbe (m)	['stʉbə]

campfire	bål (n)	['bɔl]
forest fire	skogbrann (m)	['skʊgˌbrɑn]
to extinguish (vt)	å slokke	[ɔ 'ʂløkə]

forest ranger	skogvokter (m)	['skʊgˌvɔktər]
protection	vern (n), beskyttelse (m)	['væːɳ], ['be'ʂytəlsə]
to protect (~ nature)	å beskytte	[ɔ be'ʂytə]
poacher	tyvskytter (m)	['tyfˌʂytər]
steel trap	saks (m/f)	['sɑks]

| to gather, to pick (vt) | å plukke | [ɔ 'plʉkə] |
| to lose one's way | å gå seg vill | [ɔ 'gɔ sæj 'vil] |

171. Natural resources

natural resources	naturressurser (m pl)	[nɑ'tʉr rɛ'sʉʂər]
minerals	mineraler (n pl)	[minə'rɑlər]
deposits	forekomster (m pl)	['forəˌkɔmstər]
field (e.g., oilfield)	felt (m)	['fɛlt]

to mine (extract)	å utvinne	[ɔ 'ʉtˌvinə]
mining (extraction)	utvinning (m/f)	['ʉtˌviniŋ]
ore	malm (m)	['mɑlm]
mine (e.g., for coal)	gruve (m/f)	['grʉvə]
shaft (mine ~)	gruvesjakt (m/f)	['grʉvəˌʂɑkt]
miner	gruvearbeider (m)	['grʉvəˈarˌbæjdər]
gas (natural ~)	gass (m)	['gɑs]
gas pipeline	gassledning (m)	['gɑsˌledniŋ]

oil (petroleum)	olje (m)	['ɔljə]
oil pipeline	oljeledning (m)	['ɔljə‚ledniŋ]
oil well	oljebrønn (m)	['ɔljə‚brœn]
derrick (tower)	boretårn (n)	['boːrə‚tɔːŋ]
tanker	tankskip (n)	['tɑnk‚ʂip]

sand	sand (m)	['sɑn]
limestone	kalkstein (m)	['kɑlk‚stæjn]
gravel	grus (m)	['grʉs]
peat	torv (m/f)	['tɔrv]
clay	leir (r)	['læjr]
coal	kull (ŋ)	['kʉl]

iron (ore)	jern (n)	['jæːŋ]
gold	gull (ŋ)	['gʉl]
silver	sølv (n)	['søl]
nickel	nikkel (m)	['nikəl]
copper	kobber (n)	['kɔbər]

zinc	sink (m/n)	['sink]
manganese	mangan (m/n)	[mɑ'ŋɑn]
mercury	kvikksølv (n)	['kvik‚søl]
lead	bly (r)	['bly]

mineral	mineral (n)	[minə'rɑl]
crystal	krystall (m/n)	[kry'stɑl]
marble	marmor (m/n)	['mɑrmʊr]
uranium	uran (m/n)	[ʉ'rɑn]

The Earth. Part 2

172. Weather

weather	**vær** (n)	['vær]
weather forecast	**værvarsel** (n)	['vær͵vɑṣəl]
temperature	**temperatur** (m)	[tɛmpərɑ'tʉr]
thermometer	**termometer** (n)	[tɛrmʊ'metər]
barometer	**barometer** (n)	[bɑrʊ'metər]
humid (adj)	**fuktig**	['fʉkti]
humidity	**fuktighet** (m)	['fʉkti͵het]
heat (extreme ~)	**hete** (m)	['he:tə]
hot (torrid)	**het**	['het]
it's hot	**det er hett**	[de ær 'het]
it's warm	**det er varmt**	[de ær 'vɑrmt]
warm (moderately hot)	**varm**	['vɑrm]
it's cold	**det er kaldt**	[de ær 'kɑlt]
cold (adj)	**kald**	['kɑl]
sun	**sol** (m/f)	['sʊl]
to shine (vi)	**å skinne**	[ɔ 'ṣinə]
sunny (day)	**solrik**	['sʊl͵rik]
to come up (vi)	**å gå opp**	[ɔ 'gɔ ɔp]
to set (vi)	**å gå ned**	[ɔ 'gɔ ne]
cloud	**sky** (m)	['ṣy]
cloudy (adj)	**skyet**	['ṣy:ət]
rain cloud	**regnsky** (m/f)	['ræjn͵ṣy]
somber (gloomy)	**mørk**	['mœrk]
rain	**regn** (n)	['ræjn]
it's raining	**det regner**	[de 'ræjnər]
rainy (~ day, weather)	**regnværs-**	['ræjn͵væṣ-]
to drizzle (vi)	**å småregne**	[ɔ 'smo:ræjnə]
pouring rain	**piskende regn** (n)	['piskenə ͵ræjn]
downpour	**styrtregn** (n)	['sty:t͵ræjn]
heavy (e.g., ~ rain)	**kraftig, sterk**	['krɑfti], ['stærk]
puddle	**vannpytt** (m)	['vɑn͵pyt]
to get wet (in rain)	**å bli våt**	[ɔ 'bli 'vɔt]
fog (mist)	**tåke** (m/f)	['to:kə]
foggy	**tåke**	['to:kə]

| snow | snø (m) | ['snø] |
| it's snowing | det snør | [de 'snør] |

173. Severe weather. Natural disasters

thunderstorm	torden vær (n)	['tʊrdən,vær]
lightning (~ strike)	lyn (r)	['lyn]
to flash (vi)	å glimte	[ɔ 'glimtə]

thunder	torden (m)	['tʊrdən]
to thunder (vi)	å torcne	[ɔ 'tʊrdnə]
it's thundering	det tordner	[de 'tʊrdnər]

| hail | hagle (m/f) | ['hɑglə] |
| it's hailing | det hagler | [de 'hɑglər] |

| to flood (vt) | å oversvømme | [ɔ 'ɔvə,svɶmə] |
| flood, inundation | oversvømmelse (m) | ['ɔvə,svɶməlsə] |

earthquake	jordskjelv (n)	['juːr,ʂɛlv]
tremor, quake	skjelv (n)	['ʂɛlv]
epicenter	episenter (n)	[ɛpi'sɛntər]

| eruption | utbrudd (n) | ['ʉt,brʉd] |
| lava | lava (m) | ['lɑvɑ] |

twister	skypumpe (m/f)	['ʂy,pʉmpə]
tornado	tornado (m)	[tʊ:'nɑdʉ]
typhoon	tyfon (m)	[ty'fʊn]

hurricane	orkan (m)	[ɔr'kɑn]
storm	storm (m)	['stɔrm]
tsunami	tsunami (m)	[tsʉ'nɑmi]

cyclone	syklon (m)	[sy'klun]
bad weather	uvær (n)	['ʉ:,vær]
fire (accident)	brann (m)	['brɑn]
disaster	katastrofe (m)	[kɑtɑ'strɔfə]
meteorite	meteoritt (m)	[meteʉ'rit]

avalanche	lavine (m)	[lɑ'vinə]
snowslide	snøskred, snøras (n)	['snø,skred], ['snørɑs]
blizzard	snøstorm (m)	['snø,stɔrm]
snowstorm	snøstorm (m)	['snø,stɔrm]

Fauna

174. Mammals. Predators

predator	**rovdyr** (n)	['rɔv‚dyr]
tiger	**tiger** (m)	['tigər]
lion	**løve** (m/f)	['løve]
wolf	**ulv** (m)	['ʉlv]
fox	**rev** (m)	['rev]
jaguar	**jaguar** (m)	[jagʉ'ɑr]
leopard	**leopard** (m)	[leʉ'pɑrd]
cheetah	**gepard** (m)	[ge'pɑrd]
black panther	**panter** (m)	['pɑntər]
puma	**puma** (m)	['pʉmɑ]
snow leopard	**snøleopard** (m)	['snø leʉ'pɑrd]
lynx	**gaupe** (m/f)	['gaʉpə]
coyote	**coyote, prærieulv** (m)	[kɔ'jotə], ['præri‚ʉlv]
jackal	**sjakal** (m)	[ʂɑ'kɑl]
hyena	**hyene** (m)	[hy'enə]

175. Wild animals

animal	**dyr** (n)	['dyr]
beast (animal)	**best, udyr** (n)	['bɛst], ['ʉ‚dyr]
squirrel	**ekorn** (n)	['ɛkʊːn]
hedgehog	**pinnsvin** (n)	['pin‚svin]
hare	**hare** (m)	['hɑrə]
rabbit	**kanin** (m)	[kɑ'nin]
badger	**grevling** (m)	['grɛvliŋ]
raccoon	**vaskebjørn** (m)	['vɑskə‚bjœːn]
hamster	**hamster** (m)	['hɑmstər]
marmot	**murmeldyr** (n)	['mʉrməl‚dyr]
mole	**muldvarp** (m)	['mʉl‚vɑrp]
mouse	**mus** (m/f)	['mʉs]
rat	**rotte** (m/f)	['rɔtə]
bat	**flaggermus** (m/f)	['flɑgər‚mʉs]
ermine	**røyskatt** (m)	['røjskɑt]
sable	**sobel** (m)	['sʊbəl]

marten	mår (m)	['mɔr]
weasel	snømus (m/f)	['snøˌmʉs]
mink	mink (m)	['mink]

| beaver | bever (m) | ['bevər] |
| otter | oter (m) | ['ʊtər] |

horse	hest (m)	['hɛst]
moose	elg (n)	['ɛlg]
deer	hjort (m)	['jɔːʈ]
camel	kamel (m)	[ka'mel]

bison	bison (m)	['bisɔn]
aurochs	urokse (m)	['ʉrˌʊksə]
buffalo	bøffel (m)	['bøfəl]

zebra	sebra (m)	['sebra]
antelope	antilope (m)	[anti'lʊpeˈ
roe deer	rådyr (n)	['rɔˌdyr]
fallow deer	dåhjort, dådyr (n)	['dɔˌjɔːʈ], ['dɔˌdyr]
chamois	gemse (m)	['gɛmsə]
wild boar	villsvin (n)	['vilˌsvin]

whale	hval (m)	['val]
seal	sel (n)	['sel]
walrus	hvalross (m)	['valˌrɔs]
fur seal	pelssel (m)	['pɛlsˌsel]
dolphin	delfin (m)	[dɛl'fin]

bear	bjørn (m)	['bjœːɳ]
polar bear	isbjørn (m)	['isˌbjœːɳˈ
panda	panda (m)	['panda]

monkey	ape (m/f)	['ape]
chimpanzee	sjimpanse (m)	[ʂim'pansə]
orangutan	orangutang (m)	[ʊ'rangʉˌtaŋ]
gorilla	gorilla (m)	[gɔ'rila]
macaque	makak (m)	[ma'kak]
gibbon	gibbon (m)	['gibʊn]

elephant	elefant (m)	[ɛle'fant]
rhinoceros	neshorn (n)	['nesˌhuːɳ]
giraffe	sjiraff (m)	[ʂi'raf]
hippopotamus	flodhest (m)	['flʊdˌhɛst]

| kangaroo | kenguru (m) | ['kɛŋgʉrʉ] |
| koala (bear) | koala (m) | [kʊ'ala] |

mongoose	mangust, mungo (m)	[maŋ'gʉst], ['mʉŋgu]
chinchilla	chinchilla (m)	[ʂin'ʂila]
skunk	skunk (m)	['skunk]
porcupine	hulepinnsvin (n)	['hʉləˌpinsvin]

176. Domestic animals

cat	**katt** (m)	['kat]
tomcat	**hannkatt** (m)	['han,kat]
dog	**hund** (m)	['hʉŋ]
horse	**hest** (m)	['hɛst]
stallion (male horse)	**hingst** (m)	['hiŋst]
mare	**hoppe, merr** (m/f)	['hɔpə], ['mɛr]
cow	**ku** (f)	['kʉ]
bull	**tyr** (m)	['tyr]
ox	**okse** (m)	['ɔksə]
sheep (ewe)	**sau** (m)	['saʊ]
ram	**vær, saubukk** (m)	['vær], ['saʊ,bʉk]
goat	**geit** (m/f)	['jæjt]
billy goat, he-goat	**geitebukk** (m)	['jæjtə,bʉk]
donkey	**esel** (n)	['ɛsəl]
mule	**muldyr** (n)	['mʉl,dyr]
pig, hog	**svin** (n)	['svin]
piglet	**gris** (m)	['gris]
rabbit	**kanin** (m)	[ka'nin]
hen (chicken)	**høne** (m/f)	['hønə]
rooster	**hane** (m)	['hanə]
duck	**and** (m/f)	['an]
drake	**andrik** (m)	['andrik]
goose	**gås** (m/f)	['gɔs]
tom turkey, gobbler	**kalkunhane** (m)	[kal'kʉn,hanə]
turkey (hen)	**kalkunhøne** (m/f)	[kal'kʉn,hønə]
domestic animals	**husdyr** (n pl)	['hʉs,dyr]
tame (e.g., ~ hamster)	**tam**	['tam]
to tame (vt)	**å temme**	[ɔ 'tɛmə]
to breed (vt)	**å avle, å oppdrette**	[ɔ 'avlə], [ɔ 'ɔp,drɛtə]
farm	**farm, gård** (m)	['farm], ['gɔ:r]
poultry	**fjærfe** (n)	['fjær,fɛ]
cattle	**kveg** (n)	['kvɛg]
herd (cattle)	**flokk, bøling** (m)	['flɔk], ['bøliŋ]
stable	**stall** (m)	['stal]
pigpen	**grisehus** (n)	['grisə,hʉs]
cowshed	**kufjøs** (m/n)	['kʉ,fjøs]
rabbit hutch	**kaninbur** (n)	[ka'nin,bʉr]
hen house	**hønsehus** (n)	['hønsə,hʉs]

177. Dogs. Dog breeds

dog	hund (m)	['hʉn]
sheepdog	fårehund (m)	['foːrəˌhʉn]
German shepherd	schäferhund (m)	['ʂɛfærˌhʉn]
poodle	puddel (m)	['pʉdəl]
dachshund	dachshund (m)	['daʂˌhʉn]
bulldog	bulldogg (m)	['bʉlˌdɔg]
boxer	bokser (m)	['bɔksər]
mastiff	mastiff (m)	[mɑs'tif]
Rottweiler	rottweiler (m)	['rɔtˌvæjlər]
Doberman	dobermann (m)	['dɔbermɑn]
basset	basset (m)	['basɛt]
bobtail	bobtail (m)	['bɔbtɛjl]
Dalmatian	dalmatiner (m)	[dɑlmɑ'tinər]
cocker spaniel	cocker spaniel (m)	['kɔker ˌspɑniəl]
Newfoundland	newfoundlandshund (m)	[njʉ'fɑwndˌlənds 'hʉn]
Saint Bernard	sankt bernhardshund (m)	[ˌsɑnkt 'bɛːɳɑdsˌhʉn]
husky	husky (m)	['hɑski]
Chow Chow	chihuahua (m)	[tʂi'vɑvɑ]
spitz	spisshund (m)	['spisˌhʉn|
pug	mops (m)	['mɔps]

178. Sounds made by animals

barking (n)	gjøing (m/f)	['jøːiŋ]
to bark (vi)	å gjø	[ɔ 'jø]
to meow (vi)	å maue	[ɔ 'mjɑʉe]
to purr (vi)	å spinne	[ɔ 'spinə]
to moo (vi)	å raute	[ɔ 'rɑʉtə]
to bellow (bull)	å belje, å brøle	[ɔ 'belje], [ɔ 'brøle]
to growl (vi)	å krurre	[ɔ 'knʉrə]
howl (n)	hyl (n)	['hyl]
to howl (vi)	å hyle	[ɔ 'hylə]
to whine (vi)	å klynke	[ɔ 'klʏnkə]
to bleat (sheep)	å breke	[ɔ 'brekə]
to oink, to grunt (pig)	å grynte	[ɔ 'grʏntə]
to squeal (vi)	å hvine	[ɔ 'vinə]
to croak (vi)	å kvekke	[ɔ 'kvɛkə]
to buzz (insect)	å surre	[ɔ 'sʉrə]
to chirp (crickets, grasshopper)	å grisse	[ɔ 'gnisə]

179. Birds

bird	fugl (m)	['fʉl]
pigeon	due (m/f)	['dʉə]
sparrow	spurv (m)	['spʉrv]
tit (great tit)	kjøttmeis (m/f)	['çœt̩mæjs]
magpie	skjære (m/f)	['şærə]
raven	ravn (m)	['ravn]
crow	kråke (m)	['kro:kə]
jackdaw	kaie (m/f)	['kajə]
rook	kornkråke (m/f)	['kʉ:n̩kro:kə]
duck	and (m/f)	['an]
goose	gås (m/f)	['gɔs]
pheasant	fasan (m)	[fa'san]
eagle	ørn (m/f)	['œ:n̩]
hawk	hauk (m)	['haʊk]
falcon	falk (m)	['falk]
vulture	gribb (m)	['grib]
condor (Andean ~)	kondor (m)	[kʊn'dʉr]
swan	svane (m/f)	['svanə]
crane	trane (m/f)	['tranə]
stork	stork (m)	['stɔrk]
parrot	papegøye (m)	[pape'gøjə]
hummingbird	kolibri (m)	[kʊ'libri]
peacock	påfugl (m)	['pɔˌfʉl]
ostrich	struts (m)	['strʉts]
heron	hegre (m)	['hæjrə]
flamingo	flamingo (m)	[fla'mingʊ]
pelican	pelikan (m)	[peli'kan]
nightingale	nattergal (m)	['natərˌgal]
swallow	svale (m/f)	['svalə]
thrush	trost (m)	['trʊst]
song thrush	måltrost (m)	['mo:lˌtrʊst]
blackbird	svarttrost (m)	['sva:ˌtrʊst]
swift	tårnseiler (m),	['tɔ:n̩sæjlə],
	tårnsvale (m/f)	['tɔ:n̩svalə]
lark	lerke (m/f)	['lærkə]
quail	vaktel (m)	['vaktəl]
woodpecker	hakkespett (m)	['hakəˌspɛt]
cuckoo	gjøk, gauk (m)	['jøk], ['gaʊk]
owl	ugle (m/f)	['ʉglə]

eagle owl	hubro (m)	['hʉbrʊ]
wood grouse	storfugl (m)	['stʊrˌfʉl]
black grouse	orrfugl (m)	['ɔrˌfʉl]
partridge	rapphøne (m/f)	['rapˌhønə]
starling	stær (m)	['stær]
canary	kanarifugl (m)	[ka'nariˌfʉl]
hazel grouse	jerpe (m/f)	['jærpə]
chaffinch	bokfink (m)	['bʊkˌfink]
bullfinch	dompap (m)	['dʊmpap]
seagull	måke (m/f)	['moːkə]
albatross	albatross (m)	['albaˌtrɔs]
penguin	pingvin (m)	[piŋ'vin]

180. Birds. Singing and sounds

to sing (vi)	å synge	[ɔ 'sʏŋə]
to call (animal, bird)	å skrike	[ɔ 'skrikə]
to crow (rooster)	å gale	[ɔ 'galə]
cock-a-doodle-doo	kykeliky	[kykəli'kyː]
to cluck (hen)	å kakle	[ɔ 'kaklə]
to caw (vi)	å kræ	[ɔ 'kræ]
to quack (duck)	å snadre, å rappe	[ɔ 'snadrə] [ɔ 'rapə]
to cheep (vi)	å pipe	[ɔ 'pipə]
to chirp, to twitter	å kvitre	[ɔ 'kvitrə]

181. Fish. Marine animals

bream	brasme (m/f)	['brasmə]
carp	karpe (m)	['karpə]
perch	åbor (m)	['ɔbɔr]
catfish	malle (m)	['malə]
pike	gjedde (m/f)	['jɛdə]
salmon	laks (m)	['laks]
sturgeon	stør (m)	['stør]
herring	sild (n/f)	['sil]
Atlantic salmon	atlanterhavslaks (m)	[at'lantərhafsˌlaks]
mackerel	makrell (m)	[ma'krɛl]
flatfish	rødspette (m/f)	['røˌspɛtə]
zander, pike perch	gjørs (m)	['jøːʂ]
cod	torsk (m)	['tɔʂk]
tuna	tunfisk (m)	['tʉnˌfisk]
trout	ørret (m)	['øret]

eel	ål (m)	['ɔl]
electric ray	elektrisk rokke (m/f)	[ɛ'lektrisk ˌrɔkə]
moray eel	murene (m)	[mʉ'rɛnə]
piranha	piraja (m)	[pi'raja]

shark	hai (m)	['haj]
dolphin	delfin (m)	[dɛl'fin]
whale	hval (m)	['val]

crab	krabbe (m)	['krabə]
jellyfish	manet (m/f), meduse (m)	['manet], [me'dʉsə]
octopus	blekksprut (m)	['blekˌsprʉt]

starfish	sjøstjerne (m/f)	['ʂøˌstjæːŋə]
sea urchin	sjøpinnsvin (n)	['ʂøː'pinˌsvin]
seahorse	sjøhest (m)	['ʂøˌhɛst]

oyster	østers (m)	['østəʂ]
shrimp	reke (m/f)	['rekə]
lobster	hummer (m)	['hʉmər]
spiny lobster	langust (m)	[laŋ'gʉst]

182. Amphibians. Reptiles

| snake | slange (m) | ['ʂlaŋə] |
| venomous (snake) | giftig | ['jifti] |

| viper | hoggorm, huggorm (m) | ['hʉgˌɔrm], ['hʉgˌɔrm] |
| cobra | kobra (m) | ['kʊbra] |

| python | pyton (m) | ['pytɔn] |
| boa | boaslange (m) | ['bɔaˌslaŋə] |

grass snake	snok (m)	['snʊk]
rattle snake	klapperslange (m)	['klapəˌslaŋə]
anaconda	anakonda (m)	[ana'kɔnda]

lizard	øgle (m/f)	['øglə]
iguana	iguan (m)	[igʉ'an]
monitor lizard	varan (n)	[va'ran]
salamander	salamander (m)	[sala'mandər]

| chameleon | kameleon (m) | [kamələ'ʊn] |
| scorpion | skorpion (m) | [skɔrpi'ʊn] |

| turtle | skilpadde (m/f) | ['ʂilˌpadə] |
| frog | frosk (m) | ['frɔsk] |

| toad | padde (m/f) | ['padə] |
| crocodile | krokodille (m) | [krʊkə'dilə] |

183. Insects

insect, bug	insekt (n)	['insɛkt]
butterfly	sommerfugl (m)	['sɔmər,fʉl]
ant	maur (m)	['maʊr]
fly	flue (m/f)	['flʉə]
mosquito	mygg (m)	['mʏg]
beetle	bille (m)	['bilə]
wasp	veps (m)	['vɛps]
bee	bie (m/f)	['biə]
bumblebee	humle (m/f)	['hʉmlə]
gadfly (botfly)	brems (m)	['brɛms]
spider	edderkopp (m)	['ɛdər,kɔp]
spiderweb	edderkoppnett (n)	['ɛdərkɔp,nɛt]
dragonfly	øyenstikker (m)	['øjən,stikər]
grasshopper	gresshoppe (m/f)	['grɛs,hɔpə]
moth (night butterfly)	nattsvermer (m)	['nat,sværmər]
cockroach	kakerlakk (m)	[kakə'lak]
tick	flått, midd (m)	['flɔt], ['miɟ]
flea	loppe (f)	['lɔpə]
midge	knott (m)	['knɔt]
locust	vandgresshoppe (m/f)	['van 'grɛs,hɔpə]
snail	snegl (m)	['snæjl]
cricket	siriss (m)	['si,ris]
lightning bug	ildflue (m/f), lysbille (m)	['il,flʉe], ['ys,bilə]
ladybug	marihøne (m/f)	['mari,hønə]
cockchafer	oldenborre (f)	['ɔldən,bɔrə]
leech	igle (m/f)	['iglə]
caterpillar	sommerfugllarve (m/f)	['sɔmərfʉl,larvə]
earthworm	meitemark (m)	['mæjtə,mɑrk]
larva	larve (m/f)	['larvə]

184. Animals. Body parts

beak	nebb (n)	['nɛb]
wings	vinger (m pl)	['viŋər]
foot (of bird)	fot (m)	['fʊt]
feathers (plumage)	fjærdrakt (m/f)	['fjær,drɑkt]
feather	fjær (m/f)	['fjær]
crest	fjærtopp (m)	['fjæ:tɔp]
gills	gjeller (m/f pl)	['jɛlər]
spawn	rogn (m/f)	['rɔŋn]

larva	larve (m/f)	['lɑrvə]
fin	finne (m)	['finə]
scales (of fish, reptile)	skjell (n)	['ʂɛl]

fang (canine)	hoggtann (m/f)	['hɔg.tɑn]
paw (e.g., cat's ~)	pote (m)	['po:tə]
muzzle (snout)	snute (m/f)	['snʉtə]
mouth (of cat, dog)	kjeft (m)	['çɛft]
tail	hale (m)	['hɑlə]
whiskers	værhår (n)	['vær.hɔr]

| hoof | klov, hov (m) | ['klɔv], ['hɔv] |
| horn | horn (n) | ['hʊːɳ] |

carapace	ryggskjold (n)	['rʏg.ʂɔl]
shell (of mollusk)	skall (n)	['skɑl]
eggshell	eggeskall (n)	['ɛgə.skɑl]

| animal's hair (pelage) | pels (m) | ['pɛls] |
| pelt (hide) | skinn (n) | ['ʂin] |

185. Animals. Habitats

| habitat | habitat (n) | [hɑbi'tɑt] |
| migration | migrasjon (m) | [migrɑ'ʂʊn] |

mountain	fjell (n)	['fjɛl]
reef	rev (n)	['rev]
cliff	klippe (m)	['klipə]

forest	skog (m)	['skʊg]
jungle	jungel (m)	['jʉŋəl]
savanna	savanne (m)	[sɑ'vɑnə]
tundra	tundra (m)	['tʉndrɑ]

steppe	steppe (m)	['stɛpə]
desert	ørken (m)	['œrkən]
oasis	oase (m)	[ʊ'ɑsə]

sea	hav (n)	['hɑv]
lake	innsjø (m)	['in'ʂø]
ocean	verdenshav (n)	[værdəns'hɑv]

swamp (marshland)	myr (m/f)	['myr]
freshwater (adj)	ferskvanns-	['fæʂk.vɑns-]
pond	dam (m)	['dɑm]
river	elv (m/f)	['ɛlv]

| den (bear's ~) | hi (n) | ['hi] |
| nest | reir (n) | ['ræjr] |

hollow (in a tree)	**trehull** (n)	['trɛˌhʉl]
burrow (animal hole)	**hule** (m/f)	['hʉlə]
anthill	**maurtue** (m/f)	['maʊːˌtʉə]

Flora

186. Trees

tree	**tre** (n)	['trɛ]
deciduous (adj)	**løv-**	['løv-]
coniferous (adj)	**bar-**	['bɑr-]
evergreen (adj)	**eviggrønt**	['ɛvi̩grœnt]
apple tree	**epletre** (n)	['ɛplə̩trɛ]
pear tree	**pæretre** (n)	['pærə̩trɛ]
sweet cherry tree	**morelltre** (n)	[mʉ'rɛl̩trɛ]
sour cherry tree	**kirsebærtre** (n)	['çişəbær̩trɛ]
plum tree	**plommetre** (n)	['plʉmə̩trɛ]
birch	**bjørk** (f)	['bjœrk]
oak	**eik** (f)	['æjk]
linden tree	**lind** (m/f)	['lin]
aspen	**osp** (m/f)	['ɔsp]
maple	**lønn** (m/f)	['lœn]
spruce	**gran** (m/f)	['grɑn]
pine	**furu** (m/f)	['fʉrʉ]
larch	**lerk** (m)	['lærk]
fir tree	**edelgran** (m/f)	['ɛdəl̩grɑn]
cedar	**seder** (m)	['sedər]
poplar	**poppel** (m)	['pɔpəl]
rowan	**rogn** (m/f)	['rɔŋn]
willow	**pil** (m/f)	['pil]
alder	**or, older** (m/f)	['ʊr], ['ɔldər]
beech	**bøk** (m)	['bøk]
elm	**alm** (m)	['ɑlm]
ash (tree)	**ask** (m/f)	['ɑsk]
chestnut	**kastanjetre** (n)	[kɑ'stɑnjɛ̩trɛ]
magnolia	**magnolia** (m)	[mɑŋ'nʉliɑ]
palm tree	**palme** (m)	['pɑlmə]
cypress	**sypress** (m)	[sʏ'prɛs]
mangrove	**mangrove** (m)	[mɑŋ'grʊvə]
baobab	**apebrødtre** (n)	['ɑpebrø̩trɛ]
eucalyptus	**eukalyptus** (m)	[ɛvkɑ'lyptʉs]
sequoia	**sequoia** (m)	['sek̩vɔjɑ]

187. Shrubs

bush	busk (m)	['bʉsk]
shrub	busk (m)	['bʉsk]
grapevine	vinranke (m)	['vin‚rankə]
vineyard	vinmark (m/f)	['vin‚mark]
raspberry bush	bringebærbusk (m)	['brinə‚bær bʉsk]
blackcurrant bush	solbærbusk (m)	['sʉlbær‚bʉsk]
redcurrant bush	ripsbusk (m)	['rips‚bʉsk]
gooseberry bush	stikkelsbærbusk (m)	['stikəlsbær‚bʉsk]
acacia	akasie (m)	[a'kɑsiə]
barberry	berberis (m)	['bærberis]
jasmine	sjasmin (m)	[sɑs'min]
juniper	einer (m)	['æjnər]
rosebush	rosenbusk (m)	['rʉsən‚bʉsk]
dog rose	steinnype (m/f)	['stæjn‚nypə]

188. Mushrooms

mushroom	sopp (m)	['sɔp]
edible mushroom	spiselig sopp (m)	['spisəli ‚sɔp]
poisonous mushroom	giftig sopp (m)	['jifti ‚sɔp]
cap (of mushroom)	hatt (m)	['hat]
stipe (of mushroom)	stilk (m)	['stilk]
cep (Boletus edulis)	steinsopp (m)	['stæjn‚sɔp]
orange-cap boletus	rødskrubb (m/n)	['rø‚skrʉb]
birch bolete	brunskrubb (m/n)	['brʉn‚skrʉb]
chanterelle	kantarell (m)	[kanta'rel]
russula	kremle (m/f)	['krɛmlə]
morel	morkel (m)	['mɔrkəl]
fly agaric	fluesopp (m)	['flʉə‚sɔp]
death cap	grønn fluesopp (m)	['grœn 'flʉə‚sɔp]

189. Fruits. Berries

fruit	frukt (m/f)	['frʉkt]
fruits	frukter (m/f pl)	['frʉktər]
apple	eple (n)	['ɛplə]
pear	pære (m/f)	['pærə]
plum	plomme (m/f)	['plʉmə]
strawberry (garden ~)	jordbær (n)	['juːr‚bær]

sour cherry	kirsebær (n)	['çiʂəˌbær]
sweet cherry	morell (m)	[mʊ'rɛl]
grape	drue (m)	['drʉə]

raspberry	bringebær (n)	['briŋəˌbær]
blackcurrant	solbær (n)	['sʊlˌbær]
redcurrant	rips (m)	['rips]
gooseberry	stikkelsbær (n)	['stikəlsˌbær]
cranberry	tranebær (n)	['tranəˌbær]

orange	appelsin (m)	[apel'sin]
mandarin	mandarin (m)	[manda'rin]
pineapple	ananas (m)	['ananas]
banana	banan (m)	[ba'nan]
date	daddel (m)	['dadəl]

lemon	sitron (m)	[si'trʊn]
apricot	aprikos (m)	[apri'kʊs]
peach	fersken (m)	['fæʂkən]
kiwi	kiwi (m)	['kivi]
grapefruit	grapefrukt (m/f)	['grɛjpˌfrʉkt]

berry	bær (n)	['bær]
berries	bær (n pl)	['bær]
cowberry	tyttebær (n)	['tʏtəˌbær]
wild strawberry	markjordbær (n)	['mark juːrˌbær]
bilberry	blåbær (n)	['blɔˌbær]

190. Flowers. Plants

| flower | blomst (m) | ['blɔmst] |
| bouquet (of flowers) | bukett (m) | [bʉ'kɛt] |

rose (flower)	rose (m/f)	['rʊsə]
tulip	tulipan (m)	[tʉli'pan]
carnation	nellik (m)	['nɛlik]
gladiolus	gladiolus (m)	[gladi'ɔlʉs]

cornflower	kornblomst (m)	['kuːɳˌblɔmst]
harebell	blåklokke (m/f)	['blɔˌklɔkə]
dandelion	løvetann (m/f)	['løvəˌtan]
camomile	kamille (m)	[ka'milə]

aloe	aloe (m)	['alʊe]
cactus	kaktus (m)	['kaktʉs]
rubber plant, ficus	gummiplante (m/f)	['gʉmiˌplantə]

lily	lilje (m)	['liljə]
geranium	geranium (m)	[ge'ranium]
hyacinth	hyasint (m)	[hia'sint]

mimosa	mimose (m/f)	[mi'mɔsə]
narcissus	narsiss (m)	[nɑ'sis]
nasturtium	blomkarse (m)	['blɔm,kɑsə]
orchid	orkidé (m)	[ɔrki'de]
peony	peon, pion (m)	[pe'un], [ɕi'un]
violet	fiol (m)	[fi'ul]
pansy	stemorsblomst (m)	['stemus,blɔmst]
forget-me-not	forglemmegei (m)	[fɔr'glemə,jæj]
daisy	tusenfryd (m)	['tusən,fryd]
poppy	valmue (m)	['vɑlmuə]
hemp	hamp (m)	['hɑmp]
mint	mynte (m/f)	['mʏntə]
lily of the valley	liljekonvall (m)	['liljə kɔn'vɑl]
snowdrop	snøklokke (m/f)	['snø,klɔkə]
nettle	nesle (m/f)	['nɛslə]
sorrel	syre (m/f)	['syrə]
water lily	nøkkerose (m/f)	['nøkə,ruse]
fern	bregne (m/f)	['brɛjnə]
lichen	lav (m/n)	['lɑv]
greenhouse (tropical ~)	drivhus (n)	['driv,hus]
lawn	gressplen (m)	['grɛs,plen]
flowerbed	blomsterbed (n)	['blɔmstər,bed]
plant	plante (m/f), vekst (m)	['plɑntə], ['vɛkst]
grass	gras (n)	['grɑs]
blade of grass	grasstrå (n)	['grɑs,strɔ]
leaf	blad (n)	['blɑ]
petal	kronblad (n)	['krɔn,blɑ]
stem	stilk (m)	['stilk]
tuber	rotknoll (m)	['rut,knɔl]
young plant (shoot)	spire (m/f)	['spirə]
thorn	torn (m)	['tuːn]
to blossom (vi)	å blomstre	[ɔ 'blɔmstrə]
to fade, to wither	å visne	[ɔ 'visnə]
smell (odor)	lukt (m/f)	['lukt]
to cut (flowers)	å skjære av	[ɔ 'sæːrə ɑː]
to pick (a flower)	å plukke	[ɔ 'plukə]

191. Cereals, grains

grain	korn (n)	['kuːn]
cereal crops	cerealer (n pl)	[sere'ɑlər]

ear (of barley, etc.)	**aks** (n)	['ɑks]
wheat	**hvete** (m)	['vetə]
rye	**rug** (m)	['rʉg]
oats	**havre** (m)	['hɑvrə]
millet	**hirse** (m)	['hişə]
barley	**bygg** (m/n)	['bʏg]
corn	**mais** (m)	['mɑis]
rice	**ris** (m)	['ris]
buckwheat	**bokhvete** (m)	['bʉk‚vetə]
pea plant	**ert** (m/f)	['æːt]
kidney bean	**bønne** (m/f)	['bœnə]
soy	**soya** (m)	['sɔja]
lentil	**linse** (m/f)	['linsə]
beans (pulse crops)	**bønner** (m/f pl)	['bœnər]

REGIONAL GEOGRAPHY

Countries. Nationalities

192. Politics. Government. Part 1

politics	**politikk** (m)	[pʊli'tik]
political (adj)	**politisk**	[pʊ'litisk]
politician	**politiker** (m)	[pʊ'litikər]
state (country)	**stat** (m)	['stat]
citizen	**statsborger** (m)	['stats,bɔrgər]
citizenship	**statsborgerskap** (n)	['statsbɔrgə,skap]
national emblem	**riksvåpen** (n)	['riks,vɔpɛn]
national anthem	**nasjonalsang** (m)	[naʂʊ'nal,saŋ]
government	**regjering** (m/f)	[rɛ'jeriŋ]
head of state	**landets leder** (m)	['lanɛts ‚ledər]
parliament	**parlament** (n)	[pɑːlɑ'mɛnt]
party	**parti** (n)	[pɑː'ţi]
capitalism	**kapitalisme** (n)	[kapita'lismə]
capitalist (adj)	**kapitalistisk**	[kapita'lisːisk]
socialism	**sosialisme** (m)	[sʊsia'lismə]
socialist (adj)	**sosialistisk**	[sʊsia'listisk]
communism	**kommunisme** (m)	[kʊmʉ'nismə]
communist (adj)	**kommunistisk**	[kʊmʉ'nistisk]
communist (n)	**kommunist** (m)	[kʊmʉ'nist]
democracy	**demokrati** (n)	[demʊkra'ti]
democrat	**demokrat** (m)	[demʊ'krɑt]
democratic (adj)	**demokratisk**	[demʊ'krɑtisk]
Democratic party	**demokratisk parti** (n)	[demʊ'krɑtisk pɑː'ţi]
liberal (n)	**liberaler** (m)	[libə'ralər]
liberal (adj)	**liberal**	[libə'ral]
conservative (n)	**konservativ** (m)	[kʊn'sɛrvɑ‚tiv]
conservative (adj)	**konservativ**	[kʊn'sɛrvɑ‚tiv]
republic (n)	**republikk** (m)	[repʉ'blik]
republican (n)	**republikaner** (m)	[repʉbli'kanər]
Republican party	**republikanske parti** (n)	[repʉbli'kanskə pɑː'ţi]

elections	valg (n)	['valg]
to elect (vt)	å velge	[ɔ 'vɛlgə]
elector, voter	velger (m)	['vɛlgər]
election campaign	valgkampanje (m)	['valg kam'panjə]

voting (n)	avstemning, votering (m)	['af,stɛmniŋ], ['voteriŋ]
to vote (vi)	å stemme	[ɔ 'stɛmə]
suffrage, right to vote	stemmerett (m)	['stɛmə,rɛt]

candidate	kandidat (m)	[kandi'dat]
to be a candidate	å kandidere	[ɔ kandi'derə]
campaign	kampanje (m)	[kam'panjə]

| opposition (as adj) | opposisjons- | [ɔpʋsi'ʂʋns-] |
| opposition (n) | opposisjon (m) | [ɔpʋsi'ʂʋn] |

visit	besøk (n)	[be'søk]
official visit	offisielt besøk (n)	[ɔfi'sjɛlt be'søk]
international (adj)	internasjonal	['intɛ:ɳaʂʋ,nal]

| negotiations | forhandlinger (m pl) | [fɔr'handliŋər] |
| to negotiate (vi) | å forhandle | [ɔ fɔr'handlə] |

193. Politics. Government. Part 2

society	samfunn (n)	['sam,fʉn]
constitution	grunnlov (m)	['grʉn,lɔv]
power (political control)	makt (m)	['makt]
corruption	korrupsjon (m)	[kʋrʉp'ʂʋn]

| law (justice) | lov (m) | ['lɔv] |
| legal (legitimate) | lovlig | ['lɔvli] |

| justice (fairness) | rettferdighet (m) | [rɛt'færdi,het] |
| just (fair) | rettferdig | [rɛt'færdi] |

committee	komité (m)	[kʋmi'te]
bill (draft law)	lovforslag (n)	['lɔv,fɔʂlag]
budget	budsjett (n)	[bʉd'ʂɛt]
policy	politikk (m)	[pʋli'tik]
reform	reform (m/f)	[rɛ'fɔrm]
radical (adj)	radikal	[radi'kal]

power (strength, force)	kraft (m/f)	['kraft]
powerful (adj)	mektig	['mɛkti]
supporter	tilhenger (m)	['til,hɛŋər]
influence	innflytelse (m)	['in,flytəlse]

| regime (e.g., military ~) | regime (n) | [rɛ'ʂimə] |
| conflict | konflikt (m) | [kʋn'flikt] |

conspiracy (plot)	**sammensvergelse** (m)	['samən,sværgəlsə]
provocation	**provokasjon** (m)	[pruvuka'sʊn]
to overthrow (regime, etc.)	**å styrte**	[ɔ 'sty:tə]
overthrow (of government)	**styrting** (m/f)	['sty:tiŋ]
revolution	**revo usjon** (m)	[revulʉ'sʊn]
coup d'état	**statskupp** (n)	['stats,kʉp]
military coup	**militærkupp** (n)	[mili'tær,kʉp]
crisis	**krise** (m/f)	['krisə]
economic recession	**økonomisk nedgang** (m)	[økʉ'nɔmisk 'ned,gaŋ]
demonstrator (protester)	**demonstrant** (m)	[demɔn'strant]
demonstration	**demonstrasjon** (m)	[demɔnstra'sʊn]
martial law	**krigstilstand** (m)	['krigstil,stan]
military base	**militærbase** (m)	[mili'tær,basə]
stability	**stabilitet** (m)	[stabili'tet]
stable (adj)	**stabil**	[sta'bil]
exploitation	**utbytting** (m/f)	['ʉt,bytiŋ]
to exploit (workers)	**å utbytte**	[ɔ 'ʉt,bytə]
racism	**rasisme** (m)	[ra'sismə]
racist	**rasist** (m)	[ra'sist]
fascism	**fascisme** (m)	[fa'ʂismə]
fascist	**fascist** (m)	[fa'ʂist]

194. Countries. Miscellaneous

foreigner	**utlending** (m)	['ʉt,leniŋ]
foreign (adj)	**utenlandsk**	['ʉtən,lansk]
abroad	**i utlandet**	[i 'ʉt,lanə]
(in a foreign country)		
emigrant	**emigrant** (m)	[ɛmi'grant]
emigration	**emigrasjon** (m)	[ɛmigra'sʊn]
to emigrate (vi)	**å emigrere**	[ɔ ɛmi'grɛrə]
the West	**Vesten**	['vɛstən]
the East	**Østen**	['østən]
the Far East	**Det fjerne østen**	['de 'fjæ:ŋə ,østɛn]
civilization	**sivilisasjon** (m)	[sivilisa'sʊn]
humanity (mankind)	**menneskehet** (m)	['mɛnəske het]
the world (earth)	**verden** (m)	['værdən]
peace	**fred** (m)	['frɛd]
worldwide (adj)	**verdens-**	['værdəns-]
homeland	**fedreland** (n)	['fædrə,lar]
people (population)	**folk** (n)	['fɔlk]

population	**befolkning** (m)	[be'fɔlkniŋ]
people (a lot of ~)	**folk** (n)	['fɔlk]
nation (people)	**nasjon** (m)	[nɑ'ʂʊn]
generation	**generasjon** (m)	[generɑ'ʂʊn]

territory (area)	**territorium** (n)	[tɛri'tʊrium]
region	**region** (m)	[rɛgi'ʊn]
state (part of a country)	**delstat** (m)	['del‚stɑt]

tradition	**tradisjon** (m)	[trɑdi'ʂʊn]
custom (tradition)	**skikk, sedvane** (m)	['ʂik], ['sɛd‚vɑnə]
ecology	**økologi** (m)	[økʊlʊ'gi]

Indian (Native American)	**indianer** (m)	[indi'ɑnər]
Gypsy (masc.)	**sigøyner** (m)	[si'gøjnər]
Gypsy (fem.)	**sigøynerske** (m/f)	[si'gøjnəʂkə]
Gypsy (adj)	**sigøynersk**	[si'gøjnəʂk]

empire	**imperium, keiserrike** (n)	['im'perium], ['kæjsə‚rike]
colony	**koloni** (m)	[kʊlu'ni]
slavery	**slaveri** (n)	[slɑvɛ'ri]
invasion	**invasjon** (m)	[invɑ'ʂʊn]
famine	**hungersnød** (m/f)	['hʉŋɛʂ‚nød]

195. Major religious groups. Confessions

| religion | **religion** (m) | [religi'ʊn] |
| religious (adj) | **religiøs** | [reli'gjøs] |

faith, belief	**tro** (m)	['trʊ]
to believe (in God)	**å tro**	[ɔ 'trʊ]
believer	**troende** (m)	['trʊenə]

| atheism | **ateisme** (m) | [ɑte'ismə] |
| atheist | **ateist** (m) | [ɑte'ist] |

Christianity	**kristendom** (m)	['kristən‚dɔm]
Christian (n)	**kristen** (m)	['kristən]
Christian (adj)	**kristelig**	['kristəli]

Catholicism	**katolisisme** (m)	[katʊli'sismə]
Catholic (n)	**katolikk** (m)	[katʊ'lik]
Catholic (adj)	**katolsk**	[kɑ'tʊlsk]

Protestantism	**protestantisme** (m)	[prʊtɛstɑn'tismə]
Protestant Church	**den protestantiske kirke**	[den prʊtɛ'stɑntiskə ‚çirkə]
Protestant (n)	**protestant** (m)	[prʊtɛ'stɑnt]

| Orthodoxy | **ortodoksi** (m) | [ɔ:tʊdʊk'si] |
| Orthodox Church | **den ortodokse kirke** | [den ɔ:tʊ'dɔksə ‚çirkə] |

Orthodox (n)	ortodoks (n)	[ɔːtʃuˈdɔks]
Presbyterianism	presbyterianisme (m)	[prɛsbytæriaˈnismə]
Presbyterian Church	den presbyterianske kirkə	[den prɛsbyteriˈanskə ˌçirkə]
Presbyterian (n)	presbyterianer (m)	[prɛsbytæriˈanər]
Lutheranism	lutherdom (m)	[lʉtərˈdɔm]
Lutheran (n)	lutheraner (m)	[lʉtəˈranəˈ]
Baptist Church	baptisme (m)	[bɑpˈtismə]
Baptist (n)	baptist (m)	[bɑpˈtist]
Anglican Church	den anglikanske kirke	[den ɑŋliˈkanskə ˌçirkə]
Anglican (n)	anglikaner (m)	[ɑŋliˈkanər]
Mormonism	mormonisme (m)	[mɔrmɔˈnismə]
Mormon (n)	mormon (m)	[mʊrˈmʊn]
Judaism	judaisme (m)	[ˈjʉdɑˌismə]
Jew (n)	judeer (m)	[ˈjʉˈdeər]
Buddhism	buddhisme (m)	[bʉˈdismɛ]
Buddhist (n)	buddhist (m)	[bʉˈdist]
Hinduism	hinduisme (m)	[hindʉˈismə]
Hindu (n)	hindu (m)	[ˈhindʉ]
Islam	islam	[ˈislɑm]
Muslim (n)	muslim (m)	[mʉˈslim]
Muslim (adj)	muslimsk	[mʉˈslimsk]
Shiah Islam	sjiisme (m)	[siˈismə]
Shiite (n)	sjiitt (m)	[siˈit]
Sunni Islam	sunnisme (m)	[sʉˈnismɛ]
Sunnite (n)	sunnimuslim (m)	[ˈsʉni mʉsˌlim]

196. Religions. Priests

priest	prest (m)	[ˈprɛst]
the Pope	Paven	[ˈpavən]
monk, friar	munk (m)	[ˈmʉnk]
nun	norne (m/f)	[ˈnɔnə]
pastor	pastor (m)	[ˈpastʊr]
abbot	abbed (m)	[ˈabed]
vicar (parish priest)	sogneprest (m)	[ˈsɔŋnəˌprɛst]
bishop	biskop (m)	[ˈbiskɔp]
cardinal	kardinal (m)	[kɑːdiˈnɑlˈ]
preacher	predikant (m)	[prɛdiˈkart]
preaching	preken (m)	[ˈprɛkən]

parishioners	menighet (m/f)	['meni,het]
believer	troende (m)	['truenə]
atheist	ateist (m)	[ate'ist]

197. Faith. Christianity. Islam

Adam	Adam	['adɑm]
Eve	Eva	['ɛvɑ]
God	Gud (m)	['gʉd]
the Lord	Herren	['hærən]
the Almighty	Den Allmektige	[den al'mɛktiə]
sin	synd (m/f)	['syn]
to sin (vi)	å synde	[ɔ 'synə]
sinner (masc.)	synder (m)	['synər]
sinner (fem.)	synderinne (m)	['synə,rinə]
hell	helvete (n)	['hɛlvetə]
paradise	paradis (n)	['pɑrɑ,dis]
Jesus	Jesus	['jesʉs]
Jesus Christ	Jesus Kristus	['jesʉs ,kristʉs]
the Holy Spirit	Den Hellige Ånd	[dən 'hɛliə ,on]
the Savior	Frelseren	['frelserən]
the Virgin Mary	Jomfru Maria	['jɔmfrʉ mɑ,riɑ]
the Devil	Djevel (m)	['djevəl]
devil's (adj)	djevelsk	['djevəlsk]
Satan	Satan	['sɑtɑn]
satanic (adj)	satanisk	[sɑ'tɑnisk]
angel	engel (m)	['ɛŋəl]
guardian angel	skytsengel (m)	['syts,ɛŋəl]
angelic (adj)	engle-	['ɛŋlə-]
apostle	apostel (m)	[ɑ'pɔstəl]
archangel	erkeengel (m)	['ærkə,æŋəl]
the Antichrist	Antikrist	['ɑnti,krist]
Church	kirken (m)	['çirkən]
Bible	bibel (m)	['bibəl]
biblical (adj)	bibelsk	['bibəlsk]
Old Testament	Det Gamle Testamente	[de 'gɑmlə tɛstɑ'mentə]
New Testament	Det Nye Testamente	[de 'nye tɛstɑ'mentə]
Gospel	evangelium (n)	[ɛvɑn'gelium]
Holy Scripture	Den Hellige Skrift	[dən 'hɛliə ,skrift]
Heaven	Himmerike (n)	['himə,rikə]

Commandment	bud (n)	['bʉd]
prophet	profet (m)	[prʊ'fet]
prophecy	profeti (m)	[prʊfe'ti]

Allah	Allah	['ɑlɑ]
Mohammed	Muhammed	[mʉ'hɑmɛd]
the Koran	Koranen	[kʊ'rɑnən]

mosque	moské (m)	[mʊ'ske]
mullah	mulla (m)	['mʉlɑ]
prayer	bønn (m)	['bœn]
to pray (vi, vt)	å be	[ɔ 'be]

pilgrimage	pilegrimsreise (m/f)	['pilǝgrims,ræjsǝ]
pilgrim	pilegrim (m)	['pilǝgrim]
Mecca	Mekka	['mɛkɑ]

church	kirke (m/f)	['çirkǝ]
temple	tempel (n)	['tɛmpǝl]
cathedral	katedral (m)	[kate'drɑl]
Gothic (adj)	gotisk	['gɔtisk]
synagogue	synagoge (m)	[syna'gʊçǝ]
mosque	moské (m)	[mʊ'ske]

chapel	kapell (n)	[kɑ'pɛl]
abbey	abbedi (n)	['ɑbedi]
convent	kloster (n)	['klɔstǝr]
monastery	kloster (n)	['klɔstǝr]

bell (church ~s)	klokke (m/f)	['klɔkǝ]
bell tower	klokketårn (n)	['klɔkǝ,toːɳ]
to ring (ab. bells)	å ringe	[ɔ 'riŋǝ]

cross	kors (n)	['kɔːʂ]
cupola (roof)	kuppel (m)	['kʉpǝl]
icon	ikon (m/n)	[i'kʊn]

soul	sjel (m)	['ʂɛl]
fate (destiny)	skjebne (m)	['ʂɛbnǝ]
evil (n)	ondskap (n)	['ʊn,skɑp]
good (n)	godhet (m)	['gʊ,het]

vampire	vampyr (m)	[vɑm'pyr]
witch (evil ~)	heks (m)	['hɛks]
demon	demon (m)	[de'mʊn]
spirit	ånd (m)	['ɔn]

| redemption (giving us ~) | forløsning (m/f) | [fɔː'løsniŋ] |
| to redeem (vt) | å sone | [ɔ 'sʊnǝ] |

| church service, mass | gudstjeneste (m) | ['gʉts,tjenɛstǝ] |
| to say mass | å holde gudstjeneste | [ɔ 'holdǝ 'gʉts,tjenɛstǝ] |

confession	**skriftemål** (n)	['skriftə‚mol]
to confess (vi)	**å skrifte**	[ɔ 'skriftə]
saint (n)	**helgen** (m)	['hɛlgən]
sacred (holy)	**hellig**	['hɛli]
holy water	**vievann** (n)	['viə‚vɑn]
ritual (n)	**ritual** (n)	[ritʉ'ɑl]
ritual (adj)	**rituell**	[ritʉ'ɛl]
sacrifice	**ofring** (m/f)	['ɔfriŋ]
superstition	**overtro** (m)	['ɔvə‚trʊ]
superstitious (adj)	**overtroisk**	['ɔvə‚trʊisk]
afterlife	**livet etter dette**	['livə ‚ɛtər 'dɛtə]
eternal life	**det evige liv**	[de ‚eviə 'liv]

MISCELLANEOUS

198. Various useful words

background (green ~)	bakgrunn (m)	['bɑkˌgrʉn]
balance (of situation)	balanse (m)	[bɑ'lɑnsə]
barrier (obstacle)	hinder (n)	['hindər]
base (basis)	basis (n)	['bɑsis]
beginning	begynnelse (m)	[be'jinəlsə]
category	kategori (m)	[kɑtegʉ'ri]
cause (reason)	årsak (m/f)	['oːˌsɑk]
choice	valg (n)	['vɑlg]
coincidence	sammenfall (n)	['sɑmənˌfɑ]
comfortable (~ chair)	bekvem	[be'kvem]
comparison	sammenlikning (m)	['sɑmənˌlikniŋ]
compensation	kompensasjon (m)	[kʉmpɛnsɑ'ʂʉn]
degree (extent, amount)	grad (m)	['grɑd]
development	utvikling (m/f)	['ʉtˌvikliŋ]
difference	skilnad, forskjell (m)	['ʂilnɑd], ['fɔːʂɛl]
effect (e.g., of drugs)	effekt (m)	[ɛ'fɛkt]
effort (exertion)	anstrengelse (m)	['ɑnˌstrɛŋəlsə]
element	element (n)	[ɛle'mɛnt]
end (finish)	slutt (m)	['ʂlʉt]
example (illustration)	eksempel (n)	[ɛk'sɛmpəl]
fact	faktum (n)	['fɑktum]
frequent (adj)	hyppig	['hʏpi]
growth (development)	vekst (m)	['vɛkst]
help	hjelp (m)	['jɛlp]
ideal	ideal (n)	[ide'ɑl]
kind (sort, type)	slags (n)	['ʂlɑks]
labyrinth	labyrint (m)	[lɑby'rint]
mistake, error	feil (m)	['fæjl]
moment	moment (n)	[mo'mɛnt]
object (thing)	objekt (n)	[ɔb'jɛkt]
obstacle	hindring (m/f)	['hindriŋ]
original (original copy)	original (m)	[ɔrigi'nɑl]
part (~ of sth)	del (m)	['del]
particle, small part	partikkel (m)	[pɑːˈʈikəl]
pause (break)	pause (m)	['paʊsə]

position	posisjon (m)	[pɔsi'ʂʊn]
principle	prinsipp (n)	[prin'sip]
problem	problem (n)	[prʊ'blem]

process	prosess (m)	[prʊ'sɛs]
progress	fremskritt (n)	['frɛmˌskrit]
property (quality)	egenskap (m)	['ɛgənˌskɑp]
reaction	reaksjon (m)	[rɛak'ʂʊn]
risk	risiko (m)	['risikʊ]

secret	hemmelighet (m/f)	['hɛməliˌhet]
series	serie (m)	['seriə]
shape (outer form)	form (m/f)	['fɔrm]
situation	situasjon (m)	[sitʉa'ʂʊn]
solution	løsning (m)	['løsniŋ]

standard (adj)	standard-	['stanˌdɑr-]
standard (level of quality)	standard (m)	['stanˌdɑr]
stop (pause)	stopp (m), hvile (m/f)	['stɔp], ['vilə]
style	stil (m)	['stil]

system	system (n)	[sʏ'stem]
table (chart)	tabell (m)	[ta'bɛl]
tempo, rate	tempo (n)	['tɛmpʊ]
term (word, expression)	term (m)	['tɛrm]

thing (object, item)	ting (m)	['tiŋ]
truth (e.g., moment of ~)	sannhet (m)	['sanˌhet]
turn (please wait your ~)	tur (m)	['tʉr]
type (sort, kind)	type (m)	['typə]
urgent (adj)	omgående	['ɔmˌgɔːnə]

urgently (adv)	omgående	['ɔmˌgɔːnə]
utility (usefulness)	nytte (m/f)	['nʏtə]
variant (alternative)	variant (m)	[vari'ant]
way (means, method)	måte (m)	['moːtə]
zone	sone (m/f)	['sʊnə]

www.ingramcontent.com/pod-product-compliance
Lightning Source LLC
La Vergne TN
LVHW051302080426
835509LV00020B/3108